Latino Sun, Rising

Latino Sun, Rising

OUR SPANISH-SPEAKING
U.S. WORLD

Marco Portales

Texas A&M University Press   College Station

The paper used in this book meets the minimum requirements
of the American National Standard for Permanence
of Paper for Printed Library Materials, z39.48-1984.
Binding materials have been chosen for durability.

Library of Congress Cataloging-in-Publication Data

Portales, Marco, 1948–
Latino sun, rising : our Spanish-speaking U.S. world /
Marco Portales.—1st ed.
p. cm.
ISBN 1-58544-381-6 (cloth : alk. paper)
1. Portales, Marco, 1948–   2. Mexican Americans–Biography.
3. Mexican American teachers—Biography.   4. Texas, South—
Biography.   5. Texas, South—Social life and customs.   6. Texas,
South–Social conditions.   7. Mexican Americans—Ethnic identity.
8. Mexican Americans—Social conditions.   9. Hispanic
Americans—Social conditions.   10. United States—
Ethnic relations.   I. Title.
E184.M5P675   2004
976.4'00468073'092--dc22
2004007215

Para Rita, Carlos y Marie, otra vez, once more.

Also, for all Latinos and Americans, as we

discover the strengths of our diversity

throughout the United States and the world over,

during the twenty-first century.

Contents

Preface

A Latino sun, rising, as the banner symbol for a collection of essays framing growing-up awakenings, parenthood realizations, and sociopolitical dialogues that ought to be further along in the United States may appear a rougher mix than readers of fine books appreciate. Nonetheless, that is where we find ourselves in the first decade of the twenty-first century. I never thought the day would arrive when more and more signs in both English and Spanish, now clearly the two main languages of the United States, would trumpet the idea that the sun is rising for Latinos. Some readers may be genuinely surprised by the seemingly sudden emergence of Latinos. But, most Americans have been discovering for some time that discussing the presence of Spanish-speakers in the United States today is difficult to avoid, because Latinos are virtually everywhere. This presence has been evolving since 1542 when Alvar Nuñez Cabeza de Vaca wrote *La Relación* for King Charles V, the first enormously respectful book that succinctly described in sixteenth-century Spanish the Gulf Coast region of the Américas about which I also write. Abrupt as the geopolitical manifestation of Latinos appears, statisticians of all kinds have been lately including Latinos in nearly every data bank of information about the United States. This need to catch up with demographic realities has called attention to a cultural lacuna that our English-reading public, one largely raised on what Kevin Phillips called the "triumph of Anglo-America," has not fully understood before. Notwithstanding, the 1990 U.S. Census counted 22.4 million Latinos, a population that phenomenally increased by 57.9 percent to 35.3 million in 2000, and then again to more than 38.4 million in 2003, including more than 25 million who claim Mexican ancestry.

During their heyday, the Aztecs kept calendars that observed the rise of new suns, each of which signaled different epochs. Today, it may be too early to signal a new age, but all the signs suggest that within the United States and externally, Americans and the Américas will establish totally different relationships in the twenty-first century from what has been previously the case. How the United States will change remains to be seen, but there will be many forces at work trying to exert influence to create the type of change that various people want to see. At this point, even the demographers have been too conservative in predicting population changes during the last two decades. At first, they estimated that Latinos would become the largest minority population in the United States, surpassing African Americans, by the year 2015. When realities outpaced those predictions, the year was moved to 2010, and a few years later, to 2008. Still later, the population numbers pointed to 2005. Today we know that the United States' Hispanic population exceeded the number of African Americans in 2003. That year, Latinos, which is the preferred term among most Spanish-speaking Americans, made up 12.5 percent of the U.S. population, while African Americans comprised 12.3 percent. This kind of growth tells us that the United States now largely consists of black, white, and brown Americans, a change that is sure to transform everything.

But what will such changes usher in for Latinos? How will being the single largest minority group within the United States change how we live, change the ways the rest of the American public and those from abroad perceive us? These are not questions that can be easily answered without understanding where we are, where we have been, and where Latinos need to go within the next half-century or so. The fact that as a nation the United States has not sufficiently recognized the significance of this demographic development means that all types of projected or envisioned plans need to be altered to make room for Latinos. Efforts to embrace new Latino neighbors require understanding Spanish-speaking Americans who hail not only from Mexico but also from all countries where Spanish is spoken.

Regardless of country of origin, Latinos have proven to be good, steady workers with a demonstrated commitment to improving the lives of their sons and daughters in the United States. These two traits are well known, despite, of course, difficulties often brought on by adjusting and trying to cope with U.S. customs and mores. Latinos are family-centered and patriotic. The majority support the United States, so much so that in the 2003 war with Iraq, Mexican Americans and Latinos from Central and South America volunteered to fight, confirming their citizenship or risking death to secure it. Such sacrifices have been part of history; Latino veterans and heroes abound, from Desert Storm, Vietnam, Korea, to World War II, as Maggie Rivas-Rodriguez has brought out in "World War II Narratives." This project collects testimonials that can be accessed online at www.utexas.edu/projects/latinoarchives. Behind occasional news items on Latinos, readers are learning that Latinos and their ancestors, from all indigenous groups, classes, and segments of the population, live and have lived full lives in the United States, usually and mainly away from the traditional spotlights that feature other Americans.

We Latinos engage in a variety of cultural activities that empower and help define us. Some of our people fortify themselves culturally by participating in or following sports, but also by pursuing other social and spiritual activities engaged in by all Americans. When resources are available we travel, like other U.S. citizens, generally to our home-countries but also to wherever we can, visibly diversifying American culture wherever we go. From going to see relatives and friends, to hosting their visits, to squeezing in an afternoon backyard cookout after a baseball, basketball, or football game, we Latinos enjoy getting together. These activities provide us with the satisfaction of knowing that we are contributing to the variety of ways in which people live in the United States.

The nature of how this less-heralded Latino life has contributed to American civilization is part of my reason for writing this book; the rest of my purpose is to attempt to bring Spanish-speaking American life more prominently into the twenty-first century. My life as sketched here, for this reason, is not meant to be representative, though it clearly is the result of what can be seen as a successful American education. I note this fact because traditionally it has been somewhat fashionable among Latino writers to eschew success, particularly in printed testimonials, for fear of not being perceived Mexican American or Chicano enough. In my case, I confess that even though some of my own personal plans for success have failed over the years, I have found that perseverance is generally rewarded in the United States. Striking a balance between one's true journey, calling for changes, and encouraging other Latinos has been my goal, and I can only hope I have not missed that target by much.

Events, states, and countries depicted in the following essays reference a good number of places in Latin America and make me hopeful that U.S. Latinos will see aspects of their lives reflected here. Yet no single Latino, regardless of how panethnic, can hope to speak for all 38.4 million Hispanics the U.S. census counted in 2003 midyear. Of this population, 67 percent are Mexican Americans, 8.6 percent are Puerto Ricans, and 3.7 percent are Cuban Americans. Central and South American Latinos comprise 14.3 percent while "Other Hispanics" make up 6.5 percent, likely citizens from Spain, the Dominican Republic, and the Latinos who did not identify either the country they came from or that of their parents.

Although I have resided in different regions of the United States, such as western New York, Chicago, and the California Bay Area, experiences in the places where I have lived with Latinos, including Costa Rica, Puerto Rico, and Spain, prompted me to write the following essays for readers of all persuasions. My goal has been to encourage all Americans and citizens of the world to appreciate Latino lifestyles, for, like other people throughout the globe, we Latinos are bent on living in the best ways we can muster, given our individual and different cultural circumstances. Improving education, as I point out, is front and center for most Latinos, since it is mainly through education that most of us hope to raise the quality of our lives and the nature of our contributions to life in the United States. We Latinos also seek to maintain and support our families, which is why we communally celebrate and observe all kinds of cultural and social events, including *bailes,* weddings, births, deaths, and other occasions as they arise or as needs create them. Although being a Catholic has led me to infer the importance of that kind of upbringing to what I have made of my experience, everyone knows that Latinos are members of other religions as well. We are heterogeneous; we belong to numerous clubs, organizations, and political parties, which tells us that as U.S. Latinos we seek to be woven into the social fabric of this country. We enjoy all kinds of music, including mariachi, salsa, *cumbia,* merengue, bolero, tango, classical, country, rock, hip hop, and popular music mixed for audiences with different tastes, as the Spanish radio DJs in different parts of the country daily demonstrate.

The opening morning pieces that begin this volume of essays address a handful of growing-up experiences, followed by parenting occasions, which the nature of raising children has led me to associate with the pressures of *el mediodía,* that is, noon or midday. Every family has its own rhythms, its own dynamics and patterns, and Latino *familia* life is no exception. But creating a family and then working to provide opportunities for the young while paying the bills amid life's demands is an important challenge for U.S. Latinos, especially in light of the dissolution that assails American families and individuals from a good number of angles today. Invariably our responsibilities as parents end prompting *discusiones* about public policy issues usually heard in the Latino communities throughout the country *por las tardes, después del café,* in the afternoons, after coffee with friends. Because such concerns have not been sufficiently articulated in print form, I have taken the liberty of sketching some particulars with the hope that other U.S. Latinos can further expand on these views in order to secure better attention from the media and political leaders.

These literary renditions of my perambulations aim to demonstrate that the everyday lives of Mexican Americans and other Latino Americans increasingly require the kind of positive notice that social, political, and economic leaders are now beginning to extend. I seek to encourage such attention, amplifying mutually beneficial dialogues, because the cultural gap created by the media regarding Latino issues often is ill-informed, threatening the common good. Indeed, gaining awareness of the differing cultural coordinates and the different contexts that often shape the thinking and the actions of Spanish-speaking Americans remains scarce. Even then, one essay collection seeking to remedy the fact that U.S. Spanish speakers have a little-noticed presence within the larger American family, of course, is not going to erase fractious relationships created by generations of inattention. My idea, however, is to address issues and prospects long overdue. Although Spanish has emerged as the second most widely used language in the United States, the dream of securing a respectable steady paycheck, one that provides for more attractive residences where Latino children can be educated and properly nourished as they grow, has remained a difficult goal to attain. And now, as the Latino sun continues to rise, I tender these essays to the four winds, hoping sympathetic readers will embrace the rich diversity that U.S. Latinos are capable of sharing.

Latino Sun, Rising

Title: No better friend, no
worse enemy : the life of Ge
Item ID: 33543017316340
Date due: 1/13/2019,23:59

Title: Michael Phelps :
beneath the surface
Item ID: 34028071198510
Date due: 1/13/2019,23:59

Title: Latino sun, rising : our
Spanish-speaking U.S. wo
Item ID: 34028055062781
Date due: 1/13/2019,23:59

Title: I beat the odds : from
homelessness, to the blind
Item ID: 34028076289892
Date due: 1/13/2019,23:59

Introduction

At the center of my work I have located a certain awareness that I call the Public Consciousness, which is the knowledge and general information shared by people familiar with daily life, particularly in the United States. Almost everything that registers on the five senses of Americans also influences and engages the interests of citizens from other countries. For this reason, public consciousness issues tend to attract almost automatic attention both at home and abroad. And the best way to measure and to weigh the nature of the information that engages the general public, I believe, is to examine the media in order to consider the thinking as well as the actions of Americans. For it is by studying the goals, dreams, and aspirations we spend our lives and energies securing that a society is judged, whether we find these vague criteria fair or not. Our collective and individual reactions to American life reveal the ideas, viewpoints, and intangibles that matter to us: what engages our interests, and the degrees to which we understand and the extent to which we shape and determine the particulars of American civilization.

Certain traditional issues have always captured the attention of students of the United States. When we consider the nature of the lives of Mexican Americans and other U.S. Latinos, however, we soon learn that the majority of Americans are hardly conscious of the fact that Spanish-speaking citizens are an important component of American life. Generally speaking, commentators cursorily mention Hispanics, followed by disturbing silences that do not reveal how Spanish-speaking Americans actually fit within a United States that increasingly is featuring a multiethnic citizenry. Although Latinos comprised 12.5 percent of the U.S. population in 2000, the social inertia that usually counters change has made it difficult for many citizens to realize the nature of the changes that could considerably improve life for all Americans. Changing traditions and practices is enormously difficult, and sometimes, outright resistance stymies the momentum needed to provide traction for new ideas and new ways of looking at our changing population. A new self assessment is what the United States now requires.

The Latino population is regarded as being so varied that no one Latino group understandably feels comfortable representing or speaking for other Spanish-speaking Americans. Still, the unifying experiences shared by Americans who speak Spanish provide such common ground that I do not think it is presumptuous to say that most good-willed Latinos often feel like *primos,* like cousins, when they encounter one another. Whether we are thus from Mexico or from Guatemala, Argentina, Chile, Uruguay, Venezuela, or any other Latin American country, the Spanish language and our different *hispanidades* often provide a glue that connects us both from within and without. We Latinos proudly point out that we are as diverse as our cultural roots indicate. Although American society often groups all Latinos together, we are very conscious of the cultural and geopolitical differences that distinguish us. Our foods, music, art forms, celebrations, and the histories of the Latin American countries where some of us were born, for example, are usually quite different. But in the United States many of the national and regional distinctions that separate Latinos in Latin America increasingly are seen as less significant, especially when Spanish remains the common link. Indeed, I have seen the faces of people light up, as if the sun has suddenly emerged from behind a dark cloud, when they hear someone near them speaking or addressing them in Spanish, their first and sometimes only language.

The viewpoints I feature in the following pages have been developing within me for years in a variety of ways. Readers should know, at the outset, that I have always hoped to offer positive reports about the nature of Latino life in the United States. Toward the end of the twentieth century, however, I very reluctantly determined that, although Mexican Americans and Hispanics have made great strides over a number of generations, Latinos are still not as prominent in the public consciousness of the United States as our population numbers tell us we should be. Feeling elbowed out sometimes was not what Latinos expected, but I have always believed that it is necessary to know where people stand in order to understand a country's needs. For if a situation, or state of affairs, is not being adequately addressed, perhaps we need different leaders. Disturbing as this realization may be, feeling left out has not disillusioned millions of Latinos, including myself, from continuing to work to create the best lives that we Spanish-speaking residents have been able to muster for our families, as these essays attest.

The progress of Mexican Americans and other U.S. Latinos requires a quality education that opens up the kinds of opportunities that usher in noticeable differences. In this effort, imaginative works of literature, including essays, letters, memoirs, and other writings aimed at disseminating knowledge about the cultural multiplicity of U.S. Hispanics should be particularly timely. During the last thirty years, books about the growing-up experiences of the authors have been a staple of the publishing establishment because young people have needed to see how successful models have negotiated social and cultural obstacles. I have searched for nonfiction works that address how mature Latinos address social issues, and I have found a noticeable dearth. Aside from the unrepresentative work of writers such as Richard Rodriguez and Linda Chavez, who have cast themselves as unique and exceptional, finding published materials that speak to and for average, middle-class, mature Latinos has been difficult.

I therefore begin with the autobiographical "*Sol Naciente:* Youth" section to familiarize readers with some of the shaping coordinates of my own background. The other two parts of this volume, however, endeavor to offer something considerably different in the field of ethnic writing. Although a few of the subjects addressed in these pages are already a part of the traditional discourse of the Latino community, my purpose is to invite a larger American public into a conversation. My goal, indeed, is to prompt constructive discussions about some difficult issues often avoided. Since earlier generations of Latinos were excluded from publishing their views in widely circulated venues, few of our antecedents left behind much of their history, insight, and cultural wisdom. That is why most Latinos today have very few viable means of understanding how current trends and patterns were shaped by past practices, making it hard to measure the extent of the progress Latinos think we see in the twenty-first century.

Politicians, advertising people, and survey-takers are beginning to demonstrate an appreciation for the changes that the more than 38.4 million U.S. Spanish-speakers are contributing to American culture and the economy. Latinos cannot help society more substantially if not provided with the necessary opportunities that allow us better positions as U.S. citizens. The fact that most Americans are not prepared by their education to see and to expect Latinos in mainstream society, or do not meet middle-class, better-educated Hispanics who wield decision-making and policy-setting positions across the country, has not helped. For these reasons, creating and promoting a wider understanding of resident U.S. Latinos is one of the main goals of these essays.

When *Crowding Out Latinos* (2000) appeared, I had spent a good number of years thinking about how we Latinos might cast and represent ourselves in the twenty-first century. The first essential step, it seemed to me, was to demonstrate how Latinos have worked to become regular, tax-paying, ordinary Americans. As a sequel to that book, *Latino Sun, Rising* seeks to describe, more self-consciously, how my wife and I have attempted to create our own Latino family in the United States, given the conflations and flux we experience by pursuing our Latino and American family interests. When I was a teenager I realized that some darker-skinned Latinos are not seen as the regular, everyday Americans they were taught to become by the schools in South Texas. It was then that I consciously decided to construct myself as the Mexican American that I endeavor to describe in the following pages. For, in one way or another, every person chooses how to represent himself or herself in order to develop relationships with other people.

Such a decision may not sound significant to other Americans, but how we Latinos cast ourselves, both individually and as a minority majority population group, is a serious matter. The issue usually is whether to represent ourselves simply as Americans, as most of us are, or to specify that we prefer to be known as Mexican Americans, Puerto Ricans, Cuban Americans, or Americans with roots in another Latin American country. Often what unfortunately occurs is that we represent ourselves in keeping with the way that people judge the color of our skin. If Latinos pass for white, for example, society tends to encourage such citizens to blend. If not, Latinos are taken as foreigners, regardless of whether they are U.S. residents, and without regard to how well they may speak English. When people ask me, for instance, I usually say that I am an American. Such a response usually leads people to ask where in the United States I was born, for clearly I do not look like the archetypal American. Not until I reveal that I am an American of Mexican extraction, that I was born and raised in the Rio Grande Valley in South Texas, are people satisfied. I have been extensively schooled in American literature, that is, in the literatures of the Northeast, the West, the Civil War South, and the cool, tree-filled, wetter Northwest; but, I only know something about the U.S. Latino contribution to literature because I have made it my business to discover that on my own. Americans know that there are large numbers of Latinos, particularly in the Southwest and in many other pockets of the United States. Yet most will also acknowledge that, despite the modern marvels of today's media, they have not encountered much information about Americans who speak only Spanish, or English and Spanish, on every ordinary day. This is the sad state of affairs that I am hopeful this book will partially remedy.

During my life, achieving a comfortable, personal adjustment to my own self as a U.S. Latino has not been an easy matter. In retrospect, I can now say that has been the case because our American public consciousness has traditionally lacked Mexican American and Latino success models who invite emulation. This near-zero absence of emulous figures has meant that, like most Mexican Americans, I have had to construct and fashion myself from what my parents taught me and from the great variety of images and reading materials available within American culture. Everything that I have learned from my experiences, in other words, has contributed to the Mexican American and Latino person that I have constructed. The result, ironically, is that I have often felt like the new archetypal American that J. Hector St. John de Crèvecoeur famously sought to describe in *What Is an American* (1782), a connection that surely may surprise some Americans:

> He is either a European, or the descendant of a European, hence that strange mixture of blood, which you will find in no other country. I could point out to you a family whose grandfather was an Englishman, whose wife was Dutch, whose son married a French woman, and whose present four sons have now four wives of different nations. *He* is an American, who, leaving behind him all his ancient prejudices and manners, receives new ones from the new mode of life he has embraced, the new government he obeys, and the new rank he holds. He becomes an American by being received in the broad lap of our great *Alma Mater.* Here individuals of all nations are melted into a new race of men, whose labours [*sic*] and posterity will one day cause great changes in the world. (*Letters from an American Farmer,* Letter III)

That "strange mixture of blood" that de Crèvecoeur points out, to be sure, refers to the intermarriages that occurred between Europeans and the indigenous people of the Americas. This type of new American, as we now well know, does not completely leave "behind him all his ancient prejudices and manners," for these characteristics, changed by life and education, often continue to be passed on to our progeny. Then, too, not all immigrants are invitingly "received in the broad lap" of America. Many Americans, including the great majority of Latinos, have remained less "melted into a new race of men" and women, despite the fact that the potential for "great changes in the world" are possible.

Before proceeding, I need to state that I do not mean to single out my own life, education, and progress as representative or unique. Like other Latinos and Mexican Americans who have struggled to secure the American Dream for themselves and their families, my hope is that describing my experiences in the land of my birth will be useful to other Latinos who are unsure about how they might represent themselves. The first requisite I recommend is to work on one's esteem, which is not a natural-enough process for Latinos in the United States. On this issue, there is an enormous amount of historical documentation that shows that American society has not usually embraced or made Latinos feel welcomed, often in our own land. Psychologically, history has made many Latinos more conflicted and uncertain than other Americans, whether they consider themselves Mexican Americans or Latinos with cultural roots elsewhere. They are, to be sure, Americans of Latino descent, and some feel more Mexican or Latino while others feel that they are now more American. My point is that as U.S. Latinos many have had a more difficult time maintaining and then continuing to develop an interest and pride in our own ancestral cultures, yet that is exactly the nature of the challenge that most Spanish-speaking Americans face as we move into the twenty-first century.

Like most people, I read the newspapers, and see and hear the afternoon and evening news reports. During the day I work at a university, where I teach and where I try to address contentious ideas sensibly, because I believe that sensitive, political, and downright troublesome issues ought to be discussed and not ignored. Living as an American Latino has been difficult for me, as for others, because invariably people who hear me speaking in Spanish tend to assume that I was born outside of the United States. Some Latinos were, but the great majority of us are U.S. Latinos. In the former case, I argue that we Americans need to be generous and hospitable to immigrants who have made it and who are surviving economically in this country. When America's camera eye—the same literary one that John Dos Passos invented—showcases Latino progress, successful Hispanics can be found virtually anywhere, carrying out all kinds of admirable roles. Although fortunately successful, I am also painfully aware that many of my Hispanic peers did not share my happy upbringing and subsequent good luck. The media uses examples of successful Latinos to suggest that Hispanics are making excellent progress. But such images obscure the fact that the great majority of Spanish-speaking citizens in the United States are living today on poverty-level wages, barely surviving on incomes that offer them little hope of ever reaching the great American middle class. Owning a house, two cars, and being able to rest on the weekends, with time and resources to visit friends and relatives during the holidays, is a luxury that many Latinos do not enjoy. Look at the nearest group of Latinos around; we do not have to look far to see the unattractive realities that surround most Hispanics in America today.

Depicting ourselves in positive ways within a culture that has traditionally misrepresented Latinos presents a difficult challenge. Successful Latinos have to be careful about casting themselves as exceptional, that is, as noticeably different in some discernible way from other less successful Latinos. In keeping with the American cult of exceptionalism, Latinos are learning the necessity of being unusual or different in some way in order to be successful. This means that some Latinos find it difficult to feel comfortable within American society, in part because U.S. culture does not easily embrace average Latinos, leaving many feeling left behind for sometimes feeling not American enough.

In making these opening observations, I have not been motivated by Hispanics who are exceptional and successful, by Latinos considered different and unique. Indeed, most of the books published about Hispanics are about out-of-the-ordinary Latinos, about Hispanics who have triumphed in one way or another. Rather, I have had in mind primarily members of Spanish-speaking families who do not yet feel themselves part of the general public consciousness, despite the fact that many of their ancestors have resided in the United States for a number of generations. Temperamentally I am inclined to address issues on which Latinos have not yet developed a comfortable consensus, matters that require the type of considerations I hope to communicate to readers. I believe that current and future opportunities require considerable careful attention, for the possible pitfalls are many. Dismissing past inequities is difficult, since the past everywhere explains the present. That is why most Latinos find it hard to ignore negative messages, events, and signals sent and received in all sorts of personal and public policy ways. Acting indifferently to such semiotics or avoiding or denying the cultural disregard that Hispanics have historically endured in the United States remains a challenge for all Americans. And, although Latinos understandably prefer to celebrate the advances of Hispanics, the reality is that to champion only or mainly the Latino successes is to distort the actual living realities of most Spanish-speaking Americans.

The American Dream of owning and living in decent housing, holding a well-paying job, securing a good education, and providing for the young is definitely the goal of Latinos. Compared to the lives of our parents, there is no doubt that a good number of us enjoy improved livelihoods. Yet when we consider the proportionally small number of Latinos who have learned to provide for their families versus the more than 35 million Hispanics who daily struggle to survive, good-will Americans may wince. More than a third of a century after the Civil Rights Act of 1964 outlawed the outright discriminations that Spanish-speaking citizens used to suffer along with African Americans, too many Mexican Americans and other Latinos are still waiting for equal treatment within American society.

Documenting how one Chicano grew up, how to best render the life of a Mexican American family, and how to think about some public issues in print has been an energizing experience for me. My motivating idea was to show that we Latinos have been ready to join the American family for some time—even while most of us are increasingly finding it difficult to maintain our traditions, mores, and values in order to pass them on to our sons and daughters. Most Latinos I know believe that we can be good American and Spanish-speaking citizens at the same time. We do not see the kind of conflict that some people do with our bilingualism, with functioning both in English and in Spanish, with eating hamburgers for lunch *y arroz y frijoles,* rice and beans, for supper. Many of us, of course, wish that we could communicate better in both languages, an issue reflecting the education that has been available to us. We do not believe, furthermore, that we have to stop being Mexican Americans or Latinos in order to be good patriotic Americans, as some people, including some Hispanics, appear to think. To underscore that desirable goal, we can point to our pervasive respect for education, our desire to succeed, and to our enduring, customs and ways of thinking. These characteristics have been demonstrated and they are increasingly appreciated. We now want our views to be accorded the type of attention that the larger American society will increasingly have to pay as we become regular, normal, everyday Americans.

Since our nation's past history of racial relations requires attitudinal changes that people appear to believe will somehow naturally emerge, actually making American society hospitable to Spanish-speaking citizens is not an easy challenge. Nonetheless, that is the sought goal. Although there are Latinos and other Americans who feel that the needed changes will occur by themselves, projected demographic increases among U.S. Hispanics tell us that maintaining the high quality of life all Americans desire will require some active, real work.

To encourage all U.S. citizens to see U.S. Latinos more positively, as more educated and as rising professionals, these essays are offered to suggest how the contours of almost any Mexican American's life can be shaped by parental realities and enlightened public policies. My idea here has been to highlight some matters of importance to Latinos and to demonstrate how change is simultaneously occurring and being resisted, even as we Latinos communally and individually work to define and to express our views. My main hope is to persuade readers that working to understand Hispanics at this point can only help all Americans. How else are we to move forward collectively as the great nation that we seek to enhance?

Sol Naciente:
Youth

I

Urban Renewal on the Hometown Block in Edinburg

When I was growing up in the 1950s and 60s in Edinburg in the lower Rio Grande Valley of South Texas, the federal government's Urban Renewal program came in amid much brouhaha. When it left toward the latter half of the 1960s it had transformed our little piece of land. The end of the improvement plan also ended by removing our neighbors elsewhere without noticeably helping the people it displaced. The initial and always trumpeted Urban Renewal idea was that individuals and families directly affected would be moved out of low-rent, barely livable quarters and "relocated," that is, compensated for their holdings so that they could presumably afford to buy better homes in better places. The rhetoric of the program was that the homeowners would sell their property for enough or good enough money to allow them opportunities to find more attractive homes elsewhere in Texas or in other states away from the barrios. The American Dream, in short, would be within reach for Latino people.

Urban affairs historians, planning analysts, and students of Latino history may someday see the matter differently. They will have access to information that exists in archives that preserve such records, and, depending on political lenses, they will put their spins on that social program. What I actually lived through, however, does not make me recommend the experience, and no amount of unearthed data is likely to alter how I personally feel about the changes I witnessed.

To provide readers with some sense of the world in which I was born, I want to recall what I knew before Urban Renewal descended upon us. Within a few years, this government program transformed the little block on 7th and Stubbs in Edinburg where I ran, played, and lived for the first twenty years of my life. I will describe a mixture of things as they were, as I recall them, narrated in order to record a number of points that quantitative data seldom capture. Since that life is gone, what I will attempt to remember may appear perhaps too dispassionately recalled, but that is because even after so many years I still feel oddly ambivalent about what happened and how events unfolded. Odd, because I have found that patterns connecting remembered images generally tend to unfold themselves variously with time.

First, a few useful autobiographical preliminaries. The two-bedroom, two-bath home to where I was brought a few days after being born at Grandview Hospital was built toward the end of 1946 for my father's bride, my Costa Rican mother. My mother, who is ninety-two as I write, now lives in Costa Rica again, having removed to San José more than twenty-five years ago, following ten years of living with her second son and yours truly after the death of our father. Located immediately behind a fifty-five by one-hundred-and-twenty-foot rectangle of a grocery store that my father and his business partner constructed, that house still stands in the location of my mind, even though it was razed more two decades ago. At the time of their marriage my father was thirty-four and mother forty-one. People must have said they were an older, more mature couple, and they were very much appreciated by all the *vecinos,* the neighbors among whom we lived for the twenty years about which I write.

About 1918, when it must have seemed as if the violence and the unpredictability of the Mexican Revolution would never stop, Anacleta and Ignacio Portales took their five sons from their ancestral San Luis Potosí home over to the American side of the border somewhere near Brownsville. My then five-year-old future father, second among the five brothers, came of age in central Texas, outside of Austin, in the cotton fields of the Buda area. He was to leave school while in the fifth grade, at about twelve, to help, he always said, his widowed mother. He worked very hard, rising early, denying himself the satisfactions of his business successes. By the time he was in his thirties, he was everywhere recognized as a stable young businessman with enough money in the bank to take care not only of his own needs but also those of others who asked him for help.

His bride had been visiting her fairly affluent cousin who had been sent to Edinburg by her husband to educate their two sons and two daughters. Pedro Domian, who initially was from Poland, I understand, held something like a general manager's position with the United Fruit Company in Costa Rica, and my mother always talked about the grand times that his family and everyone associated with him enjoyed. Whenever invited to visit the Domian family in Quepos or Golfito, both banana and coffee seaports on the Pacific Coast, in the late 1930s and 40s, my mother would later say, she happily went. For Domian and their whole circle of friends apparently enjoyed having great gatherings, made better by high-cost imported whiskeys that were transformed into highballs that were clearly part of the coastal life for which he generously paid. Edinburg, though, was decidedly a different world, she later averred, trying not to express *añoranza,* homesickness. It was very hot, and, in the days before air conditioning, all one could do was sit before a fan in the afternoons and look forward to an ice cream cone at the corner grocery store. When my mother asked why the Domians had left wonderful Costa Rica for Edinburg, she was told that when the family arrived in Brownsville, by way of Pan American Airlines, customs officials at the border said that was the place for the best schools in the Valley. And, in a way, what they said was true. Edinburg had the only college in the whole Rio Grande Valley, the same school that I would attend years later as a freshman and sophomore, what is today the University of Texas, Pan American.

My parents met when my mother walked the two blocks to my father's store to buy an ice cream cone to help her cool off in the hot afternoons. By then, my father had stopped milking cows before sun-up, raising chickens, and tending to the little food stands that he had enterprisingly began after leaving school. He had built several stands by himself where he sold milk, butter, bread, tortillas, and some fruits. Later he was to become the business partner of an older lady; and, at thirty-three or so, he contracted with her to build the grocery store where he would work every day for the rest of his life, except for Sunday afternoons.

The first item that appeared in the neighborhood was a big billboard that must have been about twelve by eight or ten feet. Two friends and I came home from school one day to find, in the northeast quadrant of the block, the enormous sign. From our eleven-year-old perspectives, that announcement regarding the arrival of Urban Renewal, whatever or whomever that was, promised I still don't know exactly what. All we knew is that our little parcel of turf had been designated as an area chosen for development by the City of Edinburg.

The next day, we hurried home after school, hoping to see something, though no one could have said what. On another day, I remember walking across the warm barrio dirt, wetted down by the neighbors' hoses in the early mornings to keep the dust from blowing into their homes, to look wistfully at the sign again. Other times I recall staring at the sign for some hint about the future, occasionally while driven by Dad and Mom on the way to the six o'clock morning Mass at Sacred Heart Church. There a black cassock and a white surplice magically transformed me every day for a week at a time into one of two altar boys who helped Father Poster, Father Moran, or Father McNally with the early Masses. People were summoned to these services by the tolling of bells in the church turret, the same bell tower where as a child of seven or eight I was once allowed to ring the bells. I did as told; I hung on tight, for the sound would be deafening, and I went up and down with the rope that rang them.

We had the largest altar boy association in the state of Texas, the priests informed us, a force of one hundred fourth- through eighth-graders, neatly divided into ten teams of ten altar boys apiece. For assisting with the Masses, we were annually rewarded one day out of the year with a great picnic and an even more exciting scavenger hunt in the wild mesquite country of Benson's Park in Mission, Texas. All the altar boys, including some who had written their own permission slips from their parents, piled into several buses and we were off to the area around La Lomita, one of the early missions in the area. One year, we were taken instead to South Padre Island, where sand, wind, and the sun reigned. I returned so red in the face and so sunburned that my back and arms ached when I stretched. I have since learned the best thing to do after being out in the sun is not to use soap for the first bath after that, perhaps, even for the second one, depending on the amount of skin exposure to the sun. My theory is that the chemicals in the soap combine with human skin that has been overexposed to sun to cause serious damage that scientists are now connecting to skin cancer. When it comes to the sun, I have taken more than my share of its rays, so now I tend to wear hats when I can.

At Padre Island, there were no fancy hotels then. Only a few motels frequented by the hardier tourists, the precursors of the modern-day snowbirds; that is, the people who have retired and yearly visit the Rio Grande Valley from all parts, but mainly from the Midwest. Nowadays the snowbirds form one of the more visible groups of Anglos in the towns of the Valley, especially since they move around in their RVs, their recreation vehicles. But when I was growing up I don't think we ever had even as many as three Anglos in the Edinburg altar boy organization to which I belonged. We were all Mexican Americans, and we alternately spoke English and Spanish, though all of our schooling was in English. I stayed a *monaguillo,* an altar boy, from the fourth grade, I believe, to the eighth grade, helping with the Mass, and I continued to serve periodically even into my sophomore and junior year in high school.

The events to which I want to return, however, are that for as long as half a year or so, there was no change other than the gleaming Urban Renewal sign that had been posted. And that is the way it remained for a very long time to our famished-for-change eyes. It strikes me now, as I write, that I have always looked forward to change, that I have generally sought change in life, especially when things have seemed particularly stagnant. Spanish-speaking citizens of South Texas, it has long seemed to me, have always awaited change, for life to improve, and that has been the case since before I was born. In the 1960s, even though we had no idea of what Urban Renewal would usher in, almost everyone instinctively knew that the bulldozers that appeared suddenly one day, after that long wait, were going to bring about big changes.

Aside from my Catholic school and altar boy activities, my world at that time consisted rather parochially of three-tenths of a block that variously housed, by my present count, between forty and forty-five people. The block where I lived had a *callejón,* an alley that divided the world where I had run around with my friends as a kid in half. The southern half of the neighborhood consisted of "single-family dwellings," a phrase that I first saw when my father and I read the town's newspaper, the *Daily Review,* to see what we could learn about this Urban Renewal idea. We found and read public information announcements similar to the posted ones: that our area had been designated for community development, accompanied by what I have since recognized as the usual local pride puffery often associated with such civic groups.

There were, at any rate, seven relatively modest two-bedroom wooden homes on the south side of the block and their barren-ground backyards butted up against the alley. The other half of the block was divided into twelve little houses that dotted our three-tenths of the block, while the other two-tenths or fifth was occupied by the only Anglo-American family on the block. This family, from the perspectives of some of our parents, had opened the door to our own destruction, for they had sold their home and terrain and it was on their land that the Urban Renewal sign was first posted. That transaction was a done deal, as people in Texas say. And although there was much talk from the neighbors about protesting, about "I won't sell; they can't throw me out," finally nothing emerged from the Spanish-speaking population. Mainly, I believed, no adult protested because most of the older generation could not speak English and everything in the City Council was transacted in English, despite the fact that nearly 90 percent of the people in the area spoke only Spanish. There was a sense, backed by several inquiries made at City Hall and the County Courthouse, that when the government provided "funds for improvement," little could be done. Even the courts, several lawyers and city officials were in the habit of saying, would side with the developers, and the only alternative was to sell.

No one, it is now clearly before me, stood to lose as much as my father. Our three-tenths of the block was the center of my own childhood world, but it was the sole niche my father had been able to carve out successfully for himself and his family in the United States. In this little strip of grassless, hard-ground terrain covered by a loose coat of dirt periodically kicked up by the winds of the Valley, my dad had been able to buy, through hard work and long sixteen-hour days, five little houses that he rented for $2.50 to $3.50 per week. With the exception of a one-room affair of about ten by ten feet, the other four houses offered renters two rooms—a bedroom and a kitchen. My father's business partner owned three other three-room and one four-room houses that variously rented for between $5.50 and $7.00 a week. And all of these dwellings were set in our world in such a way that we kids had a barren piece of ground, with several patches of grass that grew here and there, to play on in the middle of these clustered houses.

Although the Mexican Americans who made up almost 90 percent of the population of the surrounding cities labored and made a living where they could, a considerable amount of work on the surrounding, largely Anglo-owned farms was done by *braceros*. *Braceros* were legal green-card carrying laborers authorized to work in the United States by the Mexican government. Illegal Mexican workers, to be sure, also worked, for the continued prosperity of the Valley has always depended on paying Mexican workers, legal or illegal, very low wages. Personally, I have never been able to understand the southwestern senators and representatives who have created legislation to bar Latino workers from an American economy that cannot function successfully without such cheap labor. Aside from providing groceries to his tenants and the people who lived in the surrounding *vecindad*, much of my father's business in the 1950s and early 1960s depended both on the braceros and on the illegal laborers. Such workers labored in the cotton and citrus-fruit fields of the region alongside resident Mexican Americans like ourselves, showcasing one of the most diverse and culturally different populations in the United States.

Saturday afternoons, for example, most of field workers arrived at the grocery store from the farms—with their wives and families, if the latter lived with them in the United States, or alone, if their families had stayed in Mexico. The rest of the day was given to buying grocery goods, and to using Dad's store as a station stop where they arranged car and truck rides into the downtown area of Edinburg to buy clothes and other necessities. Many of these workers made driving arrangements with friends to the store and back to their work places, but nearly every Saturday my father and I would take four or five separate workers with their food and bought items back to the ranches around the area where they worked. There we were met by their women, children, and the barking dogs that emerged from under the mortar-raised houses where the earth was damped and cooler than the day's hot sun allowed outside. During the weekdays, when business was sometimes slower, Mom stayed at the store's counter and Dad and I prepared some cokes, sodas, apples, and other fruits into three or four twenty-five-gallon aluminum pails packed with ice. Then we headed out into the surrounding fields to sell the cold pop bottles at five cents each and to distribute free apples to the workers. My father had worked for many years in the fields in his younger days, and he once told me that when he did he often wished that someone would take the time and trouble to bring out some cold refreshments into those sun-scorched fields. He said that when one is thirsty, one is willing to pay for a coke or even a drink of cold water. But no one ever thought of bringing field workers anything. So, now that he was successful enough to have a grocery store, he could not forget the less fortunate. Frankly, I have never seen more grateful people than on the occasions when our familiar dark green pick-up truck arrived loaded with cold goods.

For several years, on the Fourth of July my father cooked *barbacoa,* barbecue, and *tripas,* or tripe, for the *vecindad,* the neighborhood. After supper, the older boys who lived on our block would light fireworks, which we continued to hear popping throughout the city late into the night. On summer evenings after work, most of the house tenants frequently sat in the shade provided by the sides of the houses and two or three medium-sized trees because the rooms were simply too hot. Outside, the southeastern winds blowing in from the Gulf gently wafted by, allowing some of the women to stop fanning themselves for short intervals. Everyone dreamed of entering homes anew that would be cool, but only the cold winter months enabled that, and then it was too cold for comfort. Neighbors would show up at the store to warm themselves by the gas stoves my dad had. During the long hot days, though, the children played outdoors while the adults talked about work, the latest developments occurring to people they knew, and what stores or employers were paying better hourly rates. A number of men, including one of my uncles, had served in the U.S. Army, and the flags displayed on the courthouse and some of the businesses reminded people of the veterans during the Fourth celebrations. Pictures taken on those days were always proudly displayed on the clothes dressers, or tucked in the little spaces between the mirrors and the wood paneling of the dresser mirrors. Veterans could be persuaded, after a beer or two, to smile when they remembered their heady, younger days in the Army, but usually they did not say much, as if the memories of those long-ago activities had not significantly impacted much of their subsequent lives. That, at any rate, was the impression the veterans left. Other than being a day when people did not work because businesses closed, the Fourth of July was not too different, for most people did not have much money and their houses had no backyard cooking equipment, as in other middle-class American households.

During the Christmas season, we bought and packaged five-pound, see-through plastic bags of apples, oranges, pears, and bananas and then distributed them to the regular store customers and to destitute families in the area. From the time that my brother and I were between the ages of seven and eleven, our mother took to dressing Eddie in a homemade Santa Claus outfit. While our cousin Santos (who ironically would later be killed in Germany, after three Vietnam tours) and I pushed, Eddie had to ho-ho the neighborhood kids and throw candy from the back of a large wagon to friends who gathered from as far away as five or six blocks.

The parents of all of these children worked in the local produce plants where they packed oranges, melons, squash, grapefruit, and whatever else was in season at various times of the year. During the summer, when fruits were scarce, the main community business was picking cotton in the surrounding farms. The trucks stopped by between five-thirty and six in the morning, and the cotton pickers would be in the fields by six-thirty or seven. The trucks returned the pickers, after working the cotton fields all day, between seven and eight in the evening. In later years, when I was twelve, thirteen, and fourteen, I also went, though not because I had to, like my friends. Since most of my neighbors picked cotton, I did not want to stay behind by myself most of the day. So I asked and asked until finally my parents relented, allowing me to spend the day in the fields, too.

I was jubilant! Now I was ready to have fun. My friends had been telling me that after they picked cotton, they jumped into the irrigation ditches, the same ones where people occasionally drowned. I could not, of course, tell my parents that I was interested in wading in the ditches that were used to irrigate the cotton fields, but that is part of the fun that I had in mind. By then I was a little older, so I considered disobeying them. Besides, I was interested in earning a little spending money. People then were being paid $2.50 per hundred pounds! Picking a hundred pounds of cotton a day may sound easy, but I soon learned how difficult the feat is. The first time I picked cotton, I turned in a grand total of eighty-seven pounds, and this was after working the whole day. My back was very sore and my neck ached! I wondered how I would be able to pick cotton the next day. But three or four weeks into the season, my young muscles had toughened, and I continued going to work with my friends. I felt less sore, and about a week after I started I had built up enough courage to take my first plunge into the ditches. After that, my friends and I graduated and regularly took to cooling off at midday in the irrigation ditches that bordered the cotton fields. Although jumping into the water was not good for my asthma, and since Mom never found out, the occasional drowning reported in other parts of the Valley did not keep my friends and me from enjoying the canal ditches at noon. What I liked in particular was the hissing sounds and the steam that came out of our clothes and bodies when we first jumped in. After wading around in the water for ten minutes or so, we emerged happy and ready to devour the tortilla and the white-bread sandwiches that our parents had made for us the night before. Following lunch, very slowly we trudged back into the cotton rows where we spent the rest of the afternoon, picking and weighing the cotton that now actually weighed less, since the morning dew on the petals had by then evaporated.

When there was no work in the Valley and little promise of anything in the immediate future, some neighborhood families packed their clothes and food and headed north on Highway 281 and others to Michigan, Washington, Illinois, and to California and elsewhere to harvest crops in those states. Sometimes the families returned in September, in time for the beginning of school. Often the fathers stayed an extra month or two; other years, the whole family would decide to stay, and I would hear later that my friends had been placed in schools in the states where they worked, since a better living could be made there. If they happened to save money, some years the extended-credit debts that my father allowed acquaintances to accumulate declined. But most of the time, these families came back empty-handed, having spent their earnings where they worked, and my father was put in a dilemma. He felt that he could not cut off credit to families that had no other recourse. "What can be done?" he would ask Mom, trying to persuade himself. So he usually ended by continuing to extend credit to families that realistically had no way of repaying him.

On Pearl Harbor Day in 1969, I received a call informing me that Dad had suddenly become ill. I drove from Austin to Edinburg in my old Volkswagen, crying a good part of the way, thinking, what would happen to the family if he died? He had never been sick a single day in his life, other than an occasional winter cold. I did not know then that by the time I was called he had already died. My brother had simply said, "Marco, you better come home." I had heard my mother crying both on the telephone and in the background. I was twenty-one. I had been keeping the accounts of the store since I was sixteen. And, during the summer, after I finished my senior year at the University of Texas, I counted six uncollectible debts of over three thousand dollars apiece, and about thirty other debts from people who owed my father anywhere from two or three hundred dollars to one or two thousand. As the store's accountant, I went out a few times to collect these debts, but I was never able to collect any of them. After my father's death, the debtors simply disappeared.

Within a year or thereabouts after the appearance of the Urban Renewal sign, the bulldozers came to life. By then all the families had sold and moved out. Some had talked of not ever moving, as I have said, but in the end the rhetoric of progress and improvement was linked too well with the idea of Urban Renewal, and fighting it died down. My friends moved all over town, and only one, possibly two families, it still seems to me, improved their lots. The rest very much landed in similar quarters. The irremediable, unalterable upshot was that our whole way of life was changed, leaving us without the family and land connections that often anchor people.

The experience, in effect, dramatically marked the end of my childhood, though I did not recognize it for that until years later. After people left and moved away, the empty houses in the neighborhood gave me an eerie vacant feeling. Nothing is as disquieting after people have left as walking about quietly and alone in a place that has previously been associated with many human sounds. There had always been the expectation that something was in the offing, that something was happening or was about to happen in the neighborhood. I remember this period in my life as constituting an early, surprising loss, a dislocation ironically not relieved by the sense that something better would materialize. What replaced our barrio was a suburban-like park, a park with green grass that erased everything that had been there before. The iron bulls, indeed, had wrought a visual transformation; they had leveled the uneven dry ground of my childhood, taking with it the first twenty years that I remember in South Texas.

I have heard that everything looks unnaturally large and significant to a child, that the adult sees everything differently, usually in smaller dimensions. Perhaps it is only as children that we see things as they truly are. As adults we become more calloused, and we notice less, sometimes not even seeing what is truly before us. In childhood, though, most things are still new, exciting, and therefore engaging, regardless of how people and things shape us up the road. After those heady years I learned to take most things in stride, as the cliché has it, but in childhood the events to which adults adjust, the realities that once carried so much importance continue to cast an influence on many of our thoughts and actions. Or so I have often thought.

Three years after the Urban Renewal sign appeared, in place of the neighborhood I have sought to describe, I could look from the window of the back upstairs grocery store office where I kept the accounting books and see a leveled green-grassed block awaiting a new fate. Everyone had sold their belongings—most losing, a few gaining—and all the houses had been disassembled with hammers and crowbars, the wooden planks carted off in trucks. I had helped some of my friends load their goods into borrowed cars and pick-ups. The better wood was sold or auctioned, and the rest given away for firewood. By the time I was fifteen or sixteen, I could be found with other teenagers playing basketball on a new concrete court with iron hoop nets. All around the court, covering the entire block, was newly planted grass, a marvel to behold, when one remembered our old bare-ground, dusty barrio.

The grocery store building served as a Boy Scout meeting place for a good ten or twelve years after we sold the place in 1970, and eventually it fell into disrepair. When I drove by while visiting from my first year in graduate school at Buffalo, it had been torn down. Rather unceremoniously, I said to myself, after the store and house had lent so much meaning to so many lives. A few years later, even the slab where Dad's store had once stood was broken into pieces by sledgehammers and power machines and carted away. It had all seemed so unalterably permanent to me. The pleasant, comfortable house where my brother and I had been raised by our caring parents survived a few years more, growing sadder and sadder in shape every time I saw it, until, finally, one day when I returned one more time, it was gone. It had been torn down.

I cannot think of our home in Edinburg without thinking of the Valley's people, without thinking of the area's economic depression that our own life struggled against so well while I was growing up. The park created by

Urban Renewal that now covers the property has become, to my way of trying to see things differently, one of Edinburg's little, uncelebrated jewels. The last time I saw it, there were several benches for picnics, swings for the children to play on, and a number of trees, two of which we used to climb when the old neighborhood existed. In one of those trees, we built our tree house. While constructing it, Manito, who was holding a big carton against the tree about twelve feet above the ground, was completely taken by surprise. When he turned to ask where he should nail it to the tree, a strong wind picked up, and before he knew it, he was sailing through the air. He did not let go of the carton box, though. He landed half-stunned on the ground, smiling, still intact. The rest of us could not stop laughing and telling the story to everyone we met, except, of course, our parents, who never found out. Everything in one way or another sails through the air like that, including the certainties that many of us cherish. Today, newcomers arriving at West Side Park in Edinburg will find a nice, quiet place to visit and relax. If you have a disposition like mine, you may even want to imagine this place as it was before it was developed and improved.

2

South Padre, Isla del Padre Ballí

S aturday morning and the mail truck pulls up to the mailbox with the day's delivery. I decide to approach the mailman to take the mail myself. Good morning. 'Morning. Among the items, a brochure advertises South Padre Island on the Texas Gulf Coast. It contains a wonderful-looking panoramic picture of the South Texas gulf waves washing up on a beach in the foreground with about fifteen high-rise hotels and condominiums in the background. The picture was taken about six thirty in the evening, judging from the rays of the sun. At that time the beach water is warm and actually fabulous. The day's glare has disappeared, the seagulls are flying about looking for the day's last meal, and the warm sand can be made to squish delightfully through one's toes. Yes, it would be great to be there, once more, I say to myself, with the evening sun reflecting a pinkish glow on the white, foamy waves that wash up against the beach.

In the early 1960s, and before any of the high-rise hotels and other developments made South Padre a vacation destination, life was different. Everyone knew South Padre Island as *La Isla del Padre,* the Island of the Priest. That was the name I heard when we were growing up. A Catholic priest had once owned the island, Father Ballí. El Padre Nicolás Ballí was one of three brothers who inherited a large tract of land from his mother Doña Maria Hinojosa de Ballí, who, in turn, had several land grants that her husband received from the King of Spain in the late eighteenth century.

According to Florence Johnson Scott's *Royal Land Grants North of the Rio Grande, 1777-1821* (Rio Grande City: Texian Press, distributed by La Retama Press, 1969), Doña Rosa Maria's name "is connected with the history of seven Spanish grants—*Llano Grande, La Feria, Las Mesteñas, Ojo de Agua* and *El Melado, San Salvador del Tule,* and *Padre Island*" (x). One of the grants extended from Edinburg to the present-day site of San Manuel, which is roughly about twenty miles. The last one listed, *Padre Island,* was La Isla del Padre. El Padre Ballí was one of several enabling ancestors whose August 6, 1828, will left large parcels of land that he both inherited and bought from two brothers and others. The recipients of this land are the large Ballí family that today numbers more than eight hundred members who live throughout the United States, from Texas to Michigan, and from California to Illinois and Florida.

Instead of summarizing events myself, a Monday, July 14, 1997, front page story written by Sam Howe Verhovek for the *New York Times* informed us that:

> In the early 1800s, Mr. [José Manuel] Ballí [Villarreal] was given a land grant by the King of Spain to a large tract in South Texas when it was part of the Spanish empire. The [Ballí] clan descended from Mr. Ballí and his wife, María Antonia Cavazos de Hinojosa, asserts that the land was ultimately stolen by Mifflin Kenedy, one of Texas's most powerful ranchers, who built a cattle empire across the area and whose own descendants later became fabulously wealthy from both the cattle and the oil and gas on the property. The Ballís are now asking for tens of millions of dollars, maybe much more, in compensation.
>
> At its core, the issue turns on an interpretation of history: Were the great Texas ranchers like Mr. Kenedy and Richard King, of the fabled King Ranch, visionary figures who tamed a wasteland with honor and grit, or were they Anglo land grabbers who used trickery and violence to rob Mexicans of their property?
>
> And, as scholars watch with fascination as the case unfolds, many say that the fact that the lawsuit has even advanced in the courts speaks volumes about the changing demographics of the region and the ways in which American history is revised from generation to generation.

Lynne Perez, a San Antonio historian and genealogist retained by the Ballí family to investigate their old land claims, said that, "Years ago, no Mexican-American family could have gone into court and demanded justice from the white establishment." But times have changed, says Don Carleton, director of the Center for American History at the University of Texas at Austin: "Hispanic-Americans in this country have a lot more political power, and this is what happens when you get political power in a democratic society." Richard Leshin, the Corpus Christi lawyer who represents the Kenedy Foundation, which is a charitable trust with assets derived from Mr. Kenedy's wealth, expresses the view that "the very principle being invoked by the Ballís could open up a Pandora's box of legal problems across the state." When interviewed, he said that:

The opportunity to attack the legal title system based on assertions about events that occurred centuries ago could cause strong disruption to the ownership of properties throughout the state of Texas.

Not so, say the Ballís, who contend that they never abandoned the land and who note that various efforts have been made by clan descendants over the years to get land back, including an effort in the 1950's to reclaim much of Padre Island, on the Gulf Coast. The bid was thrown out by a state court.

The land in question consists of "about two million acres in nine present-day counties" in South Texas. But, since Latino students of history are still engaged in doing the research, as we see, I did not know this part of the story of La Isla del Padre when I visited the island as a child.

I think I have sufficiently suggested that Mexican Americans have a long presence that is continually being revised as new information emerges. This is why the social realities of Latinos today hinge so much on the political realities that over time have shaped decisions. An August 9, 2000, Associated Press story by Megan K. Stack read as follows:

"Brownsville—A New York lawyer who swindled a Mexican American family out of decades' worth of Padre Island oil profits is worth a least $68.3 million.

The financial records of Gilbert Kerlin, 90, were displayed for an all-Hispanic jury Tuesday as the historical battle over Padre Island moved to the next phase.

The jury last week agreed that Kerlin has been cheating the heirs to Padre Island ever since he bought their title in 1938. Kerlin agreed to share any oil profits with the Ballís—but he never paid.

The jury will now decide how much money Kerlin should give the family to make up for decades of fraud and conspiracy. The 300 heirs have asked for about $11 million."

One other paragraph of Ms. Stack's article warrants attention: "Kerlin studied in Cambridge and Paris before earning a law degree from Harvard, [Ballí attorney Britton D.] Monts told the jury. The Ballís, meanwhile, were struggling to learn English and pull themselves out of poverty."

After considering the issue, the jury decided not to award any money to the three hundred Ballí family members who had filed the lawsuit. Family members generously stated that finding for the Ballís, after such a long litigation process, was enough vindication. Perhaps that is one reason why we do not have many Latino families with sufficient resources to be philanthropists.

Around 1964 or 1965, my father was approached one day by an Anglo real estate man selling beachfront property on Padre Island. I remember my mother coming up from the back of the store where our house was located to *el monstrador,* the cashier's area at the entrance of the store, with her daily three o'clock cup of *café con leche* for my dad. I was a sophomore or a junior at Edinburg High School, and, when I could, I also worked in the grocery store, sacking groceries and stocking the shelves with merchandise. I had also been keeping the store's accounting records for a number of years, or at least records of the wholesale merchandise brought in from H&H Meats in Mercedes, and a number of other wholesale businesses from Weslaco, McAllen, and Mission. I was charged by my father with keeping records of the transactions for the store accounts. I had been stamping and stocking canned goods in the shelves of the store, as I did during the hottest hours of the day when business was slow. My tired father was desultorily looking alternately at the shaded passageway that led to his well-deserved nap at the back of the house, and at the four large ten-by-eight-feet clear glass windows of the store that faced north.

In 1961, Hurricane Carla blew out the northeastern window of the grocery store. The force of the wind carried that window past my father, barely missing his head. The strength of the wind-driven rain took the entire very large pane all the way through the store, knocking food cans and carrying it above the four-foot stands of the products we sold, hurling it against a back wooden wall that finally shattered the glass into a thousand pieces. That catastrophe was followed by gallons of horizontal rain pouring in under a roof extension overhang that stretched a good twelve feet over the front concrete sidewalk entrance to the store. Later, we swept and mopped the entire store, but we continued to find tiny pieces of glass well past the event. In 1983, while living with my own family in Taylor Lake Village, which is south of Houston, Hurricane Alicia also wreaked havoc, this time to the northern part of the coast, causing $2.1 billion worth of damage. These hurricanes, experienced by most people who have lived long enough along the Texas Gulf Coast, can easily compete against the tornadoes that beset other parts of the country. I mention these two category 5 hurricanes because such super storms tend to start during the summers in the Caribbean and the Atlantic often bringing the Texas Gulf Coast into the national weather news. Since the advent of air conditioning in the late 1940s and 50s, though, Texas has nevertheless become a very popular state in which to live, as the nearly 21 million residents attest.

When I was old enough, the job of keeping our large grocery store windows clean became part of my responsibilities. I used Bon Ami soap diluted with water to wash them, and Dad taught me to use newspapers to wipe the windows clean. Nothing cleans glass as well as newspapers. I do not recall paper towels being as ubiquitous as they are today. We certainly did not stock them in the store, for who among our barrio customers would have had enough money from working in the fields picking crops to afford the luxury of buying paper towels? When I cleaned the windows I always carried a one-sided Gillette shaving blade to wipe off the particularly stubborn debris that the Bon Ami solution and the newspaper could not remove. Those were the days before tinted window glass, though it was about that time that new cars started to arrive from Detroit with a little strip of tinted glass across the front windshields; everyone thought that was the epitome of cool. Becoming "cool," indeed, was becoming the name of the American game, and Elvis Presley appealed to Mexican Americans because his hairstyle dovetailed nicely with the slick, male Mexican American hair fads fashionable then. Those were some of the popular culture things that I thought about when I was not reading the forty-eight assorted semi-monthly comics that arrived at our store. The building was rectangular, and the hot South Texas sun's light came in through eight high windows on each side. Daily we opened those windows with a long pole, letting out the hot air of the previous day, hoping that a little breath of a breeze would periodically blow through, cooling us, soothing us.

As Mom placed the steaming coffee next to him, my father told us that the man who had just left had tried to sell him land—*arena,* he said, that is, sand—in La Isla del Padre. I do not specifically recall how much my father said the man wanted per acre, but I do remember that he had been offered a parcel of several acres of land very cheaply, somewhere in the neighborhood of five dollars an acre. My father said the salesman had tried hard to get him to buy some beachfront property. And my dad did not immediately reject the idea, but finally he decided against it, reasoning that there were very few people on the island. At most, there were a handful of businesses, and he did not want to start paying taxes for "arena." He did not see much of a future in sand. Now, the offer may have been legitimate or it may have been a scam. What few people must have known at that point was that developers within the decade would start moving in and buying land cheaply, land that people like my father had turned down. At the time, my father and I did not know about the Ballí claim, so that disagreement was not an issue. What I have since believed, until I saw the contested South Padre lawsuit story in the *New York Times,* is that we should have bought and held the land, as it were, until the tourist business caught on, as the desire to own Padre Island land has since ballooned.

Today there are a number of hotels, eateries, and accompanying stop-and-shop places where once there was nothing but the hot sand, sand dunes, and beach life and vegetation for miles and miles. One large hotel, from a certain distance on both the water and from the shore, is shaped to look like a giant cowboy boot, an appropriate symbol for a Texas beach. But, if we know a little of the history of that place, after awhile the boot begins to have the type of meaning that T. R. Fehrenbach wrote about in his book, *Lone Star: A History of Texas and the Texans* (American Legacy Press, 1983). Verhovek presents Fehrenbach's interpretation in the following way:

> By 1848, with the United States having annexed Texas and defeated Mexico in yet another war, the Treaty of Guadalupe Hidalgo "confirmed all Mexican land titles in principle but could not guarantee them in practice," Mr. Fehrenbach notes. "A horde of American businessmen, squatters and ex-soldiers arrived," he added, many with various types of claims to the land. In subsequent years, many of the large ranching families consolidated their holdings, including Mr. Kenedy and Mr. King, for a period. And for decades, the dominant version of Texas history had the two and other ranchers fighting a valiant effort to claim the land and ward off the advances of cattle rustlers, many of whom were Mexican.

I suspect this is why the Mexican people and their descendants have generally been characterized in the United States as bandidos. That was certainly the way Gregorio Cortez was unfairly stigmatized in 1901, why untrustworthy workers supposedly have to be watched and supervised by, of course, the naturally more superior and upright Anglos, yes? Some readers may think that I exaggerate. But I only wish to point out that Latinos are often treated unfairly because in the United States they are suspected of being less trustworthy and dependable than Anglos. Reality, to be sure, has a way of reiterating perceptions and inclinations. Certainly, though, education, ethics, and morality should make all of us better people.

3

Largest Texas Shrine

La Virgen de San Juan del Valle

The Shrine of *La Virgen de San Juan del Valle* is the largest and most impressive church in Texas. There are other beautiful churches in Houston, Dallas, Corpus Christi, and Galveston, to name the sites of some better-known places of worship, but the Shrine of La Virgen de San Juan del Valle easily has the most uncommon history. After the untimely demise of its predecessor on October 23, 1970, years of heartbreak led to the construction of the third and present shrine. When the current church was dedicated in San Juan, Texas, on April 19, 1980, roughly fifty thousand people attended. My cousin Lupita, who now teaches elementary school in my hometown of Edinburg, told me that television news anchors flew into the airports of McAllen, Harlingen, and Brownsville from New York, Washington, Chicago, and Los Angeles. The Shrine of La Virgen de San Juan del Valle received nationwide media attention. The newspapers and television news programs carried the story of the infamous attack, bringing out how the new shrine had been constructed next to the ashes of the burnt one that is still visible about two blocks away. But that ephemeral one-day fame failed to leave a lasting imprint on the visitors, for the hoopla did not distract for long the attention of the people who truly venerate *la Virgencita*. Sometimes when occasion allows, I drive out to that neighborhood to stand on the church grounds in the late afternoon to wait for the early evening stars. When the sun finishes the day, dogs barking nearby have usually broken the connection that I have sought to establish with the past on these infrequent occasions. But the surrounding human sounds from the poor barrios help me remember with warm regard the courageous ongoing story of the people who built the shrine with their undying faith, hard work, and love and devotion to La Virgen, partly reminding people of La Virgen de Guadalupe in Mexico City.

When the current church was dedicated nearly a quarter-century ago, I was already teaching in the suburbs of Houston, with four years of graduate school in western New York and five years as a faculty member in California behind me. On that day in 1980, the opening of the new shrine in the Valley was featured on newscasts and headlines nationwide. But, having reported the news, the top names in the media who flew into the Valley for the event quickly returned to the country's old commercial centers, soon forgetting the admirable people who had put their sweat and money into building the church. Aside from the parishioners who regularly attend services and who financially support the Shrine of La Virgen de San Juan del Valle, few people today appear to know or remember its history. Yet, this Shrine is the most marvelous late-twentieth-century testament to the exhilarating, enduring faith of the poorest migrant Mexican Americans and Mexican immigrants who have long lived in the southernmost part of the United States.

I recall when I was five or six years old being taken by my parents on some Sunday afternoons to a wooden-floored, wooden-walled, stultifyingly hot church located in the small town of San Juan, Texas. San Juan is sandwiched between two other small Valley towns, Pharr and Alamo, a fact that caused the Bears football team from the area's high school to use the acronym PSJA. Today the inhabitants have other teams, I understand, but then, the only way the three little towns could sport a respectable football squad was to team up together against the larger neighboring towns of McAllen, Edinburg, Mission, Donna, and Mercedes. Ordinarily we went to Mass at Sacred Heart Church in my hometown of Edinburg, as I previously said. But several times a year, my parents would take my brother and me for what seemed like an endless car ride—endless to a pair of young boys who did not want to travel in a hot car during the days when no air conditioners were available in automobiles. The trip to San Juan, in our open-windowed, light blue tinted 1954 Chevrolet, was trial by excessive heat. That Chevy was the only car I remember that our father bought new. Two later automobiles were used cars, meaning that the fortunes of our family progressively declined as my brother and I moved through the grades of Sacred Heart School.

But, in 1954, seven years after our parents' wedding, business was still good at the grocery store, allowing my father to pay cash for the great car with the small tail fins that the 1957 Chevys featured. At the time, during Eisenhower's first term, he paid about two thousand dollars for that new car. Those were the years when the green-card bracero migrant program was still in full swing, because enlightened legislators, unlike those in Congress today, saw that such an arrangement was good business for people on both sides of the Rio Grande. Today, the Immigration and Naturalization Service, known locally as the Border Patrol, has changed life along the border, making almost everything considerably more difficult for most people in South Texas.

San Juan was only about ten miles from Edinburg, but after what seemed like an interminably long trip, my mother, father, brother, and I would eventually arrive, hot and unbelievably irritated by the midday heat. For some reason, two o'clock in the afternoon is the hour that I associate with that trip and those visits, though we likely attended Mass at four or five. Most of the time our family went to Mass at six o'clock on Sunday mornings, though other services were available at seven, nine, ten thirty, and noon. We went to the 6 a.m. Mass because, even though it was Sunday, Dad opened his store at seven, as he did every other day of the week. He did so because neighbors and customers would opportune him at home, seldom allowing him to rest. So, to reduce breakfast-time traffic one Sunday morning, in exasperation, when I must have been a baby, he opened the store, and that is what he continued to do every Sunday morning thereafter.

He could not escape because our house was located directly behind the grocery store. Although he half-owned it, he operated and managed it himself, so that even when we had clearly closed the store, neighbors felt that my father was available for their needs. My father, Toribio, was such a nice and generous man that he never wanted to turn down a person who needed a quart of milk or a loaf of bread for sandwiches. Because he parked our car in the store's garage or under a chinaberry tree next to a strip of grass by the house, everybody could see whether he was at home or not.

Customers would come around to either side of the house and the good man invariably dropped whatever he was doing to help. He crossed a little sidewalk that led to a *cuarto de tela,* a screened, concrete-floored twelve by ten partially covered room that doubled as a recreation and clothes-washing area, which led, in turn, to the back door of the store. He returned with milk, bread, eggs, and whatever other essentials customers requested. Then, of course, there was the matter of paying for the goods, and then having the proper change. To resolve the logistics of these complications, my father finally made that fateful decision to open the store on Sunday mornings. After he closed at noon, we usually ate a nice juicy steak, which Dad cut and prepared for the family from the meats he sold at the store. Our family was spoiled in that regard. We were what I would have called solidly middle class, but none of us knew enough to state the issue as such. So life went on in its own carefree way with some of the little frustrations that were not as earthshaking as they sometimes seemed to a young Mexican American boy who then believed he was as American as anybody else, as the schools taught.

Actually, families that shopped in the store barely eked out a living, and the business eventually started to fail because my father was not connected to the Anglo men who ran the Chamber of Commerce, for reasons that were never articulated by anyone. Also, if there ever was a compassionate man, Dad was that. He could not see people suffering, especially when he had some resources, so he kindly extended more credit to people than he should have. Having been quite poor when he was growing up himself, he was constitutionally incapable of saying no to families who needed food and who did not have money to pay for their basic necessities. Consequently, he drew no set salary from the store. His modest income was taken strictly for the needs of the family. Because sometimes the people to whom he extended credit did not pay, he was left in the position of being unable in turn to pay wholesalers who provided goods for the store. Much of his adult life was spent worrying about income for the store and our family. My brother and I were unaware of these anxieties, and it was only later Mom revealed that what we assumed was a good, reliably steady livelihood was in fact only touch-and-go existence. Our parents very successfully sheltered us, in short allowing us to think we were quite well off.

On certain Sundays after lunch, after a quick half-hour nap and before people came around to the house to ask for goods, we drove off to McAllen to the movies. Or we went to visit Dad's mother, the family of one of his brothers, or, to my dismay at the time, one of the Catholic churches in the Valley. Sunday afternoon was the only time my father did not work in the store. When he took us to the cinema, generally to El Rey in McAllen, which was seven miles away, the real attraction was not so much the particular Mexican film that was showing but the air conditioner. The movie house was the coolest place that our family knew. Once inside, I ate luscious hot dogs with mustard and relish, while my brother preferred popcorn and candies. We washed everything down our hot throats with a cool orange drink that was so unspeakably refreshing that even now regular orange juice pales by comparison. Every once in a while we would do something different, like drive over to Pharr, perhaps for supper, or across the border to Mexico, to Reynosa, or, to what my brother and I then considered the worst place in the world, extremely poor San Juan.

I could write about any one of these Sunday family car rides, trips that for many years were etched into my consciousness. But I choose to sketch my San Juan memories mainly because I have since completely changed my view of this landmark place in the Valley. I associate San Juan indelibly, as I have suggested, with the worse kind of insufferable heat imaginable. But to go there today, to the third church constructed for the Shrine of La Virgen de San Juan del Valle is to invite a complete surprise. A visitor, I believe, will be stunned by the sheer unexpected size of the shrine. The church appears to rise out of the surrounding agricultural fields. It is a spacious church that can be seen from the one freeway that traverses what metaphorically is the spine of the Valley, from Brownsville, at the southern tip of Texas to Rio Grande City along the river westward, and then north, turning in Pharr. San Juan itself has grown little since I was a boy, bottled up or flanked, as I said, between Alamo and Pharr. In many ways the tempo and the people that one sees have not noticeably changed either, but what has changed remarkably is the shrine itself.

The little wooden-floored church that I first knew—the one before the Most Reverend Mariano S. Garriga, the Bishop of Corpus Christi, dedicated the second splendidly built marbled church on May 2, 1954—only had about fifteen rows of pews, each seating about ten people on either side of the center aisle. There were two large fans up front, partially facing the priests as well as the parishioners, next to the door from which the priest and his two altar boys emerged when Mass began. The church was a veritable hot-house, and as soon as my mother said we were going to San Juan, my brother and I bucked and remonstrated, but it was no use. We knew we had to choose our coolest clothes. Everybody perspired there; everybody had to have either a hand fan or a handkerchief, and one of the sights that kept my attention, I remember, was to see people fanning themselves to cool off while the fans circulated hot air through the congregation and the priest droned on and on. It was purgatory for us, and Mom told us to offer our sacrifice as penance for our sins and the sins of others. There were two priests, if I recall correctly, and they both liked to speak, oblivious, it clearly seemed to me, of the faithful who unsuccessfully squirmed and otherwise signaled to the priests that enough was enough.

The priests were both committed to a dream, to the idea of building a new church in this unlikely place. Following a homily, the priests invariably mentioned, almost every time we were in San Juan, that some day the congregation would build a church for La Virgen de San Juan. "And it is going to be a big, beautiful church, for it will be built by love. God's mother deserves nothing less," they would say. It was a dream, and, even at five or six years of age, I used to look around and wonder what sort of church could be built by these poor people who were sweating and praying the rosary, everything being communicated, of course, in Spanish. Most of them were not farmers. They were the people who picked the fields—cotton, melons, oranges, grapefruits, whatever was in season. They were the kind to whom I know even my generous dad would have been concerned about extending credit. Yet these are the ones who tended to turn to my father when they could not work, when they did not get paid on time, the ones Dad helped support when their families would otherwise have gone hungry. The majority of the migrant workers were people who yearly nailed up the windows and doors of their wooden two- or three-room shacks with two by four planks before going off to Michigan, Idaho, Kansas, and California to harvest crops wherever farm hands were being hired. Tomás Rivera wrote about crop-pickers like the ones I am describing in his novel, . . . *y no se lo tragó la tierra*, which he translated into . . . *And the Earth Did Not Devour Him*. Quinto Sol Publications published Rivera's work in 1971 because it won the Quinto Sol Award for the first and best Chicano novel.

Everyone who attended those services, however, regardless of background or way of life, whether middle-class Mexican American pillars of the community or the poorest of the poor, believed in the priests. Everyone wanted a new church, especially my brother and me. Indeed, we all hoped the new church would be a better, cooler place than the oven we knew so well. I remember my parents used to say that the parishioners in San Juan sacrificed to save money for the dream church that the priests envisioned. Our own priests in Edinburg used to encourage us to contribute to our church, too, but in San Juan the nature of the devotion was different. When one is a child one notices and pays more attention to things, to particulars, than when one becomes an adult. I have found that as an adult I pay less attention to the world around, I suspect because I, like others, believe I have seen it all. Little surprises us; we have made categories for everything. Often, for that reason, we wind up dismissing what should wake us up, what should tell us that we are experiencing something different. What I used to see as a child when the baskets for contributions were passed before me is that the people in the pews took out more money and contributed more in San Juan than I saw in the other churches we attended. That was certainly the case with my own father, even though he was not from San Juan. My guess now is that he, too, like other visitors, must have felt that he had to help the poor people of San Juan, and in turn the big communal effort led by the priests to realize a people's dream for La Virgen de San Juan.

Following visits once every three or four Sundays, after what felt like many years of collecting donations, the announcement was finally made that there was now enough money to begin the church. The news was greeted with great excitement, with Masses of thanksgiving and jubilation, which, of course, brought in more money from the hard-working migrants who worked all across the agricultural fields of the United States. My sense at the time was that the priests were going to build another church like the ones that we had in Edinburg or McAllen, which were the centers of civilization, as we knew the world. So we continued periodically to attend Mass at the little wooden San Juan church even while construction for the new church was underway. I do not now recall, nor have I been able to learn, how long it took to build that second amazingly beautiful church.

Few visiting parishioners, I believe, expected to see the church that the people of San Juan eventually erected. In little San Juan, which, as I have said, is among the poorest towns in the Rio Grande Valley, those two priests succeeded in building the grandest, the most magnificent church that I ever saw until years later when I saw St. Paul's Cathedral in London. It was the most ornate, the most beautifully constructed church imaginable. Expert craftsmen were brought in to do all the finishing, inside work, and the result was like something we had never seen or dreamt. Large oil-based frescoes were painted into the alcoves and naves of the church. The central one, I clearly remember, represented God in the act of creating the universe, with the stars, and the sun and the moon, emerging out of a dark blue nothingness that served as the sky, out of the vast void according to Genesis. The biggest and the most dramatic, though, was the fresco painted over to the right side of church. This one captured a displeased God and an angel hurrying out a shamed Adam and Eve from the Garden of Eden. Behind them was the well-known Tree of Life, with the serpent partially intertwined around it, flicking its tongue at our ancestral parents as they were being ordered out of Paradise. For a young boy, that fresco, wonderfully painted so hauntingly large on the whole inside wall of the church in San Juan, was the subject of endless fascination regarding the rewards for obeying God and the punishments of hell for disobedience. Over to the side, on another panel, we could see the souls writhing in hell from the pain and the torment. Did not Christ inform us that there is a heaven in his Our Father prayer, for those who doubt? Can anyone point to a single instance when Christ failed to do right? He was always, always good, setting the example for the rest of us, who try, but unfortunately suffer periodic lapses.

The reality that shaped that wonderful church had been different. I would never have been able to imagine such a gorgeous-looking church from the matter-of-fact way the priests talked on and on while the fan droned endlessly and the poor people fanned themselves and patted their faces with their well-worn white or red handkerchiefs. Yet when the church was completed, instead of offering congregations sweat-streaming afternoons, San Juan immediately became associated in all of our minds with an extremely cool, air-conditioned afternoon. For, as if to make up for all of those other intolerably hot afternoons, the huge air conditioners in the new Shrine of La Virgen de San Juan kept the rooms so cold that women in particular took to wearing sweaters to church in the middle of summer.

It was such an awe-inspiring church that I have not been able to secure the correct words to describe it adequately. Being in the church made me feel serene and at peace with the world and myself as little else has since. One could feel God's mighty presence, and in my child's mind I somehow connected it to the quiet power of that great air-conditioning system, confidently maintaining the majesty and the coolness of the great church, which held people seriously and quietly engaged in prayer. I loved that church because when people were first introduced to it almost everyone automatically was struck by the grandeur of its size, proportion, and beauty. Its golden-laced altar prompted awe and reverence, making me increasingly aware of the indescribable meaning of the respect that the poorest people I knew had for La Virgen de San Juan.

That church marked in many ways my continuing appreciation for Catholic teachings, as well as, later, my falling away from religion during some of my college years. I have long since regretted a falling away that my mother always mentioned to me in the form of St. Augustine's life and how St. Monica, his mother, prayed him back. After I also personally defeated the misguided ideas that had deluded me into thinking that I could rationalize the teachings of being a Catholic better than the church itself, I matured and have been in the church since. In early adulthood, I thus began anew to appreciate what I had been taught as a child, what I used to take for granted, what I found out I did not appropriately value, despite how my parents had correctly raised me. Clearly I knew less when I was learning about the rest of American culture than when I was growing up, it is so easy to be sidetracked by the ways of the world.

Sixteen years after those unforgettably hot services ended in the wooden-floored church, the new dream shrine was suddenly catastrophically destroyed one Sunday afternoon. A suicidal Anglo-American pilot deliberately crashed his airplane into the church. He was convinced that Mexican Americans are poor because the church takes their money. The story that people told and repeated was that the pilot had been known to say he blamed the church for the plight of *la raza,* and that he got into his plane drunk. My sense is that any Mexican American who believes that about the church has, in effect left it. But the great majority of raza people continue to see the church and religion not as the opium of the masses, as Marx said, but as one of the few spiritual institutions that still provide solace, respite, consolation, and salvation for people less heeded by the world. The result was that the beautifully golden-laced shrine that so wonderfully embodied the dreams, sweat, and hard work of many faithful parishioners was completely demolished the instant the plane hit. Everything in the entire church was engulfed in a ball of flames; fire and black smoke visibly billowed for miles during the next few days.

The awful, indescribable destruction was communicated by a press that did not fully understand how hard the priests and the people had worked for a church that would be a fit home for La Virgen de San Juan. News accounts mentioned that the church meant so much to so many people, followed by some facts about its history. Despite the total devastation caused by the crashing impact of the plane against the roof of the church, miraculously no one on the ground was hurt. One of the priests risked his life by going into the burning church, snatching the statue of La Virgen, and successfully carrying it outside to safety. My own cousin Lupita, who was beginning her career as an elementary school teacher of Chicanitos, had just taken her Sunday catechism class out of the church into the adjoining building when the plane hit. That saved them. Besides the foundation, the only part of the church that survived the attack was the bell tower. Everything else, including the wonderful irreplaceable frescoes that were so much a part of my childhood, went up in smoke. The rubble that was left of the rest of that magnificent church, excluding the adjacent parish hall, was subsequently razed.

Recently I walked on the grounds of the church's stone foundation that once supported a beautiful marble floor. The whole rectangular measure is now exposed to the open air, accompanied only by the lone tower that stands off toward the back where the church entrance was. The artfully ornate walls that showcased the work of so many fine artisans that painted those beautiful Michelangelo-like Garden of Eden frescos on the walls of the shrine are gone, never to be seen again. Where once I remember paintings with wonderful details about the classical biblical stories, now there are only sky and trees.

As a visitor approaches San Juan from the freeway during the day, the new, larger shrine can be espied from afar. Around the colossal building the fourteen stations of the cross, each having its own space on the expansive grounds, soon become visible. Directly behind and to the south the old tower stands alone against the sky. What was once the most beautiful church in the Valley has not been totally demolished, for the remnants of that great effort by the poorest people of the United States can today be visited. Standing on the grounds of the present shrine, people can see, behind and over to one side, the old lone tower, within walking distance of the new, third Shrine to La Virgen de San Juan. At night the grounds of the new church and the shrine itself are lit from all sides. From the freeway and from anywhere that one may be in the vicinity, eyes are naturally drawn to the bigger shrine. The other tower, sole representative for some of us who fortunately experienced that first magnificent dream, know it is out there, in the dark, a solitary sentinel of a story that most people have since forgotten. That solitary, dark tower will always express the faith and the dreams of the poor Mexican American people of little San Juan and the surrounding communities. Aside from the plethora of miracles to which there are ample testaments within a special room off to the left side of the new shrine, there is one great consolation for me. Although I do not know about the weekdays, on weekends every Mass in the Shrine of La Virgen de San Juan del Valle is a Mariachi Mass. Sung by mariachi musicians and singers, Masses at the shrine offer one of the most memorable religious services available anywhere in the world today. Readers, consider taking a trip to see the shrine, for I cannot adequately describe the experience of a visit!

4

The Texas State Aquarium
in Corpus Christi

Corpus Christi is the first geographic urban promontory that people driving north from South Texas encounter. It is also one of the nicest large Texas cities on the Gulf of Mexico. I find Corpus Christi noteworthy because it is the site of the Texas State Aquarium and of a great marble and stone cathedral in the downtown area, which has been associated with this seaport resort since the 1930s. The cathedral has twelve columns that stand like sentinels symbolically posted around a centrally located sanctuary that looks out toward the east. At midmorning, a long blindingly white concrete fence can be espied sloping toward the downtown section of the city and the water, all partially protected by a three- or four-mile series of gray concrete steps. From that standpoint, Corpus Christi Bay shimmers before the visitor's eye. Invariably visitors are surprised by the sea's beauty, a luminous sight that usually is transmogrified only when the clouds and the wind join forces to dim the brightness of the Gulf, graying the world. That place always raises spirits, regardless of the mood that drives people to this unheralded splendid city on the Texas coast.

When I was growing up, Corpus Christi was our primary summer vacation destination. It was more than a three-hour drive from Edinburg in South Texas, and even though we slept most of the way, the drive was always rewarding. The trip measured 144 miles, part of the journey consisting of driving on a highway that to this day divides the King Ranch, reputedly the second largest ranch in the world after one in Hawaii. Today, when the previous day's concerns occasionally wake me at three or four in the morning, I still like to dream of the waves and the warm moist sand under my bare feet on the beach in the early morning. For me, there isn't a more inviting way to regain sleep.

Corpus Christi was the end of many Mexican American dreams. Like many Latinos from our generation, I believed it fulfilled or met most of my life's fantasies about the good life in the United States. When I was a kid my parents did not allow us to worry about the future. The future was out there, somewhere safely removed and beyond the present. What counted was the present, the next pleasure, the next adventure on a family's agenda. So long as school assignments and duties were successfully met during the year, the long three months of the summer beckoned us, enticingly. Not that we ever spent more than a week in Corpus, but we lived much of the nine months of the school year anticipating that one week.

The only bother that put a bit of a crimp in our vacations was that our mother always required my brother and me, and Dad, to visit the cathedral whenever we went to Corpus. Her point of view was that vacations were the time to be particularly thankful. Every morning, while we were in the big, bright city by the sea, and before we did anything else, we visited the great cathedral. We had to thank God for giving our family a steady, reliable living, the high point of which was our wonderful yearly vacation week in Corpus.

As time passed, I went about the business of living, of creating a life, as most of us do. After my teenage years, I actually forgot about Corpus Christi, which requires a traveler on the South Texas highways to turn east toward the Gulf, instead of naturally following Highways 281 and 77 north toward San Antonio and Austin. The highways of my life in time led me toward the University of Texas in Austin, and, later, to Buffalo, and then westward to Berkeley. After more than twelve years, one day I realized I had not visited Corpus Christi my life had been so full. It was not that I had missed Corpus Christi as much as it was the fact that the rest of the world had opened so many new perspectives for my mind. My intellectual life was unfolding, the very arena that has since engaged me most.

When I returned to Texas after four years in western New York and five in the Bay Area of San Francisco, I noticed, as if for the first time, that one does not simply arrive in Corpus. One has to plan to visit the port city. So, one July in the early 1990s, Corpus hosted the grand opening of the state's aquarium, which provided me with the opportunity to revisit my old stamping ground, this time bringing my family with me. Ordinarily most cultural plums tend to go to the larger Texas cities like Dallas, Houston, or Austin. No city by the gulf, however, is as suitable for an aquarium as Corpus Christi. The bay and the Nueces River provide an enviable estuary, making the city a natural site for just about anything that Texas may want to highlight. The idea behind the Texas State Aquarium seems to have been to help put Corpus Christi on the cultural map, to invite tourists from everywhere to flock to this great and glorious exposition of all things that live in the salt waters of the Gulf of Mexico. More than a decade after its construction, the aquarium remains a great place to see. But, like the Institute of Texan Cultures that was earlier established by the state legislature sometime in the early 1960s in connection with San Antonio's Hemisphere, neither exhibit seems to have been provided with the type of ongoing resources to allow them to continue to improve their facilities and offerings.

Nonetheless, the Texas State Aquarium offers a wonder-filled world. The concept and the execution of the aquarium are superb and not duplicated anywhere else in the United States as far as I know. When entering the cool, air-conditioned locale, a visitor immediately meets a cut-off section of the Texas marshland coastline, the area where the land first meets the sea. Much of the marine life begins here, where a good number of the smallest microscopic sea creatures thrive, that is, between and actually *within* the sand granules themselves! This is a wonderfully creative way to introduce the Gulf of Mexico to visitors. That there are such small microscopic sea phytoplankton in and around the sand particles themselves; that such living matter provide the first step of the food chain for shrimp and the smallest fish, which, in turn, serve as food for larger marine life! This concept and revelation alone make a trip to the sea exhibit worthwhile. Then there are a good number of the bigger fish that are progressively found as one wades farther and farther into the Gulf of Mexico, visiting exhibit stations that include turtles, eels, cabbage and moon jellyfish, octopi, and more.

When one enters the state aquarium, there is a petting area where children and adults alike pick up hermit crabs, whelks, starfish, crabs, and other sea creatures to inspect them and to inquire into their habits from two or three student attendants. The two-and-a-half to three-hour visit offers a fabulous way to become familiar with over 125 species of fish, oil rig marine life, fish hatcheries, and turtle and shrimp spawning cycles. This experience is the best education one could devise to impress upon people the importance of cleaning up the beaches—for human and marine life. The occasional hurricanes that hit the Gulf Coast are also not minimized by the first-rate ecosystem demonstration that visitors can see.

The Texas State Aquarium has now become one of my favorite places. Located on the northern side of the bridge, its back faces the Corpus Christi Channel. When I was a boy and we traveled from Edinburg to Corpus Christi for that once-a-year vacation, everything revolved around our beach activities in that same part of the city. Once every summer, my father used to close our family grocery store, and, for one glorious, carefree week, we would rent a little efficiency apartment in Corpus Christi! The rental place was not even air conditioned, but the fan that helped move the sea breeze through the one-room kitchenette allowed us to nap peacefully after our midday cool pâté sandwiches. As part of the bonding experience that we shared after our morning water frolicking on the north side of the Corpus beach, Mom had all of us make pâté sandwiches that we later devoured when we returned from the beach starved.

We had, of course, to begin every vacation day, alas, by visiting the great marble and stone cathedral. Mom would not allow us to go anywhere until we did. My brother and I threw some fits, but, when Dad supported her, we learned to accept that requirement, and then, oddly enough, we even began to look forward to and started to like visiting the church before doing anything else, if readers can believe that. About three or four blocks north of the cathedral, Corpus Christi used to have four or five of the tallest buildings we had seen. We liked to make believe that Corpus was our New York, and, indeed, when we walked through this particular area, the buildings felt like skyscrapers, though, at most, they must have been about twenty to thirty story affairs. Two or three were hotels, and, almost since I can recall, I remember Mom telling us that she and Dad had their honeymoon in one of the hotels that sat on the same street three or four blocks from the cathedral. She always smiled when she told us how she and Dad had been married on May 28, 1947. We know because that is the day inscribed in the wedding rings she gave us. They spent several nights at that hotel, but by the time we heard the story, the place had been sold.

What used to strike me was that on arriving in Corpus Christi, my dad always drove by the hotel, as if to say hello, and then we headed straight to the cathedral. It was not until much later, when we had long stopped our yearly summer visits to Corpus that my research interests in Latinos allowed me the following conjecture. In 1947, shortly after the end of World War II, Mexican American citizens would not have been welcomed in the best hotels in town. My parents stayed three nights, I believe, and had a great honeymoon, they suggested, but in retrospect I remember that they never really spoke much about the actual details, that is, whether they ate there, how they were treated, and whether they would ever go back. Money in the late 1940s would not have been an issue for Dad, since those were the best years for his grocery store business. Later I learned that, like African Americans in the South, Mexican Americans then had to search out restaurants, hotels, and clubs and find out whether they could stay there and how they would be treated. The truth was that my parents never went back to stay; nevertheless, we would drive by the hotel every time we arrived in Corpus on our way to the cathedral.

After our morning visit, we headed for the beach, on the north side of the bridge, about two or three hundred yards from where the aquarium is currently located. We played in the gulf waters until a little after noon, when the sun became so hot that we all had to take refuge in the fan-cooled apartment. Then, when our appetite was unbelievably keen, my brother and I would attack the cold sandwiches Mom kept in the refrigerator. There is no other way to express how we pounced on those tasty sandwiches. Those childhood days were incomparably happy ones, for, despite the hard daily work at the store, our parents always managed somehow to organize life so that my brother and I had great growing-up experiences. Most parents seek to do this, but actually accomplishing the feat is no small achievement. The challenge, as I see it, is to sacrifice, to enjoy life as much as possible within the bounds of society, and to endure by taking care of the individuals in a family. By these measures, no one has had greater parents than my brother and I. As youngsters, we did not worry much, as I have suggested, and, since we were brought up within the Catholic Church, we were shown right from wrong, and shown how to look out for the interests not only of ourselves but also of the people around us. It wasn't until I was older that I began to see the kind of hardships that our parents quietly underwent in order to provide us with the secure, stable family life that we took for granted.

The pâté sandwiches, for example, were part of the Corpus Christi experience that we associated with our vacations. To this date, even when I see or taste such a sandwich at a reception, I think of Corpus Christi. Our dad would grind up about three pounds of beef and three pounds of pork meat, separately. Then he would mix them by squeezing the two meats together with his hands. If we wanted to do the work, he would ask us to wash our hands, and then we would squeeze the stuff through our fingers until he told us to stop playing with the mix. Mom would then cook the meat in a black iron skillet, spiced lightly with salt and a little pepper and celery. My brother and I were then charged with cutting the crusts off several loaves of bread, usually named Rainbow or Holsum. While Dad minded the store, Mom, my brother, and I evenly spread out the meat on one side of the bread slices, spread mayonnaise on the other slice, closed the sandwiches, and cut them diagonally in half, before placing them back in the plastic bags in which the bread had been packaged. In separate bags, we placed all the bread crusts that we had cut, for nothing would go to waste. We took the crusts with us, too. In the late afternoons, when we were tired and somewhat sunburned from a day at the beach, our parents would take us to the three T-heads that jut out into the bay behind the seawall designed to protect Corpus Christi from hurricanes and storms. There we could always find hungry seagulls, and we threw every last crumb in the air and watched the birds fly in to catch the crusts in midflight. Every year we took many pictures of these outings, and we still have a number of photographs that serve as happy testaments to those wonderful youthful days.

The sandwiches and the bread crusts were kept in the lower compartments of the meat display refrigerator located at the back of the store. Then shortly before leaving for Corpus at five the next morning, Dad placed the sandwiches in a red-and-black-checkered icebox, along with cokes and a few Dr. Pepper soft drinks for Mom. Dr. Pepper, her favorite drink, was one of only a few other drinks that successfully competed against Coca-Cola, Pepsi, and R.C. Cola. Leaving so early in the morning was central to the excitement of going on vacation. Everything was still dark when we loaded the 1954 light blue Chevrolet with the clothes, the sandwiches, and the three bamboo fishing lines. Our parents sat in the front seats, and my brother and I, full of the excitement that we knew awaited us, scrambled into the back. The trip to Corpus took about four long hours because of the several stops that we usually made along the way. About two hours into the trip, the wind would stop blowing on our faces, which we kept by the opened windows of our un-air-conditioned car, and we would stop to eat the breakfast Mom had prepared. A little over an hour later, we would stop for gas, in Kingsville or Robstown. Then we would stop once more, where Dad felt comfortable stopping, to check the oil, the tires, to buy some candy or gum, and to use the men's room. I don't ever recall Mom using the restrooms along the way, and Dad only occasionally. Everything depended on how comfortable my dad felt about stopping to use any facilities, and it was only later that I realized we seldom stopped at restaurants along the way, though Dad always had more than enough money for anything that we ever would have needed. There were just some Anglo establishments that he would not stop at, certainly not to use their restrooms. He never said anything to my brother or me about that, but I knew some people did not look friendly enough to him. Once I overheard him tell Mom that he did not want to subject himself to people who would make what he called a face at him. I had an uncle who taught himself to disregard such slights, but Dad was different. He avoided persons who might slight him, for he was sensitive to the signs that certain Anglos sent him. At the time I found this practice a little odd because he was a fairly successful businessman. Although he was born in San Luis Potosí and was brought to the United States at five, he always considered himself a Mexican; he eventually became a citizen two years before his death in 1969. In the Texas my dad endured, during the 1920s, 30s, 40s, and 50s, widespread discrimination against Mexican people prevailed. With the election of John F. Kennedy in 1960, the only American president my father ever liked, things appeared to be on the verge of changing, but Dad was still not going to risk finding out firsthand. He wisely knew that the laws and policies may change, but the hearts of humankind often remain true to the way people have been raised and nurtured, despite whatever education they may receive. Since then, I have had a number of opportunities to see this sentiment and perspective confirmed by my own experience, unfortunately.

Dad stopped mainly at Mexican American–owned places along the way to Corpus because he felt he was treated better, was not treated impolitely or scowled at. He always paid cash for everything he bought. Now that this son often has little choice but to buy using plastic, I particularly admire his buying philosophy, which summarily said, if you don't have the money in your hand, you should not buy what you want.

When we arrived in the late morning in Corpus, the first item on the agenda was to visit San Antonio, not the city but my mother's patron saint in the cathedral, San Antonio de Padua, from whom my middle name derives. San Antonio was a great speaker, once holding fishes spellbound in some river in Italy, I understand, by the beauty and mellifluousness of his words. The idea was to thank my namesake for our safe journey and deliverance through the Texas wild bramble country, and to petition him for the litany of people and issues my mother prayed for daily. The stretch of nearly 150 miles that we traversed to arrive in Corpus Christi was one of the worst God-forsaken pieces of land in the world. My parents' ultimate nightmare was to end with a flat tire in a place where we were not sure who was likely to show up. One of my uncles related stories about what had happened to people he knew who had car trouble in those stretches of the mesquite country, and Dad also knew what such experiences could be. At his post in the counter of the store all sorts of truck drivers and customers came in to tell my father what they had heard or what they themselves experienced on the highways of Texas. The hot Texas countryside was no place for man or beast, and a good car was an absolute necessity. My father's new 1954 Chevy was wonderfully reliable. We never had a flat and it delivered us safely through many possible travails.

After praying in the quiet of that grand cathedral, we drove over to rent a place in the Seaside Apartments where, for roughly $17.50 a week, we passed the greatest week possible, annually for about ten years. The kind, old Anglo man who owned the apartments told us once that he yearly awaited our visit, always giving us one of the nicer apartments available. When we finally arrived, we breathlessly unloaded our clothes, food, and gear; we couldn't wait to rush into the water. The beach was four blocks away, but, because the sand and the sun were too hot for bare feet, we drove over in the car. According to Mom, the walk back under the Texas sun had been known to kill people weakened by the sea, the surf, and the wind. Back at the apartment, we would indulge ourselves with the cold sandwiches, which tasted inexpressibly delicious to two salt-water, wave-battered kids who stood before the rented cabana's door-length mirror looking red and tired, but ready to return as soon as allowed for more playing on *la playa*.

It was only after we had eaten that first batch of pâté sandwiches that my brother and I knew vacation time had really started for good. Happy and full, we would lie in the appropriately placed twin beds, one by a window where the ocean breeze blew in and the other where a fan stirred the air in the apartment. After discussing whether we should fish, take in a movie, or, yuk, go shopping in the downtown section of town, we would reluctantly drop off for a nap. Who wanted to waste the rest of the afternoon sleeping? But this was the part that Mom and Dad looked forward to, and, of course, we put up with the waste, even though waking up later was, I had to admit, nice. Eddie did not want to wake once he fell asleep, and he remained grouchy for an hour or two until something engaged him anew. Shopping, to be sure, would kill the rest of the day for him, and it wasn't until we went to the beach the next morning that Corpus became worthwhile again. Those naps, how-ever, were also inextricable parts of those wonderful July days, and all that could be heard in our rented apartment was the drone of the fan.

I've resurrected those days now that my wife and I have our own family, and some upcoming vacation time to spend in Corpus. Before going to the Texas State Aquarium, which is a place we hope to visit again, I will drive by the street where that hotel stood. From there, I know I can take in the beauty of the Corpus Christi sea before visiting the cathedral, a place that I hope will provide us with a satisfying quiet that is available only in a great church. I, of course, had to discover that fact for myself, even though my parents taught me that lesson long ago. Now I can only hope to communi-cate that truth to my family and perhaps to readers.

5

Solo

Chicago, Austin, London, Buffalo, Berkeley

When the home anchor has been lifted by unexpected events almost anything is possible, especially in the United States where possibilities are theoretically without limits; theoretically, because often real obstacles serve to deter individuals from achieving their full potential. That, I have learned as the years have accrued, is apparently by social design. When a state or Congress pass bills, for instance, since most of the legislators tend to be lawyers and business people familiar with interest groups, a good number of the laws and public policies that are signed are left with a few loopholes. Loopholes are allowed to remain so that some people can find legal ways of managing the things they wish to encourage or do themselves, despite the fact that laws and public policies are passed to be observed by, say, 95 percent of the population. There is much to say about how corporate America manages to take care of its own interests without looking out well enough for the public good, but I will return to this matter later. At this point, I want to continue to sketch how I managed to receive an undergraduate and graduate-level college education despite the fact that the odds were against me.

I have found out that almost any factor either within a person or from outside in society can snag a thinking young person, detaining and changing an individual's life for weeks, months, and years. For many Latinos, it can be the girlfriend, the boyfriend or friends, the grandmother, the mother, or the father who won't give the young much slack so that the latter can go off and find out things for themselves in college or in the real world. The comforts of home are also difficult to leave, since life away from the anchor of home is decidedly a risky proposition. Released and uncertain, that is how I felt for a year or two both before and after the death of my father. Like many young people in similar circumstances, I had not been preparing myself for any specific goal. Since my parents could not help me much by the time I entered high school, I was essentially on my own. I had some teachers who taught me the subjects I was supposed to learn, but I must say that I never had a guide or a mentor, someone who actually counseled me through high school or college. I was a maverick, a Latino who made it despite the expectations that most of us are not expected to be successful, though that is the rhetoric.

Since then, I have learned that most of the Latinos or Latinas who make it through school and achieve some kind of success do so because in every individual case the person is able to bring together all of his or her resources to rise above whatever obstacles exist. That was the case with me, too. What I did not know when I was going through the years that would make me an educator was that the efforts my parents had invested in bringing me up would serve me so well. The upbringing they gave me helped me most when instances in life discouraged and made me want to give up or to turn away from pursuing my dreams. Since I did not have any particular interest that engaged me when I finished my undergraduate degree in English at the University of Texas in Austin in 1970, one day I rather impulsively decided to try to attempt to change my world as much as possible. I did not know what would happen, but I have always believed that one should try and try and try again. Since this is America, somewhere, somehow, what we are after will materialize. My objective seems to have been to see if such an effort would inspire, or at least prompt me to pursue something that would improve my life prospects. The endeavor was not as selfish as it may sound, since a person has to improve his or her life in order to be in a position to help other people. The problem is that in pursuing self interests, often we do not ever find the time to help others, despite good intentions.

I now realize that what I attempted is not regularly ventured. But, being young and yearning for some adventure, after discussing the issue with my mother and securing her reluctant approval and blessing, I decided to leave the Rio Grande Valley to see if I could make a living in other parts of the world. Indeed, I recommend such an outing for those young people bent on sampling life, especially if a person is single and without onerous responsibilities. There is no better time to learn about life than after college and before professional school, I tell students. It should be known that I undertook traveling to work away from the Valley because my own future did not hold much that enlisted my attention. No one, however, could tell me to my satisfaction where I could apply for a job after I had earned an English degree—other than to study law or to try to move toward graduate school.

My father owned half of a grocery store, and following his completely unexpected, sudden death at fifty-six years of age, I could have chosen to offer to manage the store. He had worked in the store very hard all his adult life, providing our family with a respectable living as members of the lower middle class in the 1950s. The 1960s, however, were less generous to the family business, for throughout that decade the little money that he had saved during the Eisenhower years gradually disappeared. When the bracero program ended in 1964 and the U.S. Border Patrol tightened immigration restrictions, the grocery business slowed considerably, and we faced diffi-cult years. Indeed, some years toward the end, he cleared less than two thou-sand dollars after all expenses and costs were subtracted from the store's income. As the accountant for the business, I knew that for a growing fam-ily of four, such profits, after so much work, was inadvisable. During the last few years of his life, Dad worried constantly about not having enough cash on hand even to buy supplies for the store, to say little of supporting a family with growing needs.

Staying with the grocery store would have meant making some major investment decisions, and I soon came to the conclusion that the enterprise would not easily sustain another generation. Several of the bigger grocery chains, besides, were now luring most of the customers with more food choices, air conditioning, and attractive facilities. Corporate America was beginning to move into the Valley, too, and, with greater cash resources from investors, the franchises were running the mom-and-pop stores out of busi-ness. Soon the demise of the family-run store in the United States became a difficult pattern to ignore, reminding me of Bernard Malamud's fine novel, *The Assistant* (1957). For several years I even entertained the idea of becom-ing a writer of novels. I read every novel I could, especially by writers I had missed in my college English courses. I looked for but could not find a single Mexican American writer whose work was readily available. According to my analysis, after the heyday of the family store, which served my parents' generation, the avenues and paths for the sons and daughters pointed else-where. Where things pointed remained murky, but that the signs indicated away from the past was clear. So I imagined and tried to envision many sce-narios, since what frequently happens in life is shaped by what we are will-ing to conceive and to pursue. Spelling out the actual doors that I conjured up and tried would be useless; the point is that one has to keep knocking even after one has heard no eight or nine times. Eventually a door will open. It is enough to say that for some reason, everything that happens, in retro-spect, looks so inevitable, so natural.

One day when I was twenty-one I thus found myself driving to Chicago with two Chicano brothers and an Anglo friend I had known in high school. From the 17,839 inhabitants that our little town of Edinburg, Texas, had in 1968, the big Midwestern city loomed particularly large to our young eyes. Chicago is twelve or thirteen hundred miles from Edinburg, but the mileage was less important than what Chicago represented. Since the invention of the steel nail in the mid-nineteenth century—the single item, I found out, that most contributed to Chicago's enormously fast growth after the 1840s—Chicago has synonymously stood for the most American of the big cities, as I saw it. From South Texas, Chicago was more American, more Anglo, and, I believed, an even more important metropolis than New York, Boston, or Philadelphia.

I guess my sense of Chicago had to do with the sense I felt in my bones that the city came with the Midwestern accent that controlled the radio airwaves. For, on a clear night, as we used to drive around in Edinburg or sit in South Park watching a pony league baseball game, we could pick up on the car radio one single, faraway radio station in Chicago. My son Carlos recently located that station on the Internet. It was WLS Chicago, which reached 40 states, I have since learned. One of the best evening disc jockeys was Art Roberts (1932–2002); indeed, radio buffs can still hear sample late 1960s radio programs like those we used to hear more than thirty-five years ago in South Texas on www.reelradio.com/ar. Compared to the Eisenhower 1950s, the 1960s, beginning with John Kennedy's election as president, were heady years. WLS's programs were a wonderful mix of the music of the Everly Brothers, the Buckinghams, Sonny and Cher, Stevie Wonder, Diana Ross and the Supremes, Wilson Pickett, The Mommas and the Pappas, and Bob Dylan, the king of folk rock, and news and commercials, the latter often ad-libs.

It is difficult to describe just how attractive Chicago seemed to us from hot South Texas, especially since we heard periodic reports of the cold wind blowing through the city from Lake Michigan. At the time, Los Angeles and Phoenix, and the other big cities of the Southwest that have now become successful transportation hubs, did not begin to offer a comparable lure. Unlike Chicago, those cities lacked a powerful radio station that spun its magic on us as we rode around, talked, and dreamed about what we wanted to do with our lives.

Not willing to wait, we left for Chicago the day after school ended one early summer morning in June. It was around five, and the four of us spoke both English and Spanish. We were college students, moving to Chicago, leaving the Valley to try out a new life in mid-America. It was a long trip, and we had agreed to stop only for gas and food, planning to switch drivers while two slept and the third one stayed up to make sure the driver did not doze off. But around two thirty the following morning, we were stopped by two policemen in a little town in Arkansas, because, as one said, we were four guys in a Mustang with Texas license plates, and we were driving suspiciously slowly. We were, of course, driving under the speed limit because we did not want to irritate the local police by zipping through the town. We were detained for more than an hour by one of the officers while the other one checked the national wanted broadcasts to see if our car had been reported stolen.

We arrived rather uneventfully in Chicago a little over twenty-four hours later, tired and knowing not a single soul in the streets that we wistfully surveyed. Nothing is as disheartening as arriving in a large city nearly exhausted from traveling and not having a place to rest. Despite our weariness, we were excited about our prospects. We chose a motel and slept through the afternoon. Waking up in the late evening in a strange city is a weird experience, especially since it now dawned on me that we were all individually truly on our own. At most, we had one another, but we had no family in the region. There was no one else we could go to for anything. We were alone, solo, and completely free, which was both exhilarating and downright scary. One of us bought the *Tribune,* another the *Sun,* and we started looking for an apartment and work.

We ended up renting an apartment in Logan Square, which we soon learned was part of the Polish section of Chicago. Chicago, we also discovered, consists of many ethnic neighborhoods. And although we later learned about a large Latino section that was a good ways from Logan Square, we did not consider living there because we felt we had to live within walking distance of the elevated rail to work in the downtown area. There were Italian, Jewish, German, Black, Asian, and at least fifty other large ethnic sections, all of which made me realize quite early in my education that the United States is a pretty pluralistic society. America is made up of people from many countries with different customs and ways of looking at things and living. In such a world, which is basically how I have always seen the United States, cultural variety produces many philosophies, practices, and foods, and, frankly I was surprised that, like Americans elsewhere, the great majority of the people living in Chicago invariably preferred their own kind and looked askance at others. Indeed, the newspapers and the radio and television programs suggested that ethnic rivalries substantially impacted Mayor Richard Daley's town.

On the drive to Chicago we had talked of finding good positions in the downtown area in some of the many offices surrounding State Street, Wabash, or Michigan Avenue, the streets that we saw on the maps we bought. But the jobs that we were looking for, we quickly realized, did not appear in the newspapers. Almost all the posted ads were blue-collar jobs in factories or warehouses, and almost all of them required transportation away from the city's metropolitan center. We wanted to work where the hustle and bustle of the city made the city hum every day, just as Carl Sandburg had sketched Chicago in his famous poem, so we narrowed our search to that area.

Romeo, one of the friends who had traveled with me from Texas, had worked the previous year at King Arthur's Pub, a large two-part restaurant owned by a Jewish family surnamed Lieberman. So, after much unfruitful searching for several days, he and I wound up washing dishes in the Pub's hot and steamy kitchen. Until several years ago, that establishment still stood in the famous downtown Loop of Chicago. Romeo's brother Eloy, who is now a distinguished biochemistry professor at Cornell, and our Anglo friend Jan had left Romeo and me in Chicago and had driven on to Michigan where they mainly found work in the factories. There they were paid considerably better, at any rate, than jobs available in South Texas, since laborers in the northern states were usually required to become union members, which allowed them to earn higher wages.

Within a week or so, Romeo and I were promoted to busing tables; we found out that washing dishes was the preserve of certain Chicago black men who did not bus tables as a matter of pride. Busing tables required us to be out among the largely white, upper-middle-class customers wearing clean, starched, white, linen uniforms. It was clear that some of the black employees did not desire to clean and set the tables, while others did, so the owners placed those in the kitchen sink area where they preferred to wash dishes as they joked among themselves. In trying to make the best of the bad deal that life gave them, though, they sometimes ended up complaining and running into altercations with employers, with each other, with the customers, or their own families, because their existence was clearly frustrating and exasperating.

The Chicago experience, however, was so new, multidimensional, and exciting to me that I felt as if I was acting in a film. The script I was writing in my head compared my stint in the restaurant business to the young man who becomes the general manager of the St. Gregory in Arthur Hailey's *Hotel* (1965). I had seen the 1967 movie version of the novel where

Rod Taylor is the leading actor. And, being young, naive and full of life and ambition, I saw myself as someday managing or even owning a fancy hotel, restaurant, or some other similar business where big money and important-looking people came and went. That dream served me well several years.

The following summer, we took the same route, this time well aware that, in the eyes of those restaurant owners, we were never going to stop being busboys no matter how long we stayed in that particular Chicago world. The lunch manager, I have neglected to state, was a big German immigrant named Fritz, and so long as we cleaned and set up the tables for the customers, he was happy. But several squabbles arose when the hectic environment of the business picked up, and, although he was basically a sympathetic good man, he had shown that he was capable of running roughshod over the workers in order to meet the restaurant's customers with a smiling, cherubic face. Three other employees made our stay there more palatable by occasionally telling stories of past exploits and accomplishments. Wolf was the Austrian bartender whose good looks we envied. He was the Casanova who invited one or two women several times a week to sip drinks with him while he told them anecdotes of his life in Europe before he came to the United States. An older pianist entertained the evening crowds by playing just about any song that customers paid for at the large, fancy piano bar that outlined his Steinway. Lisa, one of my favorite waitresses, had the nicest personality, and she was the most efficient one, except that every time she heard the instrumental piece "Born Free," she stopped everything until that beautiful, haunting music ended.

I would have loved to study the hotel business at the University of Houston or at Cornell University, reputedly the two best hotel schools in the country. But I soon learned that such an option was not realistically available for a Mexican American in the late 1960s. The expense of attending hotel school at Cornell was just out of the question. These were the only two schools that I was aware of that, if I were to enter by some miracle, might conceivably place me on a different working plane. But unable to meet tuition and living expenses, that dream died and I turned elsewhere. Both years that I worked in Chicago I was able to clear over two thousand dollars, after paying rent and living expenses, and that was fairly good money then. We worked hard, of course, clocking in at 8 a.m. and returning to our apartment in Logan Square by subway after the restaurant closed at two in the morning. But I was young and five hours of sleep kept me living a life full of adventure; one where the great roast beef sandwiches of King Arthur's Pub kept me working full steam.

By the third summer, the year before my senior year in college, busing tables in Chicago did not seem as exotic as it had that first summer. It was plain I would never progress to anything better in that world. I would either stay there the rest of my life, or I should move into something else. For two weeks, I sold encyclopedias in the suburbs of Chicago. I was trained, told how to approach a home, and how to talk to the lady or the man of the house, to convince potential customers that an investment in an encyclopedia was the best thing they could do for their children. Since my father had bought us a set of the encyclopedia and since I had enormously profited from those books, I was convinced I could speak with conviction and actually sell some. I was wrong. They were too expensive at six hundred dollars a set, and the blue-collar families whose life I interrupted were not interested in books. The summers in Chicago were hot, the humidity from Lake Michigan at times unbearable, and after trying every day for ten days straight from 7 a.m. to 7 p.m. without making a sale, I knew I would never make it as a Willie Loman.

So I launched off in another direction, this time with the Anglo friend who had driven with us to Chicago that first year, convinced, against my parents' lukewarm protests, to see Europe. Jan had traveled through Europe the previous summer on five dollars a day, following the advice of a popular book that young student tourists everywhere were reading that summer. Not fully convinced, I nevertheless secured a very reluctant permission from my good parents and despite my own ambivalence about the business of going off to try to work in Europe, I went to Great Britain to see how people with different English accents actually lived.

We arrived at Heathrow after a long, rough but invigorating flight. Following a week of looking for work and observing the way people lived in London, my friend and I decided to stay, hoping to develop an ear for their different kind of spoken English. We had gone to Europe through a University of Texas student program, and the idea was that we were to work in England to defray our expenses. No one in Austin, however, informed either one of us that in order to work in London, a British employer had to be willing to hire us. We were given a little green card, which authorized us to work, but, as soon as the British employers saw our cards, they said that they were not interested in summer help.

Finding a job in London was a tough challenge. After four or five interviews, it became clear that if I wanted better work than another student friend had landed, in the basement of a paint factory mixing paints all day from eight to six, I would have to use some ingenuity. At the placement agency the people interviewing appeared to appraise job seekers simply by looking at them, and after two or three questions, I decided to change my approach. Since the agency employees kept the list of interview places, they controlled knowledge of vacancies; applicants could not flip through the postings to see which positions were the better ones. So, while the employee who was sizing me up was also telling me about the companies interviewing, I read his job list upside down. On an adjacent list next to the one he had, I saw that a general office worker was needed on 128 Queen Victoria Street. I had seen Queen Victoria Street on the way to the agency, so when I left that building I made a B-line to Deloitte, Plender and Griffiths, the establishment that was hiring. Mr. Trotter, the man who interviewed me, asked me how I had heard that his office needed a letter carrier. I told him that I had learned of the position from a hiring agency, as I had. He said that he had just sent word not twenty minutes before. He informed me that he could not believe how fast they were. I smiled, and, using my Texas lingo, I added that I, too, was amazed at how fast things got done in London-town. Ten minutes later, I was hired.

The accounting firm, two blocks from St. Paul's Cathedral, was excellently situated in the middle of London. My assignment was to take letters and packages throughout London either by taxi, the tube, or by walking a piece of mail to a specified location. No student who was interested in seeing the city and in getting to know as much as one can in the space of a summer could have asked for a better job. What I had not wanted was to be cooped up in an office or a basement somewhere. I also sought to avoid doing something routinely that would not have made me feel as if I was spending my summer as a college senior in one of the greatest cities in the world. My supervisor was a great help and became a good friend. He learned that I was a student on my first trip to England, and that I wanted to learn as much about the British as I could. A week into the position, he informed me, following one of my return trips from carrying an urgent piece of mail, that if I saw something I wanted to see, to stop and to take about half an hour. So long as I did not overstay, I could take quick looks around London.

My idea has always been to open up as many different avenues to life as possible. Mexican Americans seldom try to do more than what is before them, or so I believed at the time. I had looked about, talked to my parents and to a few professors whose opinions I respected, and, having spent the two previous summers in Chicago, I had crossed the Atlantic to try my luck on the other side of the ocean. I had been inclined to settle in a country where I would have to learn another language. For Edward Sapir and other linguists whose work I had read in undergraduate courses had taught me that to learn about other people one has to be able to understand and to express oneself in someone else's language. Only then, and I agree, can an individual see life from a different perspective, for a person's language and way of thinking changes everything.

By the end of the summer, with only three weeks left, my friend, and another Mexican American student who had been rooming with us in London, and I decided to cross the English Channel at Dover by boat. We then rented a Volkswagen after a week in München, and drove east as far as Vienna. From Normandy we hitchhiked through the French countryside, once being picked up by a journalist from France who had just returned from Egypt. In heading for Paris, we passed Madame Bovary's Rouen, down the Seine. The trip was wonderful; I was young; and I suspect I had a good time because I was prepared to enjoy everything. Life, I found out, can be bloomingly beautiful.

Paris was full of colors, of excitement, and I spent two happy days walking about the city, enlarging my ken. I did not particularly plan my routes, I simply went, avoiding Baedeker, consciously working to appropriate what I could of the terrain, the landscape, and everything that I saw and experienced. The people in northwestern France did not seem to like all those American kids who spend their summers hitching rides from town to town. Unfortunately, not knowing French, I was "out" with the French people, who felt then, as some still do, insulted if one cannot speak to them in their own language. I considered that experience a loss, as I consider everything that I attempt that does not, for one reason or another, work out. So, I moved onward. I simply was not prepared, and I did not have the time and the money that I would have needed, to make the effort to learn the way of the French. I also was happy that the English had been warm and generous with me, and, although I brought home no money from my general office work in London, I was pleased with the people and the friends I had made during my stay.

I was trying in effect to "do" Europe, like the American characters in a James novel, though certainly à la cheap. The idea was to see Europe in a way different from regular tourists. I had read about the countless numbers of people who trek about visiting famous places, seeing the historic landmarks, and instead of doing that I sought to avoid the touristy places. I saw many known places that I accidentally came across in my walks, such as Trafalgar Square, Hyde Park, and others, but I also recall avoiding recognized places when I learned they were in the vicinity. I sought, I now think, to see some other Europe than the one tourists regularly visit. I wanted to see Europeans going about their daily business among whatever historic sites I happened to encounter. I experienced a certain pleasure in mulling over the fact that life was being lived in the vicinity of famous sites, great places where notable events preserved by historians, novelists, and thinkers had occurred.

On the third day of our trek through Europe, I developed an unexplainable yearning to see Avignon—I suspect because I wanted to see the wall that supposedly surrounds the entire town, about which I had read. I found, however, that the wall isn't much to see. In places where the wall around Avignon has not crumbled or been removed, it is about four to six inches high, and I stepped over it, straddling both sides of the historic divide. I felt like a Mexican American Gulliver, a *bato* from the barrio who had traveled far abroad and accomplished this silly, insignificant personal feat that was hardly worth telling anyone. What a story, I remember thinking to myself. Short on money, we went to Paris, but even the coffee, which I did not drink at the time, was one dollar per cup; so, we left the bistros looking like we had seen them in the paintings of the impressionists. I returned alone to Le Havre, crossed over to Brighton—experiencing that glorious view of the British coast encountered as one arrives on the island from Normandy, thinking of Matthew Arnold's poem—and landed back in Great Britain.

I had spent nine weeks working amongst and familiarizing myself with as many European people as my meager funds allowed that summer. The second day after returning to London anew, having located a flat in the West End, close to the tube (the subway system), I emerged out of the subterranean train at the St. Paul station. It is difficult to describe the sensation of arriving, again, to a strange city, but this time, being surrounded completely by an altogether new world where I nonetheless felt unexplainably at ease. I then suddenly remembered how I had rather resourcefully obtained my position at the accounting firm of Deloitts, Plender, and Griffiths, and the whole minor miracle seemed difficult to believe.

For a young man without responsibilities, one with roots in the far away world of the Rio Grande Valley in South Texas, everything in life was grand. I had gone on swimmingly in that new country, but despite the fact that I felt as if I were very much the subject of an unannounced and unviewed film in the making, I had a gnawing concern. The more I looked at the future, the less I liked what little I could discern. I knew that I could have stayed in London for the rest of my days, working with some great Scottish friends, including Irish and English blokes, as they called themselves, who had gotten into the habit of inviting me to go pub-hopping with them almost every night. Possibly I would have married, raised a family, and grown happily old there, but that prospect made me feel as if I were trying to escape what I should be about. That scenario just didn't seem to be part of my script.

Certain things sometimes feel right and others do not. Although I had spent some fun youthful days in Europe, I came to the reluctant conclusion that England, and London in particular, was great for a while, but I was not willing to spend the rest of my life there. I had traveled about the country during the weekends a little, and my accounting general office mail-delivering position was sufficient to pay for the rent, travel to the Continent, and to pay for the evening drinking that I enormously enjoyed. Two Scottish bricklayers, an Irishman, and several other American students were our friends that summer in England. They were also our drinking and play-going buddies. But while the idea of residing permanently in London had its attractions, being raised in the very different world of South Texas made me expect more, though, to be sure, I couldn't have said exactly what.

Leaving London and my European world was not easy, for despite the shortness of my stay I had become uncommonly attached to the excitement of the busy city life, to the pubs, its people, and to their issues and ways. Air travel, however, has a way of telescoping places, and, as we know, places are as much a matter of a state of mind these days. Once back in Austin, I went to see university friends. I then went "down," as we geographically minded say in Texas, to the Rio Grande Valley to see my parents, who received me like one of the long lost biblical sons returning to the homestead, sans the big feast, thank you very much. Then I went "up" to San Antonio, but finding the wages there lower than in Austin, I returned to the capital.

I found a job at a flower and gift shop off 35th Street. I spent my weekday afternoons after classes at the university delivering flowers to people in hospitals, to happy wives romanced by apologetic husbands, and to funeral parlors. That was enough to help me with the rent and my eating expenses. Austin in 1968–70 was a great town for students, but it was beginning to develop that crazy hectic dizziness that often afflicts American cities interested in moving into the next plane of economic development.

This is not to say that I had especially seen happier faces in England, but London had more of a romantic lifestyle, or certainly that was the case for me. Although I have since concluded that Austin is one of the nicest towns to live in within the states, the Texas capital paled by comparison to London, particularly during the long, hot summer months. What I had learned is that everywhere I saw people working pretty hard, essentially to sustain themselves and their families. Most people, indeed, work to learn how to replace others. Changing things, on the other hand, requires a different set of skills, and a different purpose in life. I had not articulated things crisply to myself, despite my travels, but that is one of the main results of seeing different parts of the world. What was immediately before me were four years away from Texas, in a northern state that I never dreamt I would even visit.

Roughly about a year after my 1969 summer stay in London and Europe, I decided to attend a meeting for graduating seniors offered by the English Department of the University of Texas. I remember showing up sporting a little trimmed beard—I had been reading D. H. Lawrence and other British writers—and not being too pleased, because the professors I had studied with were not there. That told me, correctly or not, they were not among the department leaders or that they did not care much for the literal hordes of students they taught. One, I learned, was packing; he was leaving the university permanently, and he was, ironically, headed for London. The others were busy elsewhere. At any rate, the two professors charged with the meeting quickly made it plain that they would support graduate school in English, if we students were interested in teaching and scholarship. The prospect had never crossed my mind. If we were not sure but thought that we might be interested in law, accounting, or another related profession, we might also consider English graduate school.

I had vaguely entertained the idea of graduate school, but spending more years in school, after the sixteen I had already spent, especially at a time when I had begun to see myself as a world-weary, experienced traveler, was unappealing. The other discouraging point was that one of the professors remarked that the graduate schools worth going to were taking only the top students. Being a little better than a B student, since my studies had not been my main concern in life, I learned for the first time that I would not stand a good chance of being admitted. The best schools, we were informed, were considering only the top 10 percent of the graduating classes, and many of these schools looked for the top 5 percent. Michigan and Harvard and other comparable schools wanted only the top 2 or 3 percent, and SUNY at Buffalo, a school I had never heard about, but which reputedly boasted one of the best English department faculties in the country, wanted only the top 1 or 2 percent.

I recall walking away from that meeting feeling pretty dejected. Here I was, one of many English majors, a Mexican American who had received some As but mostly Bs, and no recognition, and I was ending somewhere in the top 30 percent of the graduating class. I had read a good number of books, but in a rather desultory way. I had written some good papers on subjects about which I cared to make some statements. I had by now also traveled "abroad," as the rich frat kids said, at my own expense; I had worked most of my life, even though my parents had always provided for me, but I still did not know what I was going to do with my life.

Little of course lasts longer than it has to. At the time I felt that I was at a juncture where I would be fashioning the rest of my days. Most of the doors I saw and would have liked to knock on did not look inviting. I tried a few, like interviewing for a business position, but nothing really appealed to me. I had been told no before, and would be passed by many more times in life, but I did not like to be in a position where I was asking, where I could see a "no" forming on people's mouths almost as soon as they saw me. Although I did not want to think about or to recognize it, I was very often left with the impression that I just did not fit their image of the person they were looking for to fill positions for which I felt qualified.

My parents told me that I would make a good lawyer, since I liked to talk, and I particularly enjoyed debating, though I had never studied that skill. Indeed, I considered debating to be an Anglo thing. The most I had done was to take on one of my good friends, another Mexican American, who was part Arab, and who became a champion high school debater. We liked him because he made all of us Chicanos look good. He subsequently became a lawyer and the last time I heard he was living in Washington, working with politicians. Based on several successful casual skirmishes with him, I had felt a pull in that direction, but I found that everybody was studying law. I also learned that one had to score very well to gain admission into the best schools, and knowing me, I would likely score well enough, but short of eliciting a school's notice. Smart law students, I was told, received what amounted to a commitment from some of the better-regarded law firms before they entered law school, so that a position would be waiting for them when they finished. Not having connections in the profession, and not having anyone with whom I felt comfortable enough to ask for counsel, I let this possible life go by without sampling it.

Several days after that meeting, feeling that the two English professors who ran the morning workshop on graduate information would not likely encourage a student with my grades, I filled out a form requesting information from the graduate English program at the State University of New York at Buffalo. I had picked up the form in the halls of UT's English Department; their black and orange glossy announcement caught my eye and I pulled out a form on the way out of that meeting. The materials arrived shortly, and I learned that Buffalo was indeed considering only the top 1 or 2 percent. I regretted not having taken my studies more seriously, and I moved about rather languorously for another week or so.

At the end of that time, I went to my typewriter; I clearly remember it was a cool day in early December. A few days earlier my father suffered that unexpected heart attack; the event effectively separated me from a life where I rarely worried about anything to having to consider how I was going to meet my daily and long-term needs. I typed a one-paragraph letter saying that I was interested in pursuing a Ph.D. in English. I mentioned that I had heard about the Buffalo program, and that, although I did not speak and write the three foreign languages required, I would be willing to learn two other languages. I did add, of course, that I was Mexican-American (we still hyphenated the word in those days), that I would be graduating from UT-Austin in May with a 3+ grade point average out of a possible 4, and that I was interested in applying. I sent off the letter to the graduate school office indicated on the black and bright orange poster Buffalo put out that year, and went to pick up yet another load of flowers for mothers with new babies, wives with upcoming birthdays, and hospital customers.

Several weeks after my father's funeral in December, 1969, I received a neatly typed letter from a Professor Victor Doyno at SUNY Buffalo. His letter said that just now the language requirements were being reconsidered, and he encouraged me to apply. This was early January, 1970, and the Vietnam War was being fought. Many campuses throughout the country were protesting our spurious involvement. I had marched in several rallies to protest, too, since I oppose the loss of life on any grounds, and certainly for politically clouded reasons. Things in the United States were changing, and a number of books have since described the flux and the uncertainties that people of the times felt. I was being called by the draft about that time, but I was determined to resist, even if it meant going to jail. I was not going to shoot at anyone, nor certainly try to kill another person. That much I knew. In 1973, Nixon finally brought the shooting to an end, and, here is what not too many people know: on terms that had first been offered in 1969! My cousin Santos had volunteered. He kept reenlisting, and served three separate tours in Vietnam. A number of other Latino friends also enlisted, and several were sent back in body bags, including Freddy Martinez, for whom the Edinburg city council named the street that runs in front of our old high school.

The necessary application forms to apply for graduate school in Buffalo followed, and I gathered the necessary information, applied, and went back to deliver more flowers. Those were uncertain days, for all along I kept wondering what would happen now that the war continued and my mother and brother were in Edinburg minding the grocery store and I was in Austin trying to finish my degree in the wake of Dad's death.

In late February, Romeo, who had accompanied me to Chicago and who still lives in Austin, came out of the back side of the partitioned house that we rented to tell me that Mom was on the phone. A university shopping mall now stands on that south campus site on the Texas Drag, or Guadalupe. I clearly remember being outside under a warm winter Austin sun with Lermontov's *A Hero of Our Time* (1840) and Askakov's *The Family Chronicles* (1856–58), which I had hastily read for my Russian literature class a little over a year before. Mom told me in Spanish, her only language, that she had just received a call from a professor whose name she spelled as D-o-y-n-o. It seemed to her that he wanted to speak to me. She told me that he had used some Spanish and seemed to say that I had been admitted to school in Buffalo; that is what she had understood. I was to call a number that, with difficulty, she had taken.

I was stunned. I did not know what to think. I had applied, but I did not seriously expect to be admitted. Michigan and Harvard had already rejected me with form letters, thank you. I asked her what he had actually said, and Mom became anxious and said that she was not sure, but she thought that is what he had said. I told her I would call, and I would let her know what was going on. We were both pretty excited, for I had mentioned to Mom that I would like to try graduate school, but that it did not look like a graduate school would take me. Although I had cautioned her not to raise her hopes, she had said that she would pray. When she hung up I knew she would go directly to thank San Antonio and San Rafael, the two saints to whom she has always prayed as long as I can remember.

I called the number she gave me and breathlessly asked for Professor Doyno. He confirmed that I had been accepted into graduate school in English at Buffalo. He hoped, he said, that he had not upset my mother too much with his Spanish, and extended his congratulations. Mom had mentioned he had been very nice on the telephone, from what she could gather. He said the graduate school would be writing to inform me formally of my acceptance, and that materials from the department would be included. I was, of course, elated. I thanked him God knows how many times, and told him I was very happy with the news. I believe mainstream Americans think we Latinos should emotionally restrain ourselves, but I was happy and I felt it would be improper not to let Dr. Doyno know how pleased I was. After expressing how pleased I was at being provided with the unusual opportunity, for a Mexican American, to study for a Ph.D. in English, I called Mom to tell her she had understood correctly, relaying Professor Doyno's kind words about their conversation. She said that we both now had to thank San Antonio and San Rafael, her two favorite saints, at which I know some of my enlightened university friends would have smirked, but I did. And I have done so many times since, especially when confronted by problems over which I have little control.

That afternoon, I invited Romeo and Jan West, my two Edinburg roommates, to Bevo's, our favorite student bar, to drink a pitcher of beer in celebration of the good news. At the end of May, about a week after the semester ended, I was off to Buffalo, the snow country next door to Niagara Falls. For two years I trudged through the snow when I was not reading in my apartment or reading in Lockwood Library. I was a regular Robert Frost stopping by the woods, the homes, and the buildings of Erie County, always looking in from the outside, interloper that I felt I was in that faraway white snow country. Then, one night, at a dance on the SUNY Buffalo campus, I met Rita. She introduced me to her parents and family, and I found a home. Several months later, I married my beautiful Puerto Rican wife, and we have now been married more than thirty years, all of them *años felizes,* happy years, fortunately. Two years after, with Rita's help and support, I finished a Ph.D. in English, in American literature, the result of four years in the snowiest American city. On the Southern Canadian railroad we moved across the country, and a year later settled in Albany, California, while I taught at the University of California-Berkeley. After a wonderful stay of five years in the Oakland–San Francisco Bay Area, Rita and I brought our young family to Clear Lake Forest, a suburb of Houston, Texas. We were now the happy parents of an elementary-aged son and a daughter about to enter kindergarten. We have both since struggled to pay the bills by teaching for our living.

Sol Ardiente:
Parenthood

6

Voices, Desires Being Wishful

One hot summer day, when the sun was fully ablaze and moving toward high noon, I was struck by the realization that I would not live forever. Generally, we tend to go about our daily business as if we will live forever. That is why the unexpected surprises us. Somehow we never have enough time to devote to what is important, such as building a legacy of the values, issues, and the views we hope to transmit to our children, the next generation. That particular day it suddenly occurred to me that, while representative of the Mexican American/Latino experience to the core, my life has been different enough to use my experiences to help other Latinos and maybe even non-Hispanics. Over the years I have witnessed so many things, including presentations at conferences and meetings where male and female Latinos rise to articulate positions that often leave people baffled. I believe this occurs because most Americans do not sufficiently understand the cultural coordinates and the environmental disturbances and flux that daily shape the lives of most Spanish-speaking Americans.

How Latino *culturas* interact with American culture is a vast, worthy subject that observers are beginning to consider and appreciate. Indeed, it is difficult to understand a Latino, whether Mexican American or a person from any of the twenty other Latin American countries, if we do not have a sense of the shaping environment and the language through which individuals and communities frame and interpret reality. We know that where a person was born and raised, and how he or she thinks and establishes rapport with other people largely determine how others respond. How a Latino communicates is particularly important, since English is usually a second language, often a matter of learning the right words for the Spanish ones that surface automatically.

Not all Hispanics, of course, think in Spanish before translating into English; Latinos who received an education in the United States understandably think and express themselves in English. For such *primos,* or cousins, Spanish is secondary, often being a way to establish a bond with other Latinos as occasions arise. Also, for a variety of reasons that Latinos can individually choose to explain or not, some Latinos do not speak fluent Spanish anymore. Often, it is because many are not exposed to good, articulate Spanish day in and day out, an experience that an extended stay in almost any Latin American country can remedy. For such Latinos, a forebear, either parent, grandparent, or even great-grandparent, made the decision to use only English. But, as the twenty-first century unfolds, there is little doubt that both English and Spanish will be the major languages of the western hemisphere. The signs are everywhere in the business world, in government, and in social situations. People simply have to leave their old habits and attitudes behind and notice how Latino influences are transforming American society.

Every life, of course, is unique, shaped by different influences and experiences, but, as the new century progresses, many Latinos and non-Latinos, from dissimilar life walks, are raising questions about issues, some of which have started appearing almost daily in the media. Latino media, in fact, are now drawing increasingly larger audiences, according to sociologists and other survey-takers who study such developments. An emerging new consciousness, concerned with the role of Latinos in American life, simultaneously is raising exhilaration and frustration. Exhilaration because changes are actually emerging, and frustration because many Latinos cannot forget that a good part of the twentieth century was spent waiting. We have been waiting for society and the policies of government to wend their slow way toward recognizing us as people who can definitely use help and attention with just about any segment of the U.S. experience and infrastructure.

In the areas of education, health, the working professions, and just about anything else, people are finding out that there is little reliable, useful, current data about Hispanics that informs decisions about how best to help this emergent population. U.S. Latinos are a large internal nation of nearly 40 million people of all ages who desire to be embraced as regular American citizens. We cannot and we do not want to leave our cultural roots behind, attractive as the proposition of becoming an American citizen is. Our different *culturas* are essential, inseparable parts of our identity. Today, as the Latino sun rises and shines throughout America, we are at a new juncture that brims with opportunities for forging new bonds and relationships. Soon, issues are going to be addressed in positive ways for Latinos, issues that can successfully integrate Latinos into American society.

Hoping to shape the future to some degree leads many of us to consider the past in light of the present, for it should be clear that Mexican Americans and U.S. Latinos are at a crossroads. Without positive dialogues, it is doubtful whether the nature of our lives in the United States will sufficiently serve the interests of all Americans. How the majority of us variously become acculturated, given our different upbringings, schools, and societies, and how our experiences shape us as parents and adults are issues that need concerted attention. Surveys and questionnaires are only now beginning to extract and tabulate information on young, middle age, and older Latinos. Life in a Latino household, for instance, is not all about income, number of children in the household, their ages, and disposable income. The United States is a materialistic society that measures quality of life by the number and the quality of our possessions, but how some Latinos actually learn about parenthood is not clear. The Latino home is a challenging arena, since that is where in one way or another most problems show up, or not. By carefully orchestrating several home events presented in the following pages I do not mean to suggest that these essays are more or less representative of the harder tug-and-pull lives of the majority of Latinos. Many Latino lives are beset by the dual tribulations of poverty and the lack of education that I briefly address here. Although I could have described troubled Latino lives and events witnessed over the years, I have instead chosen to describe some happier moments that my wife and I have been fortunate to have with our children. I believe parents and adults have a duty to offer their children as happy a childhood as possible, one where love, hope, and kindness to others dominates, much as my own parents offered me. The difficulties that we Latinos face in the United States I have left for the closing public policy section, which raises public consciousness issues regarding Latinos.

Mexican Americans are Americans of Mexican descent. As such, we have learned how to adjust our lives to the ways and demands of the larger American society, much as other Americans generously make accommodations for our *cultura,* in return. All citizens learn to adjust to demographic changes, but for Mexican Americans, as for other ethnic Americans, adjustment often consists of the degree to which a person embraces different ways and mores. Some forms of thinking and behavior are better suited for integration into American forms than others. The desired social objective in the United States is to find, latch onto, and create a smooth lifestyle that sustains and nourishes the individuals of a family and allows parents to provide a decent living. Indeed, being able to sustain oneself within life's flux is an admired American virtue. The majority of Mexican Americans, like most Americans, steadfastly believe in the importance of the family.

Demographically, the United States is always changing, and, although we have generally been aware of population changes, it turns out that what my Latino friends and others of my generation have been building and constructing since in the late 1960s in many ways heralds the new century. During the last fifty years or so we have been exploring and attempting to map out the terrain that most Latinos will soon follow. In effect, we have been the *adelantados,* the ones who first started to talk and to write about the nature of the Mexican American experience as a changing generational phenomenon. We have been interested in how learning about American culture and civilization will improve us as Spanish-speaking Americans. Since the Latino population has increased to more than six times that of the U.S. Jewish population, which is estimated at 5.2 million individuals, simply mentioning this fact suggests a little-known disparity when the connection between influence and education is considered. Roughly two-thirds of the Latino population is Mexican American, meaning that 12.45 percent of the U.S. population of 289 million people are now Hispanic. Yet, due mainly to the nature of the education that the majority of Latinos receive in the schools, most Hispanics find it difficult to compete for the more attractive positions. Mainstream Americans are understandably better prepared, both by education and by what in effect is general social coaching, about the U.S. infrastructure and networking.

According to the terms of the Treaty of Guadalupe Hidalgo, which formally ended President James K. Polk's 1846 to 1848 expansionist war with Mexico, Spanish-speaking Mexican citizens became American citizens in 1849, a year after the treaty went into effect. This little regarded treaty was signed in the town of Guadalupe Hidalgo, south of Mexico City. And, I suspect like most other Latinos and non-Latinos, the significance of this treaty remained unclear to me until I decided to find out why we are called Mexican Americans and how this history has made us different from other Americans. As a people incorporated into the United States by an act of war, that fact has continued to shape laws and public policies that have determined Mexican American and other Latino psychological realities.

Some people have asked, "Why don't you just call yourself an American, instead of emphasizing the Mexican part of being American?" Many Mexican Americans have tried. When Latinos who look like me say we are Americans, most people follow that assertion by asking, from where? When I answer from Texas, that I was born a Texan—not, of course, the John Wayne type that people generally imagine (media images are so powerful), but a real native *Tejano,* people nevertheless are still not satisfied until I am specific. When I say I was born in South Texas, in the Rio Grande Valley, people say, oh, next to Mexico. Yes, I say, since now they immediately see Mexico written all over me, and not the Italian, Jewish, or Greek person that they were supposing. The longest period I ever spent in Mexico was ten days during the summer of 1999. That was when the picture on the cover of this book was taken by a friend on the grounds of the Toltec ruins near the town of Xalapa. John Wayne, by the way, was born in Iowa. Most Americans continue to believe that he was born not only in Texas but also in the Alamo, the namesake of the movie that misrepresents Mexicans so badly.

I am and proudly call myself a Mexican American because historical, physiological, and psychological circumstances have created me, but many of us Latinos do not know enough about our own history because the schools did not teach us much about our past. And our parents, many of whom did not receive useful enough educations, could not help. Indeed, the record ought to show one important fact. Like countless other Latinos who went through U.S. schools, I went from kindergarten to a Ph.D. in English hearing the story of the Alamo (to which all children in Texas are subjected) without ever *once* hearing anything about the history of Mexican Americans! I find this cultural erasure in a country that borders Mexico absolutely inexcusable, but that was indeed the case. Worse, when this fact is pointed out to some educators, usually there is no response, as if to say, "and?" So what is the connection between that reality and the self-esteem of some Latinos?

It has taken me many years to recognize that we have a proud history that is not sufficiently appreciated or celebrated in this country. Indeed, our people have been cast as interlopers, as foreigners attempting to disrupt American civilization. But that is not the case. The ancestors of other Americans also arrived here looking for better lives. Yet our history books have not included pictures of Mexicans and other Latinos arriving in the States, like the immigration picture history of the Europeans who came through Ellis Island, for instance. This is a sad loss for the American historical record. Due to this cultural deletion, today's Latinos do not have social ways of commemorating events that mark when a Latino family or ancestors left the mother country and arrived in the United States. In my case, for example, I was born an American citizen, the son of a father born in 1913 in San Luis Potosí, Mexico. My mother was born in 1911 in the high plateau of Herédia, Costa Rica, the cool coffee-growing country north of Panama. Although my father and four brothers were brought by his mother and father to the United States around 1918, when it looked like the Mexican

Revolution (which began in 1910) was going to last forever, no photograph exists of the occasion. Nor do photographs exist, as far as the family knows, of my mother's arrival in Brownsville, Texas, from San José, Costa Rica, in 1946 or so. These are missing historical benchmarks that most Latino families do not possess, largely because these important events raised conflicting emotional and sociological responses in many people that discouraged recording such events during those times.

Even though I am twice a U.S. Latino, with Spanish-speaking ancestors from both Mexico and Central America, I am, ironically, today as representative and yet as unique an individual as other U.S. Latinos. Each one of us has a highly singular personal history, yet most of us are anonymously grouped together as if nothing within our different histories and lives matters to the rest of the U.S. citizenry. Yes, we Latinos generally do tend to appreciate fiestas, as the media commercials indicate. We love to be in the company of other people who enjoy a good time, but we also have heterogeneous views about politics, sports, business, and nearly every other subject, like other Americans and people throughout the world. The problem is that the media and other venues rarely invite us to discuss issues, suggesting that our views are not as important as the views of the people who are regularly asked to voice their views and desires.

In a series of essays communicating views on a variety of subjects, I hope readers see that I have chosen a conversational approach to introduce relevant information. I began by saying that most people awakening to an acknowledgment of mortality suddenly realize that time cannot be taken for granted. In my case, that realization prompted me to look at the past, and to explore what it is that my life could contribute to Latinos who would follow me. For one of the greatest vacuums or absences that I have personally experienced while living half a century in the United States is that I have always felt we Latinos have had very few social guideposts and guiding directions by which to stir and direct our lives. For that reason, I have spent a good part of my life reading American texts, hoping that somewhere, somehow, I would locate, discover, or uncover some narrative, novel, or autobiography that would usefully show us, either Latino males or females, how our lives could be fashioned within the United States. But not having found useful volumes, other than Américo Paredes's *George Washington Gómez* and Anthony Quinn's *The Original Sin* (besides others discussed in *Crowding Out Latinos* [2000]), I finally decided to write about my upbringing and adult life in the hope that my experiences will encourage Latinos to fashion new vistas. Traditionally, many avenues of American life have been left unexplored and unarticulated by Spanish-speaking Americans. We can only continue to knock outside doors until someone from the inside chooses to open them.

How one Mexican American sees developments on various U.S. fronts ought to elicit attention, mainly because there are so few useful records of how adult Latinos or Chicanos think. Having used the word, I need to explain that I believe a Chicano/a is an enlightened Mexican American, a person who has consciously decided to work to improve the world for Latinos. Over the years, I have disagreed with Latinos in leadership positions who have said, "Oh, well, así son las cosas," that's the way things are. What I find disagreeable with this position is the view that it is better not to become involved in problems that I believe should be addressed. If we don't change our realities, others will. Our children will have to go through the same experiences; they will have to put up with the same attitudes and mores. We cannot find a place for ourselves within the American Public Consciousness if we are not respected for the people we are, the people we are proud of being and the people we hope to become. There is nothing wrong with calling attention to ourselves if we do so to improve our conditions and those of our progeny and other Latinos. Indeed, part of the problem that we Latinos share in the public arena is that we too easily settle for being represented as less than we know we are. We have been misrepresented for so many generations that we are strangely reluctant to change how people portray us even though we are uncomfortable with the social caricatures used to speak for us. And because on occasions when we need to speak up we may feel ambivalent and undecided about how we can specifically change ourselves, we may remain understandably conflicted and inarticulate.

People can choose to live as they prefer, as they feel comfortable. However, I believe in making the world better for Latinos and for all other Americans. We have had many problems for which solutions have not been forthcoming because we have lacked tolerance for people of different races and for immigrants who have arrived in the United States with different cultures and backgrounds. That should not be the case in a wonderful country like the United States. Citizens and immigrants deserve better. The only way to change such attitudes is by educating people to understand and to encourage an appreciation for different versions of reality.

In a world beset by change, including the growing presence of Spanish-speaking Americans, it is time to make the U.S. world of Latinos a significant component of the larger American Public Consciousness. Although I have always had some temerity about the kind of writing that connects an individual's life with a larger public discourse, I see no better alternative than to help shape the U.S. Latino community by describing a personal road that, vague for much of my own life, has become clearer as I have heard fellow Latinos articulate similar views.

People come to terms with their mortality in different ways. In the normal course of our lives most of us do not have time to consider the legacies that we leave behind until our energies, will power, and other skills and talents are questioned by health or other considerations. I believe that once we have learned how to take care of our own needs and those of our families, caring for and improving the rest of the world beckons. We should recognize that in one way or another each generation leaves behind the stories of the struggles endured during their watch. The particulars of every generation end by defining the nature of the contributions, shaping, in turn, the lives of the next few generations, members of which will either be empowered or not, successful or not, rich, middle class, poor, and famous or infamous. Anchored where we have been taught to live or where our lives have placed us, given our education, skills, and backgrounds, most of us end by typifying a generation, contextualizing the stories that journalists and historians record.

Some lives, of course, claim more attention than others, and self-writing brashly says that my life warrants notice. We can take the first-page challenge in Rousseau's *Confessions* (1782) and ambitiously itemize and detail particulars. But at some point, even in Rousseau, declarations about the self tire readers, appearing hollow, leaving us with chary words that underscore human pretensions. José Guadalupe Posada, the Mexican lithographer made famous by Diego Rivera, for that reason drew skulls and skeletons in his little flyers. These he freely gave to passers-by, reminding all who saw his drawings that, regardless of social and cultural differences, someday everyone will be equally deceased, replaced by another generation.

For this reason I endeavor to inscribe Latinos, particularly Mexican Americans, into the story of our time in a different way from the typically American. Although my own life in many ways is unorthodox, I write partly to show readers that Mexican Americans vary tremendously, a fact not sufficiently understood and appreciated by North American culture, as Octavio Paz referred to the United States. Although Mexican Americans are found in nearly all of the professions in all parts of the United States, we are characteristically not viewed that way today. Rather, we are generally seen as poor and barely able to subsist, and, although unfortunately that portrait is largely true, Mexican Americans are not all contained by that image.

The part of the world that I know best is Texas and the surrounding region, and that is why most of these essays deal with the Southwestern part of the country. Although there are ample signs that the world is discovering both the quiet beauties and the challenges that Texas and the Gulf of Mexico pose for the United States, too many people ironically appropriate this region of the world without meaningfully interfacing with its large Mexican American population. Since "snowbirds" and other northern visitors have been visiting the Rio Grande Valley and other parts of Texas, New Mexico, Arizona, and the entire Southwest in growing numbers during the last quarter-century, this book seeks to enlarge the scope of life that such visitors encounter. The goal of *Latino Sun, Rising* is to invite the world to recognize that there is a growing middle class of Mexican Americans in the United States with recognizable needs and hopes that are not insuperable if the rest of the American family helps.

In looking over this particular piece, I am struck by my several attempts to establish rapport with an audience that may still remain unclear about the opening autobiographical chapters. Since life in South Texas shaped me, I proceed by suggesting how and why the Texas Gulf Coast area engages my life and interests. By continuing to move from the personal to larger issues, I hope to suggest the nature of some of the difficulties that Spanish-speaking citizens face. Reconciling our more private life to the experiences of our public spheres is where the voices of Latino adults are largely absent. I don't, of course, expect all Latinos to agree with my views, since one of my intentions is to broach subjects and to show that we do have views. My main intention, though, is to prompt discussion of issues not sufficiently considered part of the normal American dialogue that the media shape, often without considering Latinos.

Deciding on a writing voice is easier when the audience is clearly defined. When one writes for readers from the four winds, however, the task challenges, because, regardless of strategies, the avenues for self-definition, given the voices and issues previously employed and associated with Chicanos, constrain instead of opening new doors. Look, rather, at *The Education of Henry Adams* (1907), an autobiography that features and simultaneously effaces the author's life. Better yet, let us return to Rousseau's opening quip. Boldly asserting himself, Rousseau challenges all future writers to be more honest and more forthright—before he hides behind the masks he creates to tell his story. As an American of Mexican descent, as a member of a race of people progressively writing from voices other than the ones so far devised, few of which are known to American audiences, finding the appropriate words and signals, after considerable thought, is central to the task.

When I began these essays, a number of voices automatically arose before me, clamoring for use. Some Chicano texts urged militancy, others counseled ridiculing standing realities, while still others advised creating guilt or further dissatisfaction. Dismissing a good part of the Eurocentric and Anglo worlds on the grounds that such social constructions have not been kind to mestizo people has also emerged, ready for use, but these worlds, too, proved unsuitable because such voices did not altogether arise from our struggles. As descendants of the indigenous people of the Americas, Mexican Americans and other Latinos have a long history of marrying the conquering Europeans in the wake of Columbus's 1492 arrival. Like most people, though, Mexican Americans and Latinos have developed ways of communicating with different audiences, and that is why writing a different kind of book has prompted me to move in a number of directions within the same volume. I, too, seek the larger game that Mark Twain pursued, but even making such a statement introduces the risk of endearing one to some audiences while alienating the work from the eyes of others. The literary voices available to Latino writers, in short, pull and push in a number of directions; thus, devising the necessary coalescing words that will enlist the attention of all audiences and soothe readers is not an easy matter. Fortunately, the desire to communicate more about how American Spanish-speakers feel about issues that daily affect life in the United States has prevailed, shaping my language and rhetoric.

Although I feature the lives of the people who live north of the Gulf of Mexico, the main purpose of these pieces is to show that Tejanos are part of the larger American population. Personal essays are included because most nonfiction books do not sufficiently detail the lives of authors who attempt to alter opinions. Thanks to editors, such books these days are too neat, offering rounded-out, nicely tucked rhetoric, leaving readers without a good enough sense of the shaping, creating writer. Artifice that too obviously insists on looking natural makes me uneasy, for as Walt Whitman suggested, consistency constricts, instead of affording people the liberating opportunity to express themselves. Like that Walden sage, I also pay attention to how a writer describes himself or herself, which partly explains several of the short chapters situating me at home in the warm, beautiful Texas Gulf

Coast. Highlighting South Texas and the Rio Grande Valley permits imaginative visits to other places and permits the broaching of issues that I hope readers will pursue further. When considered, credibility in writing, after all, is largely based on the nature of the relationship that unites readers to an author.

During the last thirty years, the place where I was born has received increasing attention. The Edinburg-McAllen and Harlingen-Brownsville areas are known as the Rio Grande Valley, a land that produces some of the best oranges and grapefruits in the country. Cotton, of course, is the principal crop. But the actual people, I believe, are the least recognized product. *El Valle es la pura mata, como dice la gente allí*. The Valley is the place where a good number of our country's Mexican Americans are produced, and I use the word cautiously, because, as in the case of other questions, people are also shaped and turned out by the history and the circumstances of a region. Historically, little educational attention has been placed on the people of the Valley. We have not been taught, nor have we sufficiently learned, how to teach ourselves to provide better lives for ourselves and our progeny. I now suspect that is partly why I left the Rio Grande Valley for Chicago in 1968. Shortly after returning from England, I made what I considered the rather risky decision to pursue a Ph.D. in English. Since then, the United States has changed considerably. Yet the school preparations available to the youths of the Valley have changed little, despite the understandably positive statements made by the educational leaders of the area.

People from the Valley may take issue with this assessment, for, like people from other areas, citizens of South Texas and the Southwest in general also like to point to the many school improvements that have been made in the last two generations. I have in mind, however, not the growth in school buildings, but the actual teaching. What we need, to be sure, are educations that will make a discernible difference demonstrated by how lives unfold.

So, one bright Saturday morning when everybody was busily preparing for the week or the month and years ahead, it occurred to me that at some point in our lives most of us feel the need to reconnect with the place where we grew up and with the people there. This realization resulted from the ten-day trip to Mexico City, Puebla, and other Mexican cities that I previously mentioned. That visit allowed me to see my role in life, as well as my time, place, and state of mind altogether differently. Instead of focusing attention on how we Latinos are all different from one another, I suddenly saw how we all remain products of forces that have shaped our immediate histories and environments, regardless of dissimilarities.

Like the U.S. Latinos that I met in New York State, California, Arizona, New Mexico, and elsewhere, Mexican Americans from the Rio Grande Valley are more alike than different. From the U.S. 281 bridge span in Pharr, which connects the main towns of the Valley, I looked out at how the twenty-first century was starting that day when I was brought up to consider our direction by the fleetingness of our lives. Looming above the many-hued green spring trees and the residential roofs, my hungry eye was caught by the taller palm trees, the water towers of the neighboring towns, and the church steeples spread out against the horizon, as if an artist had sketched them along the business thoroughfares. The understanding of my own mortality, under a blinding sun, at such a place, and after countless learning and travel experiences, instinctively made me pull over to the side of the freeway, absorbed in my mute epiphany. Life had brought me full circle, for I realized that now it is my turn to expand the Latino story, furthering the legacy, creating new doors.

7

Education

First Priority

Most Latinos love children and are especially interested in being good parents, in providing not only so-called education for children but also the best quality educations that can be afforded. We know that the best way to improve our children's chances for success in America is by offering them an education that is capable of changing their lives. If education does not change their lives, what is the point of spending years in the classroom? Unfortunately, too many of us have lacked the resources necessary to provide quality educations for our children, which is to say that the education most of us have attained has allowed little progress. Nonetheless, as the Latino population increases, all Americans need to understand that educating Latino students well will place them in positions to improve their lives, and all of our lives.

Since roughly the end of World War II Latinos have theoretically had access to the same education as other Americans, but in actuality the educations that Latinos have received have failed to provide us with quality job skills. The media, too, remain inattentive to and unconcerned with Hispanic realities and needs, undermining, by such indifference, the very dreams that many Latinos try to pursue. Even though the issue has been repeatedly brought to the attention of leaders who control the media industries, CEOs have shown that they do not know how to change to represent Latinos in positive ways. Worse, they appear quite reluctant to hire the people who can teach them. I remain confident, however, that this situation will change in the near future. Media industry leaders seem to believe that Latinos in the United States simply ought to be grateful for being implicitly included as part of the American Way of Life, without being explicitly included as Americans. Such attitudes would continue to relegate us to the marginal roles and positions that we have traditionally occupied. We need to have our faces and the faces and bodies of Latinos on the screens of America, just like other Americans who are now embraced and championed. The schools and the media, the two most important institutions that daily promote active participation in the American community, have been failing Latinos, even though Hispanics have called such injustices to the attention of leaders and the public policy people responsible for treating and extending equal opportunities to all Americans. In light of these realities, it is difficult to emphasize U.S. Latino progress, which may explain why most Latinos appear to prefer to live quiet lives away from the hubbub that nourishes and sustains the rest of American culture.

Look, for instance, at most U.S. Latino youths today. What I see is not the same confidence and zest for life exhibited by other American kids. Too often what I notice is their lukewarm, lackluster involvement in everything from academic school activities to sports to the nature of their everyday participation in American life. I am not saying that the Latino population does not include well-adjusted and successful children and adults. What I am saying is that for every flourishing Latino, there are twenty to thirty others whose lives remain untouched and engaged by American life. If we expect such citizens to secure good jobs, to pay their fair share of regional and federal taxes, and to contribute to American society, then our schools, the media, and how we portray and represent Latinos in our country's national life need immediate improvement.

By not articulating how American Latinos have been treated and viewed since the end of World War II, we leave the next generations of Hispanics with the misfortune of experiencing the same type of marginalized participation in American life that baby-boomer Latinos know all too well. Because we have not been sufficiently encouraged to be players in the making and the sustaining of American life, today an inadequate number of Latinos have the needed clout to make a difference. How can we shape the kind of political and public policy decisions that all Americans need to meet the demographic requirements of the twenty-first century? These are issues that need serious, concerted attention.

8

Puerto Rico or Houston

The Caribbean or the Gulf?

Rita and I were married in February of 1972 at St. Vincent de Paul Church on Main Street in Buffalo, next door to Canisius College. Rita selected the readings for the service and we had a beautiful late afternoon Mass with the actual ceremony occurring right before the offertory. By the time our wedding party marched back down the aisle toward the front door of the church, Rita and I happily beaming as new wife and husband, a light snow was falling and the weather had turned colder. The cracked sidewalks were slippery with ice, and I remember that Rita took hold of her mother to ease her down the steps, and then, to prevent a possible fall, they held onto each other as we made our way to the wedding car. To help, I opened the back door, seated them together, and then jumped into the front passenger seat. That's the way we went off to the reception.

Rita's parents overrode our desire for a small wedding; they convinced us that we needed to invite "a few friends." It turned out that more than three hundred people showed up for the wedding reception at the Buffalo Puerto Rican Center. We enjoyed every minute of it, and by the time we left, toward one in the morning, we were deliriously happy and it was snowing furiously fast, as blizzards easily take over everything in western New York. About three that morning, still under blizzard conditions, Rita and I arrived in Toronto for our honeymoon, the wind howling through the downtown buildings as we made our way with her luggage into a hotel that I had reserved in a street off Canada's longest *calle,* Yonge Street. I say Rita's luggage, because, when I went back to the car to bring in my suitcase, I discovered I had left it in Buffalo!

We first went to Puerto Rico in December of 1972, following our wedding that previous February. Like some Mexican Americans, I suspect I was a little anxious about visiting Puerto Rico, particularly during the holidays. I had heard that the island was very hot, and I had become used to the wonderfully beautiful snowfalls of Buffalo at Christmastime. Puerto Ricans, I also knew, tend not to pronounce the last syllables of their words, which I always found an interesting dialect of Spanish. Rita and her family did not lop off the ending of their words, except for a word here and there, but that practice sounded oddly attractive to me because it was so different to the ear. Also, since I occasionally mispronounced a Spanish word, Rita's mom always corrected me, saying that, as a professor, I did not ever want to be embarrassed for not saying a word correctly. I appreciated her tutoring, and took her lessons in good humor, since I have always been the type of person who willingly takes instruction wherever offered me.

I had learned that Mexican Americans and Puerto Ricans use similar words differently. For example, Mexican Americans use *ahorita,* which is a more casual version of *ahora,* to mean right now or immediately. Puerto Ricans use *ahorita* to say in a while, after they finish doing something else. *Ahora* for Puerto Ricans, then, means now, immediately. Rita's father, affectionately called Tati, I believe was a descendent of the Taino Indians, the native inhabitants who lived on the island of Puerto Rico when Columbus sailed into the Caribbean. He and I went through a very comical series of misunderstandings when I first met him. We were in his parlor, and his wife, Nani, Rita's mom, had asked us to drive to the store to buy some grocery items for the Sunday afternoon supper that, following our marriage, became a regular family weekend gathering at their home on 310 Chestnut Avenue in Lockport. Lockport, known for being the birthplace of the writer Joyce Carol Oates, and the home of Jack Kemp, the football quarterback and legislator, is where the famous Erie Canal was opened in 1825, about thirty miles north of Buffalo.

We were watching the Buffalo Bills on television, as we did throughout the football season. I asked when we would be driving to the store to bring the goods that Nani needed for the supper. Tati said *ahorita,* which to him met in a little while, likely during half-time. For a Mexican American like me, however, *ahorita* meant now. So, I jumped up from the sofa where, as Rita's fiancé, I had sat rather uncomfortably watching a game that I was not following too closely. I walked toward the closet to put on the all-purpose Navy pea coat that I wore for the four years I lived in Buffalo. Rita's father asked me where I was going, so, of course, I told him to the store. He said don't worry, we'll go in a little while, again ending by using the word *ahorita.* But instead of having the desired effect of making me take off my coat and sit down to watch the game again, as Tati intended, his use of *ahorita* again set me in motion. I got up again and was ready for the trip to the store. I believe we went through one more version of this misunderstanding before I figured out that we were both using the same Spanish word, but that our Puerto Rican and Mexican American meanings were totally different.

We had a similar experience with the word *guajolote,* which is the Mexican American term used to refer to a turkey, as in the Thanksgiving turkey. When I first used the word, everybody looked at one another, and I wondered if I had used a bad word or if I had unintentionally insulted someone. Then I saw that Rita's brother Mandy, who is now a policeman in Tucson, Arizona, and her older brother Frank, and their wives, were looking at me funny, one signaling something to the other. It was not until I asked what they called a turkey that I was informed that the correct Spanish word for turkey is *pavo.* And they were right. *Pavo* is in the Spanish-English dictionary, while *guajolote,* over which they could not stop laughing every time I said it, is not. I suspect that *guajolote* may be an onomatopoeic word, likely from Nahuatl, one of the several languages used by the Aztecs, or from some other language belonging to the indigenous peoples of the Americas. Here I was, a graduate student studying for a Ph.D. in English, using a word in Spanish of which I did not know the origin. Until I met my Puerto Rican wife's family, it had never occurred to me that a turkey in Spanish might be something other than a *guajolote.* This was an education, suggesting that we obtain an education any number of ways, both inside and outside the classroom. I have since learned, for example, that the English words chocolate, chili, and tomato are derived from Nahuatl, which begins to suggest that many other words have likely been lost.

Puerto Rico was hot, but the people were so friendly, and the *pastel*-eating Christmas gatherings were so merry that I fell in love with my wife's island and the Puerto Rican way of life. We talked about virtually everything, including politics, though Rita's family had warned me to talk about anything except that, it was supposed to be such a volatile subject. And it was, but I have found that, if approached respectfully and in a serious way, most people will feel comfortable talking about many issues that otherwise are not easily discussed. During the most recent of our three trips to Puerto Rico, taken during the last thirty years (we have not been able to afford more), we drove through *la Calle Ashford,* which is one of the main streets that runs lengthwise through the casino Condado section of downtown San Juan. That is *the* political street, we found out, where, during elections, people who have a stake in the outcome turn up to display the banners and the campaign signs of their party. We found it great fun to see the gusto with which Puerto Ricans divide themselves into the three reigning parties. Some Puerto Ricans fervently desire U.S. statehood, while others are committed to remaining a U.S. commonwealth, and a third, still smaller group, are insistent on securing Puerto Rico's independence. The U.S. Congress, as some political observers know, is directed to have a plebiscite every ten years on whether new states are to be admitted into the United States. And throughout the ten years, the three (or more) Puerto Rican parties lobby, discuss, argue, and make their cases to the general population, giving us one of the best demonstrations of democracy in action anywhere in the world. The best time to see the political action on Ashford Street, though, are the months right before the November vote every ten years. I have not been there during other elections, but knowing the fierceness of their political views, I suspect all elections are sights to behold. During the political season, the Puerto Rican scene is very interesting to watch, for Puerto Ricans take their politics seriously, but, thankfully, they usually remain civil and respect differences of opinion. This, at any rate, is what we saw the last time we were on Ashford Street.

When we first visited Puerto Rico, there was no island-wide freeway system to speak of, and driving from one side of the one-hundred-mile east-and-west island took more than three hours, depending on the amount of traffic on the highways. When we last visited Puerto Rico, however, twenty years later, we drove on two of their three new main freeway systems, called Highway 1, Highway 2, and Highway 3. Moving from one side of the island to another or north and south, say, from the capitol San Juan, which is located in the northeastern part of the island, to Ponce, on the southwestern end, takes about an hour and a half or so, again, depending on the traffic leaving metropolitan San Juan. Ponce has a great art museum and the drive there from San Juan on their modern freeway system is wonderful and well worth the trip. Over the years, we have also visited El Yunque, Puerto Rico's famous rain forest, and Luquillo, for its serene beaches. But most of our trips we have spent our time on the western end of the island by Quebradillas, Rita's birthplace and early childhood hometown. On the other occasion, we were just south of that where some of her relatives rented a cabana, and we witnessed the fishermen bringing in their hand-drawn *tarayas* or their *chinchorros,* the two words Puerto Ricans use for nets. In one of their hauls, I saw a *taraya* full of fish, the wonderful sight silhouetted against a blinding setting sun.

In 1979, when we left the Albany-Berkeley area of California, I was fortunate to have an offer of a teaching position from the University of Puerto Rico in Río Piedras. My wife and I were quite interested in the post because teaching in Puerto Rico would mean that we would establish our family in the Caribbean. We would be within easy reach of the U.S. mainland as well as Costa Rica, where my mother was thinking of removing to at that point. But when we inquired about the price of buying a home and raising a family in San Juan, we learned from Rita's relatives that real estate prices on the island were high. Violence that year was also escalating and appeared to be out of control, just as it had been in New York City throughout the 1970s and the early 80s. The University of Puerto Rico also, unfortunately, was not in a position to help us pay for our moving *gastos,* whereas the University of Houston at Clear Lake provided me with half of our moving expenses. Since our daughter and son were two and four at the time, after considerable soul-searching, we felt we had to chose to bring our family to my home state of Texas, where my brother and his family also lived, and where my mother was staying at the time. The Clear Lake-Seabrook area, we learned, had schools that were relatively good, and this was the most important factor that shaped our decision. Being in close proximity to good schools has always been a primary consideration for our family, as it generally is for most Latino parents who have the opportunity to choose. So we chose Houston, the nation's fourth largest city, and the Gulf of Mexico area became our family's home. We would be the next generation.

9

Apples after School, and the Alamo

This essay is not about picking apples in Washington State in the afternoons after school, as one of my students who is studying in Texas from the Northwest thought. Picking apples along the freeway and the country roads is where he generally sees Spanish-speakers in that part of the country, he explained. I told him my essay could deal with that reality, since during World War II that was the region of the country where many Latinos were brought in to help. Starting in 1942, the U.S. government and the Mexican government agreed to a mutually beneficial project called the Bracero Program. This international agreement legally authorized Mexican laborers to work in the United States for a number of years, picking the crops and making sure that the railroads were running well for the war effort. Resident Chicanos as well as green-card carrying braceros worked in these and other low-paying jobs, generally in the western states, until the program was terminated for political reasons in 1964. Today, our immigration problems largely stem from the inability of both countries to work out an agreement that would again be mutually beneficial.

Like most of the other reflections in this volume about how one postmodern Mexican American lives, this essay seeks to provide a glimpse into the nature of my family life in Texas. I offer a look into my home life to show how my wife and I consciously worked, when our children were younger, to encourage them to feel good about themselves; we paid attention to what was going on in their heads and tried to build their self-esteem. This is an issue that Latino parents, like other minority parents, too, have to work hard at because there is so much in American society that does not encourage them, like, for example, the seemingly harmless comment made by my otherwise intelligent student. It is very difficult for many Latino youths to see, imagine, and to represent themselves proudly as Spanish-speaking people because where Latinos usually have to work is almost automatically associated by many Americans with an unattractive quality of life.

My wife and I, as teachers, have not had enough to provide the kind of opportunities that we would have liked to offer our family. Nonetheless, we are thankful that we have been able to live a middle-class life. Still, it is true that the great American middle class has been dwindling, from every sign that I have seen since the 1980s. Corporate America has simply dried up the American Dream for too many people, and the credit card has been the main instrument and culprit. Through this tool, which the big-money people have learned to use by taking over and hobnobbing with the government to write laws and policies that favor them, big business interests have effectively siphoned off savings and whatever other funds the middle class used to have. What we average Americans have been left with are essentially debts, for even what used to be our ability to move and to see other faraway places has been progressively restricted and curtailed. Indeed, it seems that every time state legislatures or Congress work for our supposed benefit, we end up paying more and more fees, even though we are continually told that taxes have been lowered or in some way curtailed. To be sure, I want the record to state that I dislike being so negative in a book where otherwise I champion American opportunities. But I have set my heart on being straightforward and honest in these pages, and that is what I have reluctantly concluded, given what I have experienced.

One afternoon around four o'clock several years ago, though, I had the luxury of sitting at the kitchen table to wait for the return of our son and daughter from school. On that particular day our children were still in the elementary grades, and we were at a period in our lives when we were working on developing little family rituals to bring us closer together. Due to our desire to nourish such efforts, which replicate the weekends that we spent with Rita's parents and the families of her brothers and sister when we were both graduate-school students in Buffalo, we have often continued to cook outside in the backyard. Rita also has always cooked a good hot *olla de arroz* and *frijoles,* a rice pot and either brown or black beans, following recipes from our Puerto Rican, Mexican, or Costa Rican families. To help, I usually set the table for supper, and rinse, or wash the dishes after our family get-togethers, a task that over the years has earned me some good-natured ribbing from a number of predictable quarters.

On the occasion I have in mind, I had already finished grading most of the student papers that I would return to my class the following day. I had begun at six that morning, and, although I still had some other reading to do, committee materials to prepare, and errands to run, both before and after supper, I had taken a few minutes to enjoy the interval just before our children's bus was scheduled to arrive by the cul-de-sac opposite our house. To provide the kind of immediacy I want to convey, think of the humming air conditioner that is cooling the house. It has been humming that way all summer, day and night. Indeed, I have been concerned that it may go out any day, that we won't have enough money to repair it. I have two or three other issues that I will forego mentioning, other than to say that they also require money that we simply don't have. One can only charge so much. Still, if we can make it to the end of September, when I will have an extra twelve hundred in my paycheck for the coming year, we should be okay. Still, I know two other Latino families who are having it worse, one with an unexpected operation that is not covered by health insurance, and the other having to finance a family trip back to Mexico to see aging parents. When the second family returns, the kids will be behind in school several weeks, Rita mentioned that the other day. When I compare our situation with theirs, I am thankful.

It is early autumn, and the school year started a week ago. For their afternoon snack, I am paring some Jonathan apples that usually arrive in our part of Texas this time of the fall. The bus has just left my daughter in front of our house, and my son will arrive soon. The moment forecasts some well-earned parental pleasure, what with the work at our different schools, taking care of the needs of the house, and settling into being part of the Houston-Seabrook everyday scene. We have been in the area seven years, but somehow we still feel like new arrivals, as if we moved from Albany, California, only a year or two ago. Since my teaching schedule at the university is more flexible than Rita's, I have developed the habit of waiting for our children's return from school on the days when I do not pick them up myself. Being a parent in what people tell me is postmodern America is difficult, what with all the running to the organized programs for children that is required. I remember when we were kids, no one organized our play activities. We simply played in the barrio neighborhood, so long as we did not go out into the streets. I am the type who likes being at home with my family, because I thoroughly enjoy the moments with my spirited children. In this case I am also listening to Modest Mussorgsky's *Night on Bald Mountain* on the CD player in the adjoining piano room, which lends a funny contrapuntal tone to the following parlor-room scene.

When Marie enters, I tell her that the apples I have been cutting are so good they make me want to write an essay or a poem on apples. I ask her if she would like to see an essay written by her father on that subject. She smiles and says yes. She then takes two of the apple slices I have placed on a plate, and zips by to pick up her piano books. She is in the fourth grade, and I will drive her over shortly to Mrs. Madge H. for her lessons. Several times a year, Mrs. H. kindly arranges recitals in her beautiful home by the lake on Sunday afternoons, and the parents of the students are invited to hear the pieces that the students are studying. In two or three years, Mrs. H. will think Marie good enough to enter some competitions, including one in Dallas. She will bring home several first place trophies and other second and third place finishes. Needless to say, I cannot play a note, though our whole family loves music. We are very impressed with her teacher and are thoroughly pleased with the relationship that our daughter has developed with Mrs. H.

Writing an essay should be something like composing a piece on a piano, I say to myself. Before her next birthday, she will write two emotionally moving melodies that wonderfully engage memories of our one family visit to Costa Rica, in 1984. Due to family needs and expenses, we will not have money for a second trip for almost fifteen years after that one, but her composition will continue to stir memories of that visit for many years. My wife and I have long hoped that she will one day win a scholarship to study music somewhere, preferably in the northeast where I have seen how the long, cold winters promote more reading, music, and other indoor activities not sufficiently embraced in cities and living spaces where the day is long and most human activities revolve around escaping the heat of the sun into cooler, air-conditioned rooms. Among the nearly three thousand books that I have bought since my college days, I have several long shelves of essay collections penned by some of the best handlers of the language. The books are in the built-in bookcases in the den next to the fireplace that we fire up on cold December or January days. Our home, our biggest investment, is attractively nestled among the pin-oaks in a Houston suburb next door to the Johnson Space Center in Taylor Lake City. This Seabrook community is built around a lake that slowly empties out into the Gulf of Mexico, on which shortly I have more.

In a first-rate piece of writing, I appreciate a willingness to follow an author's carefully crafted words. I especially like a fine eye for pictures made from ideas communicated with a certain smoothness arising from the nature of the very language employed, suggesting a well-developed sensibility that brings out details affecting the relevant senses. That, I believe, is what the better essayists in one way or another wring from life again and again. The task is something like choosing the excellent apples from the ones available at the local farmers market, cooling them in the refrigerator, and delierately paring them for the enjoyment of children coming home from school, or of friends and neighbors. The right selection of the juiciest apples is like the inimitable notes of that Mussorgsky composition on the CD player.

My son, Carlos, arrives shortly. He is in the SIXTH GRRRADE, as he proudly belts it out when I exaggerate the question, what grade are you in, son? It *is* a big step, the first year out of elementary, and probably the most important, since he and his friends are beginning to wake up to the fact that they will too soon be adults. Preparing schoolwork for six or seven teachers, all asking for assignments with different, specific directions is an altogether novel challenge for an eleven-year-old young man. Responsibility is what the teachers emphasize this year, they have told us. And that is good, when the parents are available to back up the curriculum.

But what happens to youngsters whose parents do not know what the school agenda is? That is the case with many Latino parents. Mom and Dad or the single parent are simply not at home; or, when they are, they are too tired to cut and pare apples for the children when they arrive in the buses in the afternoons. When my son arrives, he rushes into the cool air-conditioned room, pushed indoors by the day's momentum, his books in the satchel on his back, his face flushed from the hot bus ride. There is the motor and the brakes. In less than a minute, the bus moves off to drop the neighbor's children, and Carlos enters, beaming, excited. Yes, those apples are pretty good, Dad. Thanks!

Today he has a Social Studies exam that needs to be signed and returned. He received a 93, and, of course, I told him that his mother will be as pleased as I am with that kind of school work. Shows that he will do good work later when he is a big guy, I add. He is studying King Tut, the Egyptian boy king, among other subjects these days. Everyone knows he is eleven, but when I ask, he smiles, smirks and says "eleven plus." He will be twelve on December 12th, *el día de la Virgen de Guadalupe.*

We have now forgotten that several years ago my wife and I had to visit with his teacher. Here is the type of incident that we Latinos are good at blocking out, I guess, because dwelling on it would bother us continually. He came home one day while he was still in kindergarten or the first grade, and, while I was washing the dishes, I heard him say that the Mexicans were bad people. I stopped and said, what? The Mexicans were the bad guys at the Alamo, he repeated, while he was coloring. That was what he was being taught. We could not, of course, believe that teachers in Texas were still unaware of history and teaching that one-sided, simplified view of the Alamo. But here it was, a whole generation after I had heard the view as a student myself, and in our own home. I eventually found out that Mexicans and Mexican Americans also defended the Alamo, but not until I had spent some years reeling under that misinformation, feeling personal disrespect, self-dislike, and general unworthiness.

Fortunately, now as professional teachers ourselves, we felt comfortable questioning the teaching of such a biased perspective, and we did. Rita called his teacher that same evening, and the following morning we met with her before the beginning of classes at eight. Walking into the room, I also noticed that she had the story of Little Black Sambo very prominently displayed for her students. I inquired about that, and she told me the students love the story. I told her that there were a good number of better stories about young African Americans written, since that would provide her students with a better sense of blacks. I added that I would look into it and suggest several titles for her. I later called her back with some titles, but she left me feeling that I had interfered with her teaching instead of thanking me for trying to bring her out of a racist past that she apparently had been blithely promulgating. Where are the colleges of education that they do not instruct teachers better, I asked my wife? Why do they still allow such psychologically destructive ideas to be taught?

And, we ask ourselves, what happens when Spanish-speaking parents are unaware that their sons and daughters are being taught ideas like these? No wonder some Latinos and African Americans wind up confused and conflicted. Some even end up disliking and disrespecting themselves and their own race and ancestors. Whenever I bring up issues like these, most Anglos and Latinos want to talk about something else, mainly, I suspect because they are in a state of denial. They do not want to recognize and admit that some of the materials and views we are teaching students can be harmful and hurtful, especially to minority students who have been entrusted to the care of the schools. We need to talk about more positive things, they tell me. Why dwell on the negative—as if I am the one who first created the negative images and as if I were the one continuing the situation. Forget about the past, they say, today the world is different; things have changed. But because I often encounter such experiences, I remain unpersuaded. I just wish we could, I respond. The world around us badly needs education.

Our son then tells us that today he and his friends ran what they call the Amaya Mile. The surname of his coach is Amaya, and he is the only Mexican American coach at his school. Has he forgotten about the Alamo, I wonder? What does he remember; did he try to block out the story, as I tried to for years? If you are a Mexican American and live in Texas, you are going to hear about the Alamo, and likely from someone who uses the event to show how the Anglos beat and drove out the Mexicans. Carlos fortunately learned, but what about the Anglo and the African American kids? They will go through school and on to college where they might learn otherwise, but I would not bet on that, since I teach such students. So Carlos ran the Amaya Mile, which they are required to run every day during P.E.

When I was in the sixth grade in 1959, we did not have a coach at Sacred Heart School in the northern part of the Rio Grande Valley. During recess, which was at ten fifteen or so in the morning, we would quickly choose teams and play until after the bell rang twice. Only one or two more batters could hit before we had to sweatily trek back into the classrooms. Panting and huffing, we returned to the science class. But it was the seventh grade that I actually recall. I remember T. L. who had the nicest *ojos borados,* gray-green eyes. I was particularly aware of this one girl at thirteen. I can see us working on an experiment we had to present to the rest of the class. That year T. L. had the nicest, lithest body around, and all the boys envied the fact that I had drawn her name as my science partner. I don't remember if she had a boyfriend at that point. She would though, marrying later while we were still in high school. A high school older guy would come by on the street side of our school in his big, red truck—but all of this is immaterial to the year I am concerned with here. That would happen about three years later. Between the row of chairs by the Venetian glass windows that flanked a whole side of the classroom and the counter shelf on which we carried out our experiments, there was space for only one adult. There T. L. and I brushed and awkwardly bumped against each other as opportunities arose. There among the plant cells, the chlorophyll, and the issues that we were expected to talk about for our science project, the working space forced us to lean against each other, both of us smiling at two or so in the afternoon while the teacher worked with other students.

F. S. was a *pachuco,* though, a *chuco,* as we were in the habit of saying. In the sixth and seventh grades he was at the juncture where he was just beginning to rebel against the way things were set up for Mexican Americans. By the time he left the eighth grade, he was a full-blown pachuco, and he sported the pointed-toe shoes and the baggy khaki pants that reached down to his back-heels. He positioned the waist of his pants midway between his belly button and his crotch, supported either by a white- or silver-colored thin belt, or, at other times, no belt at all. F. S. and I were both headed to the public high school across town, where our class of roughly twenty-eight Catholic school Spanish-speaking friends would be swallowed up into a class of more than four hundred freshmen. But I began to say that by the time F. S. and I got there, we would be on essentially different paths. I would be enrolled for College Prep courses, and he would be placed on the vocational track by the school counselors who never asked him anything about his life. They simply assumed that would be the best place for him, and he didn't care a fink. During our freshmen year we still saw each other walking through the halls. I would make an effort to find him to see what he was up to, but we both knew that we already were on separate tracks, and that the friendship we had enjoyed in the sixth and seventh grades was gone.

In those grades we had been great friends, and, since he was the oldest member of the class at fourteen and fifteen, when I was twelve and thirteen, the others and I looked up to him. He could out hand-wrestle all of us, except A. G., who was a plumb, cherubic-like *guero*. A. G. was so strong that twice that year he bested F. S. But after that, F. S. reestablished himself in the event. He was also king of the dirt mound that workers had left behind the school, and, he was the second-fastest runner. I was the fastest, but only for a month or two, or, at least that's what F. S. said, for I won three races. That is primarily why I enjoyed a measure of respect from F. S.

The rest of our little group admired F. S. because on Saturday afternoons and sometimes on Sunday evenings he was permitted to go into Beto's to play snooker and eight ball. I would not be allowed there until I turned fifteen or so. By then F. S. had gone up north to Michigan and had either stayed there to work, likely in the fields or at some corrugation factory, where some of us would later work, or, he would periodically disappear, appearing to some of my friends here and there occasionally. By the time the rest of us were ready to graduate from high school, no one knew what had happened to him. I suspect he went on to live a life like Turo in that fine story by Saul Sanchez called "Esperanza and 'Turo.'" This story can be found in a little-known collection of short stories called *hay plesha lichans tu di flac* [*sic*] (1977), that is, I pledge allegiance to the flag.

Yes, paring apples in the afternoon for your children in Texas can prompt all sorts of other stories that bring out patterns. To see the patterns, though, one has to have been around for a good while; otherwise, everything looks new. Things look like they are occurring for the first time. Being around for a good while allows us to compare what we went through with the events that we read about in the newspapers and that our own sons and daughters tell us about daily, which we hear if we but ask. Most of the time, of course, life doesn't allow us much time to ask, but that should not keep us from doing so as often as we can, since life goes by so fast and our children are young today and young adults tomorrow. One always ought to hope, of course, for better instruction and more enlightened books, but, regardless, students are always learning something, given the way things are. The challenge is to pare apples and to wait, wait to see what stories our children *may,* for one reason or another, tell us. We need to listen and we need to act if we are to make their world better than ours has been. I would hate to think that we have not succeeded in changing the world for the better for them. It so badly needs that.

10

Harvard Visit

Several years ago I visited Harvard one afternoon following an interview for a faculty position at another nearby college off the River Charles, as a Boston singing group calls that waterway. I mention the fact because there is a certain romance to moving one's family because a professorial appointment has materialized at another college or university. The idea of securing a faculty appointment in the Boston area is especially attractive. Indeed, I suspect nearly every professor's dream at some point is to teach, if not at Harvard, at least within the Harvard-Boston rim, keeping college instructors thinking that someday, perhaps, a prized faculty appointment there may actually materialize. Judging from comments I have heard on various campuses where I have taught over the years, I would say teaching at Harvard is a widespread higher-education fantasy. This second visit to Boston, however, brought me, rather abruptly, to consider some inchoate ideas that I have previously broached and which remain difficult to express.

My first visit to Boston was interesting. I went to the puritan capital, an unlikely place for a middle-class Mexican American from South Texas, to see the city and to call upon a publisher to discuss the possible publication of a book. I had allowed myself the luxury of an extra day, and, following coffee and a breakfast biscuit at a McDonald's, I turned up a street toward Boston Common. It was exactly ten thirty on a glorious morning, and the streets and parks were full of people enjoying the weather. I was two hours away from Melville's Arrowhead, close, I later found out, to Thoreau's Concord, and within driving distance of the famed sites of Hawthorne's haunts. The day was a lovely New England summer day, but I was feeling a bit queasy, surrounded by so much history that so many writers of that area have worked so hard to create and then to sustain so that New England would be associated with America's best writers. That, indeed, is part of what I call the social infrastructure. I remember thinking that I wish we Mexican American Chicanos had a widely known, comparable history that could be easily pointed to at this time in our cultural life, something that most people would immediately recognize as being unmistakably Mexican American. Yes, we do have some books that might be recognized, but we are still largely in the process of creating ourselves and digging out our heritage from the musty records that lie forgotten in dusty archives, courthouses, and other historically unattended to places, like family attics. I recall ending somewhat consoled by the thought that, like other Latino writers, at least, I was then engaged in preparing several projects designed to encourage people to look at U. S. Spanish-speaking residents differently.

A security officer, sitting at the door to the basement of a warehouse, surprised me. A quick check of the address in a card I was carrying told me I was at the right place, but, from his reaction, my presence seemed to indicate that perhaps I had made a mistake. I asked him if I could see an editor that I had contacted from Texas several days before. I had envisioned a comfortable anteroom, perhaps with a dull red or green leather sofa, and two or three soft-light lamps appropriately placed on side tables in a classily decorated waiting room. But the publishing house looked more like the rented warehouse it was, and the presence of a guard did not help. The publishing firm was an old, respected establishment, but all the signs appeared to indicate hard times, tough streets, don't trust anyone, particularly would-be authors. Why the armed guard? Without saying anything, he was point-blank asking me: who are you, and what would *you* want here?

Three awkward questions later, the editor I had buttonholed by long distance reluctantly took an elevator down to the lobby to see, as the guard phrased it, this guy who wants to talk. We prefer to see the manuscript or a prospectus first, he said. He had told me the same thing during the call, and I had informed him that I was almost finished, that I might be traveling to Boston, and that I was interested in meeting and leaving my proposal or the actual manuscript with him, whichever he preferred. This is highly unusual, he added, and, although I could see that they would want to evaluate a book project when the author was not around, I had hoped at least to meet him, since I was in town. Editors need to be objective in evaluating proposals, he continued, and meeting with prospective authors like this is not going to help either of us.

What I should have countered with, I thought to myself, as I walked out into the bright sunlight, is that my life and experiences have prepared me for seeing some highly different realities that I have not read about or heard articulated in American life.

On the return flight, I took out a sheet of blue paper on which I jotted down what I had experienced during my three-day trip to Boston. One must understand that from Texas, a trip to Boston, at today's travel costs, is not an easy endeavor. I had applied and had been invited to interview for a teaching post, which is to say my flight and one night's lodging would be reimbursed. That is about the only way I have been able to travel to different parts of the country since I finished my dissertation in 1974. I had just finished teaching the two regular summer courses that I usually teach, again, to pay family bills, and I had also decided to use the occasion to explore as much of the Boston area as I could sandwich in during my stay. In the early 1980s I had taken a quick trip to The Houghton to research the question of why Sarah Orne Jewett herself had not included three sketches that her publishers included in the 1896 edition of *The Country of the Pointed Firs* following her death. Because my essay disturbed the Jewett scholars who controlled the journals, my interpretation went unpublished, but my reason for mentioning this fact is that my research work on Jewett on that first visit had kept me in the library, so I did not see much of anything else. At that point, I had been to Boston, but had left with the sense that someday I would return to spend more time looking at life in the New England area.

On the blue paper before me, I now wrote the following words: Boston; Harvard; Boston College; Boston University; Radcliffe; MIT; Houghton Mifflin; phone calls to Julio and Kathy; Widener Library; Harvard's English Dept. and Creative Writing; film: "A Room With A View"; Loney Music School; Eliot House; Harvard Square; Thoreau article to NEQ at Northeastern University; The Coop; Harvard Motor House; Boston Subway; Buses; Charles River; Univ. of Mass./Boston; Logan; high real estate prices, very high real estate prices, too high, really; great submarine sandwiches; almost no Chicanos, from what I saw; some Puerto Ricans (which I would report to my Puerto Rican wife); better loan rates; excellent cultural opportunities for the young and parents who can afford them. I then itemized the names of people I had seen/met/and failed to see, most being on vacation. Work that ordinarily would have taken me a week and half or two, I compressed into three warm July days that provided me with a pretty fulfilling sense that I had spent several great days in Cambridge and the vicinity.

Although I had lived for four years in western New York while I attended graduate school in Buffalo, for a number of years I had wanted to see the seasons change in New England because I suspected they would be different there. I had seen the seasons change in a few movies about the Boston area, but, on the large screen, of course, everything looks better than in real life. In July, however, Harvard looks much like other campuses, that is, everything moves slower, mainly because the university itself appears to be at rest, breathing slowly and seemingly recuperating and fortifying itself for the onslaught when students return in force in the fall. During the days I was there, most of the professors were away. The secretaries told me they are off writing books. One secretary told me the scholar I asked for was off to England, France, South America, and, when he returned, he was headed for some other out-of-the-way place in Vermont, Maine, or New Hampshire, where the weather is bracingly cool, unlike Texas. If I was lucky, all we could afford for the summer were a few days in Galveston, where the sea breezes, thankfully, did clear my head. Others, like me, occasionally work a job interview or a conference to see what this mother of all colleges is contemplating, content with imagining how this first American institution of higher learning functions in October or March, when the students are in full siege during two of the prettiest months.

In late July the back streets surrounding the campus can offer the visitor a wonderful walk beneath the numerous trees that cast beautiful shades on the roots that have cracked the sidewalks. Needless to say, I enjoyed walking everywhere during that energizing summer visit. Such places are not easily found in Texas, I remember thinking, although we do have some surprisingly attractive areas, like the Blanco River area by Wimberley, the Guadalupe River in San Marcos, and even the Seabrook estuary where Clear Lake meets the Gulf of Mexico. All the great Tejano summer areas in my mind are associated with being next to a river or a lake or the ocean. "If they but knew it," Ishmael says at the end of the first paragraph of that great romance on whales, "almost all men [and women, too, I suspect] in their degree, some time or other, cherish very nearly the same feelings towards the ocean with me."

Circumambulate the city ["the insular city of the Manhattoes"] of a dreamy Sabbath afternoon [he continues]. Go from Corlears Hook to Coenties Slip, and from thence, by Whitehall, northward. What do you see?—Posted like silent sentinels all around the town, stand thousands upon thousands of mortal men fixed in ocean reveries. Some leaning against the spikes, some seated upon the pier-heads; some looking over the bulwarks of ships from China; some high aloft in the rigging, as if striving to get a still better seaward peep. But these

1

102   *Sol Ardiente:* Parenthood

are all landsmen; of week days pent up in lath and plaster—tied to the counters, nailed to benches, clinched to desks. How then is this? Are the green fields gone? What do they here [*sic*]?

Ishmael goes on for two more inspired paragraphs, which readers of *Moby Dick* (1851) can visit at leisure, ending with that fine sentence, "Yes, as every one knows, meditation and water are wedded for ever."

Harvard and its vicinity would be great, I said to myself, but I suspect I would miss the long Texas summer days when the beach following a particularly hot afternoon is quite simply spectacular. I particularly love to see the evening tide when the sun lowers itself. *Apagando el día* it slowly turns off the day along the oceanside, and the daylight lengthily disappears. That part of the day is one of the nicest times, and I would recommend it to any person interested in musing about anything one desires. Thinking about Boston and Harvard oddly made me want to drive to Padre Island or to Corpus Christi to sit under a beach umbrella. So long as the gulf wind offers a moderate breeze and is not bent on blowing down all the beach tents and tarps on *la playa,* this is the place to be during the summers in Texas. From that vantage point, seeing the great wide expanse of the ocean before one and hearing the waves lap up against the vast sandy beaches of the Gulf is one of life's incomparable experiences. Then there are the star-studded Texas skies that my wife and I love. From our back yard in central Texas, we can see the ever-present scintillating sentinels virtually every night during the warm summer evenings. But during the coldest winter months we periodically step out to fill the bird-feeder; oddly, I found myself missing that whole world while on my trip to New England.

II

Fishing at the Point in Seabrook

The day arrives when fishing presents itself as the best way to find some relief from the Houston area humidity in early August. By then, the backyard cookouts and the fireworks of the Fourth are a vague memory. The neighborhood's American flags, however, still wave to the little breeze that occasionally wafts its way through the oak trees and the sizeable two-story houses of the Clear Lake area. Although we have lived nearly twelve years within five miles of the Gulf of Mexico, work and the activities associated with raising a family have not often allowed fishing. Altogether I think we have fished only three times; today is one of those times. The first time occurred about a week after we moved our family to Clear Lake Forest in Taylor Lake Village, the suburb next to the NASA Johnson Space Center where most of the astronauts raised families in the 1950s, 60s, and 70s. Even today, half a century later, several astronauts continue to reside in Taylor Lake. On an afternoon, one can often see a lone hero running during the hottest part of the day, sweating profusely, working to stay in shape, hoping to be selected for the next space trip. Training and waiting for a space assignment is rougher than it seems. Despite the aeronautical successes, now on exhibit in the area's space museum and on NASA's Internet site, what the world vividly remembers, unfortunately, is the January 28, 1986, Challenger disaster, which affected nearly everyone in the Gulf region and beyond. Then, on Saturday, February 1, 2003, the Columbia space shuttle once more disintegrated before the eyes of thousands, eliciting awful emotions and memories.

When I taught at the University of Houston at Clear Lake during the 1980s, astronaut Story Musgrave was one of my students. I recall him for three reasons. The first is that he was the astronaut with the most actual space flight experience; he had a long and distinguished space career. The second item is that he once told a group of students that when he circled the earth in one of the spacecrafts, what he thought about was Walt Whitman's poetry. I have always considered that remarkable—that a scientist and astronaut, as he is circling the blue earth, would not be thinking of all sorts of scientific issues, but instead about the beauty of Whitman's poetry. Blue was the color that prevailed. He had enrolled in a course on Whitman shortly before, and, from the height he was at, he said the earth looked like a big, beautiful blue balloon. The sight reminded him of Whitman's poems. The third memory I have of him is that, like Charlie Bolden, who was the first African American astronaut, and also a neighbor who lived three houses down the street, Story accepted my invitation to meet my family. He came to our house one hot summer afternoon and spent a little over an hour talking to my son, daughter, and wife. We did so many things when we lived in Clear Lake that I had actually forgotten Story's visit to the house. But my children, now grown, who work and have separate apartments that we periodically visit in Houston, still remember that event very fondly. No doubt they will tell that story better someday.

If you are from the Texas Gulf Coast, the idea of catching a good-sized perch or a three- or four-pound redfish is never too far out of mind while one drives about the area. On the grill, in the backyard, under the pin-oak trees on a muggy Seabrook afternoon, one quickly learns that few pleasures compare to cooking a pair of freshly caught, nicely cut fillets, even if the fish have been bought at the seafood places of the area. A few very cold bottles of Bud Light that have been marinating in an ice cooler on such occasions will not hurt either. The area's humid weather is particularly stressful during the first few years, especially when one has become used to the natural air conditioning that the Pacific casts over Berkeley and the Bay Area. But after a few summers, a person learns to savor the rich mixed beauty of a summer morning, heat, fish, backyard pool life, and a rising or afternoon sun that periodically breaks through the piney woods of southeastern Houston.

At the Point, where the boats of the Houston-Clear Lake backyard tend to cruise by, out into the estuary, bound for the open sea, toward the serene, *azul* waters of the Gulf, I realize, while musing over shrimp and beer, that we verily fish nearly every day of our lives. We fish, of course, for different things, but we nonetheless cast our reel, hoping to bring some dream into our ken. As my son and I cast our fish poles against the rippling waves raised by the wake of the passing luxury boats, I momentarily lose touch with the impulse that actually brought us to fish one particularly hot afternoon. I am taken, rather, by the sight of the great variety of human beings promenading on the platform decks across the water on the tourist side where our family has often enjoyed a repast of cold shrimp many a weekend before. People in bathing suits float by on their flamboyant yachts, liberated, carving out independent trails toward the sea, some to return before sunset, others intent on spending the night anchored out on the dark waves under the Texas stars. From there one can see the lights of the homes along the coast, a West Egg sort of comforting thought in this Gatsby-like splendorous Texas Gulf world. But most people who have the wherewithal to buy or to rent these large powerboats tend to tear through the water, single-mindedly bent on leaving the land far behind as quickly as possible. The idea seems to be to clear their heads with the salve of the salt water, the ocean's wind and waves tearing against the sides of boats that furiously churn up the water into white spray that shoots up and falls irregularly behind, grace that only some beholders espy. It is a new *que díos los bendiga* religion, may God bless them.

That day, perhaps fifteen years ago, my fourteen-year-old son and I took a place between two fishermen posted as the sentinels on the north and south side of the Point. One cannot ruminate on too many things without being distracted by countless particulars of the scene when fishing is the order for the day. After I had had my fill of the passing vessels and the human vanities displayed, after I had considered the cost and the efforts required to put up the type of indifferent fronts readily seen, I turned my attention to my fellow fishers. These seemed truer human beings, part of the indigenous surroundings, grafted natives, if we must, and not the passing visitors flaunting their worldly success for the rest of us to covet.

We were, in all, about eight hopeful fishers, spaced among the rocks and the pilings that memorably mark the land's end at the Point. The evening before, my wife and I had enjoyed a grilled trout and a red snapper at the Brass Parrot, one of the restaurants fronting the waterway across the span where the boats make their very public exits toward the sea. She had remarked that the land on which we were now fishing was available. Indeed, the "for sale" sign she had seen was twenty yards behind us. Someday soon, the Point would be sold. And, to tell the truth, the land across the point that I speak of has since been turned into the Kemah Boardwalk. The area is about as close as it can be turned, in Texas, into something like a San Francisco pier. The Boardwalk, at any rate, is sensibly designed to bring out both tourists and area residents like me. And since it is planned well, the opposite side still provides quiet pleasures for a fisher or two who may want to muse while casting a line into the Gulf of Mexico.

About an hour before lunch, a commotion over to my left drew my attention. It was an African American woman who had been fishing there. Her line had somehow unbelievably snagged a seagull. The poor bird was squawking and making awful sounds. The woman was visibly upset, and, I will write it as people say, she was beside herself. A young Vietnamese fisherman, from the nearby community of recent immigrants who had settled in the Seabrook area after the end of the Vietnam War, had gone to the woman's rescue. He was bending over some broken wooden boards, reaching over the railing, extending his arms over into the water, trying to untangle the poor screaming bird. The woman held onto her line, but she couldn't help much, scared as she was by the situation, which had simply surprised all of us.

I moved over the rocks and made my way toward them. Reaching out into the water with the Vietnamese man, I also attempted to disentangle the fish line from the seagull's feet and trapped wings. But fearing that the young Vietnamese man might well be flipped into the water himself, I motioned him to lift the line so that together we could free and relieve the bird over on the rocks. The more jagged rocks were simply making our footing too difficult. He did so, and, holding the bird's head with one hand, he continued working to free the line, which was ensnared around the two wings and one of the bird's legs. Seeing that he could not do both, I took the initiative of holding the bird's head, and, as soon as I did, the seagull quickly bit my right thumb, rather fiercely, I thought.

Since I had not experienced the bite of a seagull before, I didn't know what to expect. The pressure its beak exerted on my thumb was something like that of a clothespin pinching a finger. And the wonder of the experience was that I did get one of the best looks I ever will at the bright, orange-red mouth and throat of a seagull. I would never have expected to see that five minutes before when I had been musing about the boats that parade up and down the estuary. My Vietnamese friend continued to work to remove the line and to help me with his left hand. Several minutes later, he held the bird cupped in his hands for one brief moment, and in the next second he threw the seagull up into the air. Everyone watching this totally surprising drama followed his actions, expecting to see the seagull flying away, but the bird fluttered, flew a bit, and then fell, right shoulder first, into the water. The three of us and several of the other fishermen and spectators from both sides of the Point who were observing this live scenario, saw the bird float, boatlike for a time, before trying once more to fly. After several unsuccessful attempts, it lifted itself, like a sputtering plane, and flew off to join, we knew, its watery avian group.

While walking back to our fishing posts, the woman and I talked about the event that had joined us. I was relieved and even exhilarated by the turn of events, for, due to the bite from the seagull, I now found the slight pulse on my thumb a comforting and oddly unexplainable nudge of my mortality. Not that there ever was that much danger of actually toppling over into the water, though for several moments it had looked that way. I stayed around and wondered why some people have to fish, why others like me will try to fish, why yet others boat, and why some people choose to jump in to help while others prefer to watch. It took a seagull entangled in a fish line to cause three lone sentinels of three different races to interact on that day out at the Point.

About ten minutes later, the Vietnamese man circled back around and coming up by the "for sale" sign, I saw him approach. He told me, in difficult-to-understand English, that my line wasn't set up correctly, that I was apparently scaring the fish away with the floater or bobber that I had positioned near the hook, and too close to the line's weight. I suppose I could have taken issue with him, but I asked him instead if he would help me re-arrange the line. He quickly placed the weight at the end of the line, and pulled off the hook, which he then placed about five feet above the weight. He took the bobber away and handed it to me. Then he asked me for a shrimp, which he inserted with the main body trunk first into the hook so that the shrimp's tail pointed up on the spiked tail of the J of the hook.

In broken English he told me that there were good fish at the Point, but that fishermen do not know how to fish, that Americans can't fish. I asked him for his name, and he said it was Dan. He may be right, I thought, and he was right as far as we were concerned. We had already been fishing over two hours, my son and I, and our fish bucket was still empty. I asked him if I was now ready to cast my line, and Dan said yes, moving his head down once toward his chest. I flipped the line toward the rippling waves, trying to show my son and Dan that I could at least cast halfway decently. With the larger weight that the Vietnamese fisherman had placed at the end of my line, the line sailed out beautifully over the water, toward the waves left by the wake of a passing boat.

Dan told me also that the rod I had was no good, and he gave me to understand that I would not be able to feel the tug on the line well enough. He leaned over the boards where he stood toward the water and felt the line with what, for the first time, I saw was a badly calloused forefinger. Dan continued talking and with the waves and the breeze, I could not understand if he was trying to tell me that he had caught two thousand pounds of fish this past week, or if that had been the high mark of his fishing career. I also wasn't sure if he was saying that he would take me fishing "for free" or "for a fee," but since I would be moving inland to College Station from Taylor Lake Village to teach at a larger public university soon, I did not pursue the offer. Enough to say that Dan was a wonderful human being, helpful, engaging, and full of information about fishing and the sea that made me direly lament that I do not speak Vietnamese and that he did not speak better English.

I went over to the car and came back with Gatorade drinks for all three of us. Dan pulled up the line and brought in a good-sized crab. I then cast again and several minutes later brought in a two-and-a-half-pound perch! After being at the Point all morning with nothing for the effort! I cast again, and, feeling a nibble on the line that now ran over my forefinger, I reeled in to find a redfish just slightly above the required twelve-inch length.

When I went back to the car, I passed the line over to my son, and, on returning with some sandwiches, saw that Carlos was bringing in another redfish! An African American boy about seven years old had been standing off to the side watching us. When I returned to the car, I had asked him to hold my son's pole, which Dan by now had also arranged with the weight at the end of the line and the hook again about five feet above that. I asked him to reel in the line and he brought in a small three-inch catfish that his mother and older brother captured in a picture. This fishing expedition had certainly turned out beneficial for all of us. Originally, I had thought that I would simply go out to the Point and spend the morning taking some sun with my son, watching the boats with names like "Mother's Mink Coat," "Our Legacy," etc., but actually catching a few fish for the backyard grill was better.

Dan changed my perspective that day. He made me think more about the lives of the people who daily depend on the Texas coast for a living. That is why a hurricane can be so devastating in the Gulf areas where flood insurance is required. I thought I would ask Dan if he might know something about fishing in fresh water, where I would be living, but I refrained. I suspect he would have wagged his head quickly to and fro, once, and then said something like, "no, salt water better."

12

An Aztec Reverie

The rising sun, as I have previously suggested, appears to me as the ideal metaphor for the Latino/Chicano situation today. In *A History of the Aztecs and the Mayas and Their Conquest* (1967), Alfred Sundel wrote:

> The Aztecs—linguistic relatives of the Hopi, the Shoshone, and the Comanche of the western United States—descended out of the arid Mexican northwest. They were typical of the many backward nomadic tribes who filtered down into middle Mexico from the upper regions of the North American desert. The Aztecs finally came to rest in the twelfth century in the Valley of Mexico, where they slowly rose to power on the wings of a 2,800-year-old cultural heritage.
>
> The Mayas were of the southeast, far more populous than the Aztecs, their origins unknown. They lived mainly in the lowland rain forests, but several Maya tribes climbed up into the rugged heights of the Guatemalan Cordillera. The first important period of the Maya was from A.D. 325 to 900, the classic phase; their second period, almost without memory of the classic, was highly infiltrated by northerners loosely called Toltecs. The Mayas of the second period were a product of Maya-Toltec culture fusion, both in the lowlands of Yucatan and in the highlands of Guatemala.
>
> By 1500 the main mountain-lake culture of Middle America, centered in the Aztec-dominated Valley of Mexico, held sway over many—but not all—of its neighbors within a radius that extended beyond the mountains enclosing the Valley. (12)

When the Mesoamerican people flourished, in the time before the conquering Hernando Cortés arrived in Mexico in 1519, the theory is that the Aztec people were already living in their Quinto Sol period, the Fifth Sun.

Legend has it that the first four suns, each of which represented a substantial epoch within the Aztec period, had been respectively destroyed by water, wind, fire, and the earth itself. What is remarkable about the origin myths of the Aztecs is that these stories have survived in a number of different versions, and the legend continues to tease the minds of *raza* people who live in various parts of the country, particularly in the Southwest and Mexico. Some of the attempts to reconstruct unwritten Aztec chronicles and chapters destroyed by the Spanish conquerors are available today by searching for "Quinto Sol" on the Internet. But, as far as I have been able to ascertain, there is no one widely accepted version of the Aztec story, including the Quinto Sol events. What is known is that much of the world of the Aztecs has been lost, and archaeologists, historians, and other scholars have been trying to piece together that civilization for more than a century. We do know that they occupied the central valley of Mexico and the surrounding areas roughly from 1200 until Cortés conquered them in 1521.

Despite the amorphousness of the legend and the destruction inflicted by the Spanish soldiers on the Aztecs, it is amazing that both events continue to exert a strong fascination on the minds of the Mexican people and many Mexican Americans. Both groups feel a special tie to an indigenous people about whom we do not know enough. The encyclopedia says that the Aztecs "belonged to the American Indian race. They were sturdy people with dark skin, straight, coarse hair, and broad faces," wrote Gordon Ekholm in the 1973 issue of the World Book. Some Latinos even see a form of ironic retribution in the current Latino population explosion affecting the United States and Mexico. Still, the issue is not to feel pointlessly vindictive about a past that is part of history, but to push forward with ideas that will nourish all the people of the Americas, and, indeed, the world. Regarding the world's population, as we know, the 6 billion mark was passed in 1999.

The first shadowy, obscure ancestral culture that eventually gave rise to the grand Aztec civilization that greeted Cortés is believed to have been destroyed by torrential rains. When we visit the tropics today, we can still experience instances of those apocryphal rains in the sudden downpours from which, if we are standing in the rainforests of Mexico or Central America, there is little relief. According to the story, great rains followed by immense floods destroyed an antediluvian world that appears to have been the biblical analogue to the Old Testament story of Noah. The society and culture that followed, or the second sun, in due time was annihilated by winds, by tempestuous hurricanes, and cold glacial formations of ice and snow. The next or third civilization of the sun was extinguished by fire, by volcanic eruptions, lava rain, and burning ashes spewed out from a scorched and scorching land. The fourth sun, the legend continues, was erased by earth, by a land supposedly unable to control its own development. This last clause leaves us wondering what such a scenario might mean. Then, in the wake of the decline of the first four suns, a new people somehow emerged, nomadically to make their way toward the central Mexican plateau. We presume that these events occurred from what today would be the U.S. southwestern areas, Yucatán, or perhaps from Central America. This last group went looking for and in time established a Quinto Sol, a new fifth sun, a sun that would shine and exert its influence upon the Aztecs and their descendants.

In the Aztec chronology, the Quinto Sol period was the heyday of the Aztec people, the epoch that the conquering Cortés and his soldiers mercilessly did what they could to obliterate. Does such a history mean that a Sexto or a Sixth Sun is in the offing? That, of course, depends on a person's perspective. What is clear is the idea that a series of rising suns are definitely associated with new hope, with a different kind of life symbolically represented by the everyday rising of that wondrous celestial orb. As shown by the way of life of the Aztecs and the indigenous people of the Americas, our mysterious antecedents, we Latinos today have to learn not only how to survive, which we have clearly demonstrated, but also how to thrive.

It is important to recognize that we Latinos have not yet learned how to use the schools to help us succeed well enough in society. Therefore, we still need to provide ourselves with the education necessary to thrive socially and economically. Despite our hard work, the support required for successful adaptation to American civilization has not yet been developed. Despite the fact that we have been part of the Southwest for centuries and part of the United States for more than 150 years, the social infrastructure needed to help Latinos advance has not yet materialized. Although we Latinos are Americans because of geopolitical history, we have not discovered how to live in the United States as average, taxpaying, middle-class citizens. Latino unity and success are particularly difficult to achieve because of the different national histories, and communal and family stories.

Most Latinos who have "made it" in America have done so mainly by relying on themselves and their own resources. This fact suggests that such Latinos have a maverick streak, which means they seem to prefer doing things alone, even though they are amply aware of the fact that the rest of the Latino and American communities are also very important to their lives. A number of Latinos who make it for that reason are inclined to say to other *raza* members, "See, I did it by myself. You can also be successful."

But too many Latinos have not been provided with the necessary tools for becoming successful, even though they have been trying to succeed in the United States for several generations. This means that they obviously just have not yet received the right combination of education, opportunities, and the means to capitalize more productively on their own talents and skills. I make this statement because too many Latinos today remain stuck, earning minimum-wage-range salaries, working in less than middle-class employment positions, not having yet made it into the professional ranks. Most Latinos have not learned how to harness the necessary resources available in American society to promote success either for themselves or their families. But Latinos can do so, especially now that we are beginning to analyze what it is that constitutes success in the United States, and how it is secured.

In *Crowding Out Latinos* (2000), I explained why Latinos have not been as successful as we might be. My diagnosis as the last century closed and a new one started was that Latinos are still being elbowed out, even as our numbers are growing. People have since asked what my proposed solution is to improve the lives of Latinos. I have resisted an answer, waiting to see if people agree with the diagnosis or my interpretation of the past. What I have since found is that Latinos are so optimistic that even when we have suffered setbacks and when presented with negative evidence, we continue to insist on seeing a new Latino sun, one that continues to rise day after day. This consistently positive attitude is exhilarating. I have found such a view of life wonderfully promising and refreshing. Nonetheless, we Latinos need real help. We cannot wait to educate our children better. And, to achieve that goal, my wife Rita and I have finished *Quality Education for Latinos: Print & Oral Skills for ALL Students, K–College,* a book manuscript that analyzes the psychological school environments that Latinos face. What we attempt there is to articulate what we need to consider doing as a society with vested interests in Latino youths to help them overcome traditional obstacles. Our objective has not been to assign blame, but to describe the nature of the education that Latino dropout students have experienced. We then offer a series of constructive ideas designed to help all members of society educate Latino and non-Latino students so that all young citizens can attend college, should they later develop that desire.

The Latino community has been asking for help and support for more than a hundred years, and it remains to be seen if such help will be extended, either by the American people directly or from the government. The immediate solution for Latinos, as I see it, is to learn how to succeed with whatever outside help is available. That is what history has taught us. We need to improve our minds so that we learn to use everything we can from our past and present condition to help us meet the exigencies of the world of the Internet where the rest of American society already lives.

The objective should not be to jettison off our past ancestral ties, which are already skimpy enough, but to work to understand our ancestors better, and to accept our history in order to serve our current and future needs better. The world ushered in by the Internet, in effect, offers yet another opportunity, another sun, another universe that threatens to overwhelm the Latino people once more. This time, though, we are also likely to affect American civilization: we will either help American society see a better day, or we may weaken and possibly contribute to undoing it. One reality is certain: U.S. Latinos will either learn how to thrive or the quality of our lives will not sufficiently enable us to help the rest of the residents of this country. For, just as the previous five suns saw the different destructions of the antecedents of the Aztecs, those indigenous Mesoamericans who married and cohabited with Europeans are the root ancestors of a good number of Latinos today. As such, Latinos have found it particularly difficult to make progress, because the competition for resources both here in the United States and throughout the world is intense and unrelenting. Thus, despite the fact that life and history tend to move in cycles, as Boethius (475–525) pointed out in his justly famous book, *The Consolation of Philosophy,* Latinos, like everyone else, have no choice but to find out what it takes to be successful and then to trudge. Indeed, to live is to struggle toward a better future.

Regardless of the actions of human beings, the sun will continue to rise according to fixed, immutable laws. Early mornings, when it bursts forth on the horizon or behind the clouds, signaling the day, that is the same sky, the same light the Aztecs saw. To capitalize on opportunities, conscious attention to what the day offers while the sun traverses the sky is required. For, by the light of the rising of the sun, we should soon see how our wits, talents, and skills will effectively help us to contribute and to transform American society. There is nothing quite like studying how the dawn turns into day, and how the day offers us challenges for our energies and dreams. But if we are busily engaged in other activities that do not promote the common and the public good, we will surely miss how our days can be used to advance our ends. The sun, instead, will remind us of the lighthearted busy old fool that John Donne saw in "The Sunne Rising," when he imagined seeing it peeping through the windows of our minds.

Everything depends on the nature of our minds. On July 25, 2000, the country's newspapers carried a story about the latest research findings regarding Alzheimer's disease. Researchers claimed they have discovered that the brain is not only the center of the nervous system but also a very powerful muscle that can be trained to continue to grow and to generate new connections, even when the old links will not function properly anymore. If exercised during the early years, the brain apparently continues to work and remains actively engaged long after researchers and scientists thought it declined. As long as a person exercises it, scientists now believe that the brain will continue to function in all sorts of different ways. The enlightened objective is always to open up new vistas, views that offer us new ways of thinking and living, if we but make the effort to use what life has taught us over the years. I mention these findings while musing about the Aztecs because it seems to me that, like our ancestors, Latinos have to continue to learn how to engage our minds to surmount both individual and collective problems. Only then can we progressively improve our lives, those of our children, and the lives of everyone else in the world. That, indeed, is the most American as well as the basic, most steadfast characteristic of our indigenous ancestors: to try and to try, repeatedly, until eventually a better way is discovered and successfully disseminated to everyone.

Since the Spanish, European, and Asian people mixed with the people of the Americas, the need for this kind of cooperation has very slowly become clear to all civilized men and women. History amply shows us that violence, dissension, and destruction lead to further conflict. For that reason, people need to know that the world can only be improved when groups of people who have lived with strife are provided with the necessary means to pursue avenues consciously designed to create better human lives.

13

Mi Tierra *in San Antonio*

"Mi Tierra," which means "My Land," is one of best twenty-four-hour restaurants in San Antonio, that enormous, up-and-coming *pueblo* of the twenty-first century. There are many good eateries throughout the eighth largest city of the United States, but because the people of San Antonio usually do not think of their town as a large metropolis, even the more popular places do not stay open late into the night. The bohemian, noisy life I enjoyed when I visited Europe as a senior student continues to appeal to me, and should to other Latinos. London, Munich, and Paris had some great late-night places, and U.S. Latino life is moving in that direction, too. Although parenting and midlife have changed my interests, there is a certain charm that I still associate with restaurants that stay open late at night or that never close. After-dinner outings, after all, are central to Latino culture. Late-night establishments tend to lend an air of big-city life to Texas, and I suspect that San Antonio will progressively change and nightlife will flourish much as, say, in Miami. One can only hope that its small-town atmosphere remains protected at the same time though, so that both its small- and large-city qualities can attract visitors.

Saturday mornings I like to go to a neighborhood Mexican restaurant that prepares what might be called a Latino mulligan, *un caldito* that warms me up nicely for the challenge of the week. I am a *caldo* aficionado and would gladly take a bowl of hot soup every day of my life, if I could find it. In San Antonio I can always find soup, as I can in Austin, especially at a corner family restaurant on Cesar Chavez wonderfully named Juan in a Million.

But one of my favorite places is Mi Tierra. This *restaurante* is walking distance from the downtown Riverwalk Mall, and closer to the largest of the San Antonio Franciscan missions, San Fernando Cathedral, which, built in 1731 when San Antonio was known as San Fernando, is the oldest cathedral in the United States. According to an article in the *Bryan–College Station Eagle*, Saturday, January 23, 1999, page A11, written by Suzanne Hoholik, the cathedral in effect serves as the city's living room. Rector Virgil Elizondo, author of *The Future Is Mestizo: Life Where Cultures Meet* (1988), is credited for the accomplishment of opening the "cathedral doors to people of all faiths." The San Fernando Cathedral is an impressive eighteenth-century church that houses, among other holdings, a sarcophagus reputedly containing the remains of Davy Crockett. The Alamo, located in the same downtown neighborhood, also encourages a short walk for a cup of coffee, preferably at Mi Tierra or the Menger, the latter being across the street from the place where the Alamo battle was fought between February 23 and March 6, 1836. The Menger is the hotel where Teddy Roosevelt recruited soldiers for his famous July 1, 1898, charge up San Juan Hill in Puerto Rico. This was the same Roosevelt who served as U.S. president from 1901 to 1909, who lost his sight in one eye while boxing with a military aide in the White House in 1905. He also encouraged the type of xenophobic hysteria that later appeared in a reference to the "Colored Empires" in Fitzgerald's *The Great Gatsby* (1925), making statements like the one he made in 1915: "There is no room in this country for hyphenated Americanism. The only absolute way of bringing this nation to ruin, of preventing all possibility of its continuing to be a nation at all, would be to permit it to become a tangle of squabbling nationalities." But when have newly arrived immigrants to the United States squabbled? In fact, most immigrants have been so happy to arrive in the United States that the general response has been one of necessary adjustment.

Mi Tierra recommends itself for family outings because its cooks maintain one of the best menus in San Antonio, including a tasty bowl of *menudo,* which rivals their *caldo.* As I understand it from a friend who is a member of the League of United Latin American Citizens (LULAC), Mi Tierra has a basement where the cooks and the bakers prepare their delicacies. The restaurant is so popular that visitors usually stand in line to obtain a sitting, but that is just another way of waiting while customers watch the interesting goings-on, which continually engage attention. Another of my favorite dishes is their well-prepared *lengua,* or tongue, especially when served with hot corn tortillas. I rank this plate second only to the hot green chile stew available at Tia Sophia's in Santa Fe, New Mexico, another great restaurant to which this Latino loves to take family and friends when in the neighborhood. In the Alamo City the mariachis and the *cancioneros* promenade through the restaurant and the Mercado area, singing *corridos, guapangos, boleros,* and other Tejano favorites, requested or not. A festive atmosphere in the city's Mexican market pervades the air. If no fiesta is visibly in progress, a good reason for something approximating one soon emerges.

Next to the Rio Grande Valley, San Antonio, like El Paso, is one of the few large cities in Texas where Mexican Americans feel comfortable and at home. Dallas, Houston, Austin, and Fort Worth have pockets where Latinos feel *en casa,* too, but other sections in these cities still make Spanish-speakers feel less welcome, despite the fact that larger numbers of Latinos are increasingly populating these Texas communities, too. Although Anglos still control many Chicano lives in this great city, San Antonio amply provides the type of environment that Chicano writers and artists need if Latinos are going to capitalize on past history in order to construct a better future for all people.

In a few words, I believe that Mexican Americans and other Latinos in Texas and throughout the United States are bereft of a useful, energizing past. Because we have been educated in public and private schools that have not particularly focused attention on how Latinos fare in the educational enterprise, not too many of us know enough to have insisted on learning about our immediate and long ago past. And we do not know more because we have not been taught and have not sufficiently recorded the history of our past ancestors. Here and there, yes, but not in ways that have been successfully disseminated to the whole American and Latino population. Although Mexican Americans have lamented the absence of an empowering past and accompanying narratives, continued neglect suggests a resistance to teaching a history that separates rather than unifies Americans. Personally, I do not believe that knowing the Latino contribution to the history of the United States will divide us any more than people already are. In fact, good history lays out the facts, encouraging people to understand the past and to appreciate one another more.

As Latinos, those of us who are products of the education system are taught to know as much as other Americans about the pilgrims, the Puritans, George Washington, Thomas Jefferson, Lincoln, and the Roosevelts. Ask us, though, about the contributions of Latinos to American society, and most of us cannot mention a single Mexican American hero or leader. This situation is sad but not surprising, since only recently have a few, less available school textbooks pointed to some contributions by Chicanos. That, at least, is the impression I have—that a handful of Mexican Americans are worth remembering, largely because they were exceptional in one way or another. But the presence of the majority of Mexican Americans remains unremarked and seldom mentioned.

When walking around San Antonio, for example, only a few historical sites of *Tejanos,* the native Hispanic Texans, are encountered. Other than that, Tejanos or Chicanos are not credited for making much of a historical impact on Texas. Within the last twenty years, a new generation of historians has been working to provide Latino Americans with a different sense of our past, of our accomplishments. Someday the names Arnoldo de Leon, David Montejano, Armando Alonzo, Rodolfo Acuna, Guadalupe San Miguel, Andres Tijerina, Gilberto Hinojosa, Carlos Blanton, and others will be better known. When the works of these and other writers are taught in the schools, then the younger X Generation of Chicanos will begin to notice that they cannot sufficiently understand the past and develop the future unless they know our cultural roots.

Mi Tierra is a forty-plus-year-old establishment, and it is a wonderful place to begin a few days' stay in the old Mexican metropolis of central Texas. I say San Antonio is an old Mexican city because the public relations people in charge of attracting tourists frequently downplay just how Latino San Antonio is. But that is also the case with Houston, Austin, Dallas, Fort Worth, and most Texas cities. In almost all of the tourist guide magazines, Latinos are barely included, if at all. The reality, however, is very different from the advertisements designed by corporate America and the people who have the resources and therefore wield power and influence.

For example, according to the 2000 Census, San Antonio has 671,394 Latinos, 371,911 whites, 78,000 African Americans, and 23,341 Asian American and other citizens. Houston has 730,865 Latinos, 614,621 whites, 494,297 African Americans, and 113,848 Asian American and other citizens. Dallas has 422,587 Latinos, 417,401 whites, 309,547 African Americans, and 39,045 Asian American and other citizens. Even Austin has a sizeable Latino population with 200,579 Hispanics, 353,706 whites, 66,738 African Americans, and 35,539 Asian American and other citizens. Despite numbers that clearly show how Latino these large Texas cities actually are, at most I usually find maybe one or two pictures of Latinos in their fifty-plus-page tourist publications. And the fact that one or two pictures of Hispanics are now included is a relatively new development. Before that, Mexican Americans rarely appeared, though we clearly make up sizeable populations in most of these Texas cities.

Like Los Angeles on the western coast, in many ways San Antonio and the whole state of Texas is already living where the future of the United States is going to exist. In 2003, demographers informed us, Latinos became the largest minority in the United States, surpassing African Americans. That means the iconography of this country has considerable catching up to do, as the slang-users say! How soon will San Antonio be allowed, by the powers that are in place, to assume its rightful place in the new American galaxy? *¡Arriba con San Antonio!* It is time to move all Latinos who still live in the barrios of the last century into the twenty-first century!

14

Indian Trails and the Texas A&M/UT Presidential Corridor

A few months before the George Bush Presidential Library was dedicated at Texas A&M University, on November 6, 1997, the section of Texas State Highway 21 that connects Bryan–College Station going west to Austin was named the Presidential Corridor. The Texas State Legislature officially made the decree, and, shortly after, two or three signs were placed along the highway between the two cities to commemorate the fact. Motorists familiar with the highway know that about one hundred miles separate the Lyndon Baines Johnson Presidential Library located on the UT/Austin campus with its George Bush counterpart at Texas A&M. What is less known is that from Bryan–College Station, Highway 21 going east toward Nacogdoches and beyond, to New Orleans, was earlier also known as El Camino Real. Several waist-high marble markers prepared in English in 1918 and placed by the Daughters of the Republic of Texas alongside Highway 21 point out that El Camino Real became known as the King's Highway sometime after Texas joined the union in 1845.

Nacogdoches, recognized as the oldest settlement in Texas, and named to honor Native Americans of the same name, is also the seat of Stephen F. Austin State University. Like Sam Houston State University in Huntsville, Stephen F. Austin and several other smaller state public campuses touting historically venerable names suggest how academic power and Texas opulence work. I would love to say that these two campuses and all Texas colleges and universities are part of a first-rate higher-education system, comparable to those developed and better funded by California, New York, and Pennsylvania. But unfortunately higher institutions in Texas have long been overlooked by a state legislature that has not been able to figure out how to finance the very schools that can well serve as the best economic and social investment instruments for the future of our people.

While my wife Rita and I were on the Nacogdoches campus to speak at a conference, we looked into three or four classrooms in one of the main buildings. We could not believe the poor condition of the tables and desks. I know for a fact that the classroom equipment removed from larger campuses like Texas A&M and the University of Texas-Austin is in considerably better condition than the classroom furniture and the technology used by students attending Stephen F. Austin State and Sam Houston State Universities. That should not be the case. Such waste and ineffective distribution of resources shows, unfortunately, that in Texas, state public institutions depend on the lobbying support they can muster and wield on the state legislature. But the legislators by law meet for a spring session only every two years, and most of the time they have historically shown that they are not too interested in talking about the state's most important issue, education. Indeed, I have visited with a few politicians myself, and, despite election-year promises, every time I bring up education issues, their eyes glaze over. Once, a representative actually turned on me and challengingly asked where "I" expected to find the money for an idea I was proposing. I countered with, "But I thought that was your job! Weren't you elected to take care of Texans? I don't think you are hearing when I tell you that Education is what we need!"

Being a Tejano, I dislike pointing to drawbacks in Texas, but Texas legislators simply do not appear to have the type of short- and long-range visions that the growing population of the state needs. Since almost everything addressed is approached piecemeal every two years, the serious issues frequently receive stopgap measures meant to keep things rolling. This leaves business and corporate America with the resources and the time to befriend the legislators and to build support for other interests. My sense is that the legislature needs to meet every spring, since, with 20.8 million Texans, the state has grown in altogether different demographic directions that are not even being considered. Traditionally, the idea has been to respond to the political agendas of conservative legislators who are very much into preserving what they like themselves; but, the new needs of the parents and their young progeny, particularly that of the Latino population, are education, education, and education. Nothing else is going to provide us with the type of advantages that are so badly needed to improve the quality of life in Texas and the Southwest.

Education is central to everything that Texas needs, but since this is a much larger issue that needs considerable attention, here I can only suggest that the changes made in the future must include the state's Latino population. The growth in the state's population is among Latinos, which means the future of Latinos is what the Texas legislature has to place front and center on its agenda.

Since the schools do not teach Texas history, I have had to learn on my own that the Nacogdoches Indians once formed part of the Caddo Indian tribes who lived in the piney woods of east Texas. That was around A.D. 800, or about 800 years before the first explorers from Spain arrived and claimed Texas for the Spanish crown. A recent drive on El Camino Real to participate in a conference on diversity at Stephen F. Austin State in Nacogdoches made me aware that east Texas is a beautiful part of the country. The area has abundant rivers and lakes, and the countryside is filled with shady places to stop by the side of the road. One can hardly enjoy a drive through the area's green scenery without thinking about the region's little appreciated past.

Before the arrival of Spanish explorers and missionaries at different junctures throughout the sixteenth and seventeenth centuries, the Caddo Mound Indians and other Texas Indian tribes made trails or footpaths through the woods all the way across the Sabine River from French New Orleans. The latter city was founded by Spanish settlers in 1718, whereas San Antonio was founded around 1691. Some maps refer to this passageway as the Old San Antonio Road, but since the Native American inhabitants of Texas did not have a print culture, no one appears to have recorded the name or names they used to refer to this initial trail or trails. When the Spanish crown renamed the Native American footpaths El Camino Real, that, of course, imposed a new order on the people and a roadway that would have been the fastest and most direct route connecting these two seventeenth- and eighteenth-century cities. This history, however, has long since been lost or glossed over, transforming the Nacogdoches Indian footpath or trail to what became the Spanish El Camino Real. In due time, this same roadway was renamed the King's Road, the English translation of the Spanish name. Sometime after, the road apparently was renamed just plain Texas Highway 21. Today, El Camino Real runs close to my own backyard in Bryan. By driving west on the Presidential Corridor from Texas A&M, we arrive in Austin, and then on to San Antonio. By traveling east, in the direction of New Orleans, motorists will end driving through Nacogdoches, and perhaps pay a well-worth-it visit to the Caddo grounds to learn about our Native American past.

15

Among Mullets, One Galveston Summer

When summer arrives, Galveston is like a fresh-squeezed drink of cool orange juice offered when the Texas heat is about to turn unbearable. *¡No mas!* people appear to shout in unison. Then, together, everybody, it seems, bolts out toward the island. Take U.S. Highway 45 from Houston to the Gulf Coast any day during the summer, but especially Fridays and during the weekends, and hundreds of people will also be inveterately driving toward the ocean. All will be hauling boats, surfboards, tents, lawn chairs, and any other sand and water accouterment that can be taken on the freeways. Leaving Houston and the hot interior Texas lands for the Gulf breezes of Galveston, where the temperature is usually about ten degrees cooler almost any day between May, June, July, and August, affords a much-needed release for people residing in the country's fourth largest city and the surrounding communities. Summer in Texas actually begins sometime around April, occasionally even in March, and usually it extends well into September, despite the fact that the schools tend to require students to return to their desks shortly after the middle of August. Following the long summer, activities on the island decrease; commerce dwindles; and the hurly-burly commotion that crowded the seacoast town slackens. Summer is over; the hurricane season has begun.

Mention Galveston on a hot day and people who have caught the sea breezes on Seawall Boulevard even once will invariably smile. The island is not yet like Cape Cod, many will thankfully agree. It is still accessible, people love to watch other people, and the traffic keeps moving. During the height of the season, good overnight accommodations can be difficult to find. Galveston is particularly great in the summer because all kinds and types of people can be seen whiling away the days engaged in activities from horseback riding to surfing, water skiing, and taking the sun on Steward Beach or on the west side of the island. The rich, the super rich, the poor, the middle class, and people from all quarters throughout Texas and the rest of the country take whatever transportation they have and head out toward the water. Once there, the waves, the sun, and the ocean take over; everybody becomes a lighter version of the person he or she was on the mainland.

Galveston has been attracting visitors like a starfish on the beach since the native inhabitants first crossed from the Texas mainland. The island has a great history, a little of which is known. For example, Galveston was the place where in November of 1528, Alvar Nuñez Cabeza de Vaca shipwrecked what was left of an ambitious Spanish expedition of five ships. Along with six hundred soldiers, Cabeza de Vaca left Spain on June 17, 1527, to explore the land from the Río de las Palmas (the Rio Grande) to the Florida cape for the king. By the time Cabeza de Vaca and his men discovered they were on the island of what is now Galveston, it is not certain how many men were left. We do know they lost their last European clothes there, and that only four of the survivors eventually found deliverance, after having hiked naked through the Texas wilderness west to near Baja California for more than eight years, arriving in Mexico City barely able to walk. Cabeza de Vaca's wonderfully succinct memoir of his desperate search for food, relief, and the way back to civilization in a wilderness inhabited by both hostile and generous native tribes offers a great experience for readers with an imagination. His narrative is one of the best records concerning the natives who peopled Texas when Europeans first arrived in the New World in the sixteenth century.

But what do we know about Texas and the Gulf Coast from, say, 1540 to about 1776, when the Declaration of Independence was written? For over two hundred years, or longer than the time the United States has been a country, Texas life apparently amounted to the nature of the relations that developed between the Spanish traders and settlers and the Native Americans of the area, historians infer. It was not until the nineteenth century, when Tejanos sought to separate themselves from Mexico mainly because Mexico did not pay attention to their needs in the vast, too-far chaparral country north of the Rio Grande Valley, that the Texas saga enters our consciousness again. The area was first explored thoroughly in 1747 when an expedition led by a proven Mexican military leader named José de Escandón brought 765 soldiers into the region between the Rio Grande and the Nueces River, where Corpus Christi is currently situated. Armando Alonzo's *Tejano Legacy* (1998) details some of the specifics involved in this interesting venture beautifully.

By highway, Galveston is roughly three and a half to four hours north of Corpus Christi, and these two Gulf cities are the largest summer resorts along the Texas coast. From either urban center, one can walk on the beach northward or southward to the heart's content, feet in the warm waters of the Gulf or only a few steps away in the warm sand, as beachcombers prefer. In certain places in both residential communities, beachfront homes look out toward the water, but the public beaches fortunately belong to anyone who happens to walk by, barefooted or not. Depending on what people seek, there are many miles of heavily populated, lightly populated, or nearly and even deserted beaches.

For a number of years when our children were young, my wife and I planned our budget so that we could spend a week, or at least a few days, in Galveston after I finished teaching a summer class I usually offered. One summer, when our son and daughter were twelve and ten, we rented a beachfront house in Galveston with the Steins, a family who lived two houses over. Our children were in school together, and since we could not afford to rent a house by ourselves, we joined the Steins for what turned out to be a great vacation on the island for both families. The Barraterria House in Pirates Beach on the west side of Galveston Island at the time rented for $750 from 2 p.m. one Saturday to 10 a.m. the following Saturday. So, for one glorious week, we enjoyed a wonderful space of time that allowed both families to relax, to fish, to cook out, to run to the beach in the early morning, or to tiptoe as fast as possible at high noon toward the water. Little, I believe, is as pleasant a family outing as renting a summer home where one can see and hear the waves wash against the seashore in the morning, noon, afternoon, evening, and way into the night. The rhythm of the sea and the seagulls against the sky, cloudy or clear, invites the appreciative soul to while away the day in fancies and daydreams, indulging itself to the heart's content.

We took in a number of the attractions that Galveston offers, including a film shown by one of the pier establishments next to the University of Texas–Galveston Medical Center of the disastrous 1900 storm that killed six thousand Galvestonians and left eight thousand homeless. That in part is why the U.S. Army Corps of Engineers built, between 1958 and 1962, the famous Galveston Seawall, to protect the "Queen City of the Gulf" from similar natural disasters. For an exhilarating experience, whenever I have the time, I enjoy walking from the fish pier on 91st Street west toward the end of the Seawall, where residents and tourists camp out in their R.V.s, enjoying the panoramic view of the sea all along the shore. On that particular vacation, we also went fishing with the children at 9 p.m. after the sun set, and stayed until a little after eleven thirty, catching several perch on the 61st pier where fishermen and women walk out a good ways to cast their lines out to sea. At night, with the wind blowing in our faces and under the lights provided by the pier management—what more can a fisherman want by way of enjoying a family outing with wife, friends, and the kids? Indeed, when we looked around, we saw that several other Mexican American and African American families, mainly, but also some white Galvestonians, are part of the local regular fishing culture of the area.

The best time to go into the water, as far as we were concerned, was in the late afternoon, after 5 p.m. Once on vacation, everyone quickly developed a new schedule. I started walking to the nearby store early every morning. I was there to buy the Houston and Galveston newspapers and a half-gallon of orange juice for the early risers. I would return to make the coffee for the caffeine takers, all adults. We heard from newscasts that it is best to avoid the water and basking in the sun from ten in the morning to three in the afternoon when the ultraviolet rays are strongest. During these middle of the day hours we drove into Galveston to run errands or stayed around the veranda that encircled the beach house, listening to a music tape or playing a game of Monopoly. Sitting on the second-floor veranda, looking out to sea and feeling the breeze blowing salt against our faces was indescribable. Like most of its neighbors, the house has a beautiful elevated second-story porch where one could well spend the day reading, listening to music, or watching the waves lap up on the beach. A good number of activities, like preparing the fish lines, blowing up the rubber tubes and the raft, and other such tasks kept us involved at other times that vacation week.

Just now, in going out to extend a tarp over our German shepherd's kennel, which is on the back patio of our house in Bryan, I thought of the fun we had setting up the same blue tarp on the beach when we were in Galveston that summer. With the wind flapping strongly against the twelve-by-twelve tent that I had bought at a sporting goods shop, tying the sturdy nylon cover to the yellow plastic stakes that we had to hammer into the sand now sounds easier than it was. Fortunately my wife and our friends and kids helped, and during the rest of the week the protection afforded by our blue tarp against the sun was grand. Several times we walked what we figured were two or three miles down the beach, and from that distance, we could still make out the blue tarp, like a faraway blue dot dabbed against the horizon as an impressionist painter would have placed a blue dot on a canvas.

The best experience that I remember, to cut to my purpose here, is that we would go into the waves, pulling a rubber raft that trailed behind us, around 5:30 every afternoon. My daughter and son would jump inside the raft and I would pull them and the two Stein boys, who had waded in on rubber tubes, to the point where I could barely touch the sandy bottom. About six, foot-long fish could be seen from here swimming toward the shore for their evening meals. These fish, commonly called mullets, aren't appreciated by fishermen, but they provided us with enormous fun. There were literally hundreds of them in the area, in schools of forty or fifty apiece, and being out in the water among the mullets was an incredibly exciting experience. I had bought two large Chinese fish nets at the same Academy Sports and Outdoors store where I secured the blue tarp, and the nets were so good that all I had to do was drop them in the water and I could scoop up around me at least one fish every time. Now, once I caught a fish, the problem was what to do with it out there where the water was at the level of my chest.

The first time I caught a mullet, I jokingly told the kids that I was going to throw it into the raft with them. Well, before I could say anything else, my son and daughter jumped out, head first from opposite sides of the raft, into the water. Fortunately the water was not deep, and both came up laughing, water gushing from their mouths, splashing wildly as they strove to reach the sandy bottom where they could run toward the shore. From then on, I could not persuade either of them to climb into the raft again, so I turned the raft into our fishing pail. The game then became how many mullets we could catch and throw to swim around in a raft that no one was willing even to look into, because as soon as the fish saw any one of us they would try to dart out. With the waves beating against our suntanned bodies and the seagulls looking for their watery suppers, we enjoyed some of the best times that I can remember out on the beaches of Galveston. The experience was so good for the entire family, in fact, that whenever we have been able to afford it since, we still look forward to returning to spend a few days in Galveston, or Corpus or elsewhere on the Texas Gulf Coast.

16

Disney World Florida Trip

Ahhh, *¡La Florida!* The land that Alvar Nuñez Cabeza de Vaca and his soldiers of fortune first espied from the bows of Charles V's armada, the same ships that were wrecked off Galveston Island in 1528. During the next eight plus years, Cabeza de Vaca and his men were enslaved by various Texas Indian tribes, before becoming traders and then prayer or medicine men, the last allowing four survivors to work their way northwest toward El Paso and beyond. When they found no India waterway back to Europe in that direction, they turned south and ended up walking into Mexico City, where they reported their travails, suggesting in the process that they had seen great wealth in the distance in present-day New Mexico and Arizona. It is the story that opened up the Spanish exploration of the Southwest, a legend that continually titillated explorers for more than four hundred years, until air conditioning made the southwestern United States habitable in the 1950s. On the eastern coast of what is now the United States, Spain also took Florida from the four largest tribes then living on the land—the Calusa and the Tequesta in the south; the Timucuan in the central peninsula; and the Apalachee in the northwest. This appropriation occurred in 1513 when, looking for a fountain of youth, Ponce de León landed on Florida's east coast and claimed the region for Spain. But it is Don Pedro Menéndez de Avilés who is credited for driving out the French, who contested the area, and for founding St. Augustine in 1565, regarded as the first permanent white settlement in the United States.

Today, U.S. Interstate 10 heading west from Houston goes through the American Southwest, including the major cities of San Antonio, El Paso, Tucson, Phoenix, and into Los Angeles. All of these cities have sizeable young Latino populations, suggesting that the number of Latinos is likely to continue to grow in these large, urban centers. Going east from Houston, though, Interstate 10 bypasses New Orleans, taking travelers to Pensacola, Tallahassee, and into Jacksonville on the eastern Florida coast. Although our family has not traveled by car directly east of Mobile, which we once drove through on our way to visit our newly married niece Laura in Atlanta, we did fly into Orlando one time.

Orlando, county seat of Orange County, Florida, with an 18.8 percent Latino and 18.2 percent African American population, is pretty diverse. I was not surprised at the African American numbers, since Orlando and Eatonville are the locations for Zora Neale Hurston's famous rediscovered 1937 novel, *Their Eyes Were Watching God*. But the Latino population, I confess, was unexpected. Most Latinos in the Orlando area, I understand, are Puerto Ricans and Cuban Americans, and since the 1999 median household income for Orlando is $41,311, compared to the national average of $41,994, one surmises that the county residents are solidly ensconced in the U.S. middle class. The percentage of the persons living below poverty level for the county is also 12.1 percent, in keeping with the national average of 12.4 percent for 1999.

Although I set out to discuss our one-time family trip to Orlando, I will add that I have twice also flown into Miami. Once I attended an American Studies conference there, and stayed at the classy Fontainebleau Hotel, an experience worth repeating. The next time, I discovered that *La Calle Ocho* is one of the main hot spots for Spanish-speakers. La Calle Ocho is somewhat like Mission Street in San Francisco; it is a U.S. haven for resident Cuban Americans as well as all visiting Latin Americans. Since Castro took over Cuba, the Cuban American community in Miami has removed itself so successfully into the city that most people would be pleasantly surprised to learn that it has only been there roughly forty years, or two generations. Miami has been Cubanized, if we can say that, and it is as great a Latino place for all Spanish-speaking people as San Antonio, or, in different ways, as Santa Fe or San Diego. At this point, I will stop, but only because I do not want to slight other towns and cities, since I eschew writing a tourist piece.

Florida was admitted into the union in 1845, the same year that Texas became a state. In 1819, Spain turned Florida over to the United States, following the defeat of the Seminole Indians the previous year by General Andrew Jackson. Congress declared Florida a territory in 1822, and its population has been growing steadily since. In 1990, Florida had 12,937,926 people. In 2000, the Census counted 15,982,378 people, for a 23.5 percent increase. This means that Florida is now the fourth largest state, surpassed in population only by California (33,871,648), Texas (20,851,820), and New York (18,976,457), again according to the 2000 Census. I mention these numbers because after the 2000 presidential election, which the U.S. Supreme Court decided in favor of George W. Bush, most observers are very interested in seeing if the sizeable African American and Latino populations of Florida will emerge as deciding factors in future twenty-first-century elections. On this matter, time will tell, and observers are mindfully watching political developments in Florida.

But I began this rather long digression not to discuss Florida politics, but to record a more provincial family vacation that we took to Orlando, which is closer to the Atlantic Ocean than the eastern shores of the Gulf of Mexico. Toward the middle of the northern part of the Florida peninsula there is a certain room next door to Disney World, at EPCOT's famous Journey into Imagination, where the public is invited to make its own music. Modern technology is transforming the way we live, and engineers, as Thorstein Veblen predicted, show all the signs of being the new trendsetting leaders, the people presenting society with new ways of doing things that in turn present new problems. By bodily moving under colored lights reflected off the floor, people walking through the room activate non-stop cacophonous sounds designed to entertain them. A souvenir I bought on the Orlando grounds says that in this room visitors can "conduct the Electronic Philharmonic." When one stands and moves under the four groups of spotlights, which otherwise shine on a dark carpeted floor, the strings—the violins, the violas, the bass, and others—play. When another group of lights are activated by human motion under them, the trumpets, the French horns, the trombones, and some percussion instruments are heard, signaling the presence of a wide array of symphonic instruments. Other lights arouse the woodwinds. By stepping on the lights on the carpeted floor, instruments alternately emit their prototypical notes, and visitors marvel at the advances of science, enjoying the wildly discordant notes emitted from the place.

On entering, the novelty of the idea seizes one's attention. Moving into the spirit of the experience one mid-August day, I hopped about back and forth, along with my wife and children, attempting, in frustration, to "make" the best music we could. The point was to combine, say, the beat of the drums with a trumpet or two, after which the violins might be brought in center stage and allowed to take over. That, at any rate, is what we tried to orchestrate, once we saw the music possibilities of the room. A few good notes is what everyone seeks to get off before someone else enters the room and begins to play his or her own notes. Then there are the kids who hopscotch through the room on the way to the special-effects video production room, and the other wonders of this futuristic journey into the imagination.

The physical impossibility of running from the violins to the woodwinds and on to the horns while other people in the room are also variously creating their own music notes, along with the fact that the lights are meant to be heard individually, kept us from achieving Beethovenian heights. Like other vacationing family members trooping through, though, I dutifully hopped here and there, enjoying myself with the children, trying to listen to single notes amid the din.

When the novelty of how the electronic lights worked was over, I found myself close to the exit door. Vacationers were still streaming in from the entering door, the room was full of people stepping on the lights, periodically forcing another family or a group of people to leave, moving on to the next exhibit. Engaged in their various antics and poses in the effort to play some discernible tunes, the people passing through the room offered themselves for all sorts of analogies. They struck me as metaphoric representatives of the larger humanity. At that particular time and place, the conceit seemed appealing because I have always enjoyed mulling over what life presents, like countless meditative characters in literature.

The occasion, indeed, offered a choice morsel, for that large, dark room lit by twenty or more colored lights invited twelve to fifteen individuals of all ages to prance, cavort, and to quick-step in various ways to express their joy, surprise, glee, and general enjoyment. The moment appeared especially expressive because it dramatically represented humanity in its great variety. In our own ways, every one of us—and the sheer immensity of how many people we really are in the world never ceases to amaze me—work daily at capitalizing on our experiences. Some of us, of course, are more successful than others at securing attention and getting rewarded, but many more labor behind the scenes wondering how they can make music out of the motley group of instruments and materials that they are handed at birth.

17

The Rain-Blessed Mountains of Costa Rica

I suspect most readers, certainly most Latinos, have a favorite country that is either the land they hail from or the country or region in which they feel comfortable and at home. I also believe that for most Americans that choice place is understandably connected in some way to Europe, a continent that has cultural attractions found nowhere else on earth. When considering a north-south hemispheric axis, however, one of my favorite countries is Costa Rica, my mother's native land. Costa Rica is one of the two smallest countries in the Western Hemisphere, but being small seems to have concentrated everything attractive about the tropics in one place. Where else can one see the natural beauty of towering mountains and swelling rain forests that often reach well into the clouds? It is also home to the famous tucan, the Quetzal, and hundreds of other rare birds that live among thousands of exotic trees, wildlife, and orchids. And the warm coastal beaches attract surfers from around the globe.

Costa Rica, indeed, is so unique that at one point, several hours by car out of San José, the teeming capital can be seen sitting on its high plateau surrounded by even higher mountains. From that spot there is a highway that travelers who need to reach the Pacific Ocean do not soon forget. On a clear day at El Cerro de la Muerte, a cliff referred to as the precipice of death, a highway erected along the backbone of La Cordillera de Talamanca, tourists can look back to see the road where their vehicles wended their way through the mountains and observe a remarkable sight. On one side, far below and reflecting the rays of the sun, the sparkling Caribbean will be seen. At the same time on the other side of the land, tourists will espy the vast Pacific. Talk of upstaging Vasco Nuñez de Balboa (1475–1519), the Spanish explorer disturbingly credited with discovering the Pacific. This is a sight that certainly would have made many natives before Balboa smile!

Costa Rica is one of the most charming countries of the Americas in part because the people are so polite and considerate, a result not only of their genial nature and the country's excellent year-round weather but also of their education and healthy respect for others, whether residents or visitors.

Whenever I visit, I usually walk the streets of San José, from Guadalupe to Aranjuez, where my mother's ancestral house was built around 1920, downtown toward the city's imposing cathedral, across from El Parque Central, literally the center of the country. There, when I visited as a youngster, I remember listening to the San José national band. At the time, during the 1950s and early 60s, it used to play the Costa Rican national anthem and the music of the country's composers along with medleys from the marches of John Philip Sousa (1854–1932). Our parents worked and saved to be in a position to take us to our mother's country for a month's vacation every four years. Those long-awaited vacation months are among the finest experiences that my brother and I had.

During the month, we were able to see how the residents of an entire country made up of Latinos interfaced with one another daily. What I now realize is that we were exposed, among many other people, to a Latino lawyer, a dentist, and a female medical doctor—all members of my mother's family. These people in turn knew others who were doing well enough economically to travel to Europe and the United States every year or two, allowing us to see a well-adjusted Latino society where stability reigned. We also met and were familiar with the struggles of our middle-class cousins, and saw firsthand the financial concerns and living conditions of the working class. We visited the *mercado* and traveled up and down the country, seeing urban and rural people and enjoying the whole experience, since at the time the only experience we could compare with Costa Rica was our home area in Edinburg. Costa Rica, at any rate, was a world peopled by the kinds of individuals whom we did not at all see in South Texas. To this day, I know that traveling to my mother's native country opened our eyes to the possibility that Latinos everywhere could also be as successful and as enterprising as any other people, given the proper education and opportunities.

Costa Ricans boast one of the highest literacy rates in our hemisphere, variously measured above 85 percent. The country has no military or service requirement, and education has traditionally been the primary responsibility of the government, making it one of the most pro-American and stablest republics found throughout the Americas. Costa Rica, in fact, attracts so many people from both neighboring and far-off countries that during the last twenty years or so immigrants, particularly from neighboring Nicaragua and El Salvador, have destabilized and seriously compromised Costa Rica's future. Its social health service, as well as a host of other public offerings, amenities, and service utilities that used to offer most of its citizens a highly attractive quality of life without unduly overtaxing them, has been experiencing financial difficulties for some years. But although many of its public services have been seriously challenged, the Costa Rican way of life is successfully communicated by its now famous motto of "Pura Vida," which means "Pure Life," or "all of it is life." The mindset highlights the upbeat philosophy of the people and the wonderful environmental resources for which Costa Rica is known throughout the world.

Once, while driving directly north from San José with two of my first cousins, Guido and Alberto, I counted crossing twenty-five different fresh-water tributaries in the space of less than one hour. We were headed for a day's outing to Guanacaste, the warmer cattle-raising and agricultural region of Costa Rica, and I was absolutely stunned by the frequency of running cool-water streams over which Guido's Isuzu Trooper passed every two or three minutes. Driving over several of these streams reminded my *primos* of stories of when they were growing up. Their father, who was the dentist of the family, my Tío Rafael, my mother's third youngest brother, used to take them, I enviously learned, to swim to cool off in several of these same streams in areas where the water pooled, sometimes allowing them even to fish. Imagine that! I was from South Texas, where, if it does not rain, one sees water about as often as one encounters it in the deserts around Tucson. And here were my cousins telling me about the different kinds of water holes that they have always enjoyed, depending on what they felt like doing! It was enough to make even the adult in me want to cry for the injustices unevenly parceled out both by geography and culture, childhood is always so unforgiving and great. Along with the excellent Costa Rican cuisine, which is too varied and numerous even to list, and the great weather, one hardly knows what to describe. Then there were the jaunts to the Caribbean or to the Pacific and the trips to see the volcanoes—the Poas, El Irazu, and the Arenal, all of which we visited on various trips. I hope readers can see why I found and find the country so attractive. The last volcano, the Arenal, is the volcano that these days still puts on a lava show almost every night. What other comparable piece of real estate on earth offers so much in such a concentrated space? Ah, I have often felt that life offers too many amenities to the lucky Latinos who live or who visit that postage-size mid-America country.

I have lately come to the conclusion that fresh water is Costa Rica's greatest resource. Due to the fact that I teach nine months out of the year, I have visited Costa Rica only during the summer months. Summer in the United States is when Costa Rica experiences its winter months. Winter there means the rainy season. When I have visited now as an adult for a week or two, I usually try to accomplish whatever I set out to see or do before three or four in the afternoon. After that, in June, July, and August, it usually rains the rest of the evening and into the night, often not stopping until midnight or the early hours of the morning. The next day, though, because the Costa Rican countryside is so hilly, having deep valleys and huge blue-green mountains that cover a person's normal ken, a country full of natural crevices and fissures, the rivers and tributaries quickly take most of the rainwater toward the two seas, seldom allowing flooding. Every morning when I am there I awake to a country that feels new, that smells fresh and clean, since, of course, it has usually rained for seven or eight hours straight the previous evening. Go to most tributaries in Costa Rica the day following one of their regular famous rainstorms, and you will see wonderfully cool fresh water flowing out to the Caribbean or to the Pacific!

Since good, clean water is now at a premium almost everywhere in the world, certainly in the southwestern part of the United States, given our population's inexorable movement toward the desert areas, I sometimes wonder if a small country like Costa Rica could help by capitalizing on its natural resources. Like Mexico, Central and South America have many amenities that could find markets in the United States and abroad, but the challenge is to find out how to market products mutually beneficial to many different people. Perhaps one day some forward-thinking entrepreneur, or group of enterprising business people, for example, will harness Costa Rica's most abundant resource and find a way to bottle that wonderful clear-running water. After all, Costa Ricans use water from their abundant rains to irrigate rich coffee crops, ranked among the world's best brews by those who know. Then we have their bananas, strawberries, and literally hundreds of different lush vegetables and produce unheard of in the states. Even then, there is always enough rainwater left over to travel all the way down from the high mountains and its cloud forests to the two coasts. Imagine what such possibilities might do to our north-south hemispheric commerce, and for all of the people of the Americas!

18

Projecting Consciousness in Maximum Security

Life makes many claims on people's consciousness, and, like many, sometimes I think that there are areas of the mind that we do not fully know. Even though different stimuli enlist the attention of our five senses almost everywhere we turn, we can see that some of us variously inhabit parts of the mind that are less understood. We know that there are many levels of awareness, and, in order to function in our daily lives, most of us are prompted, by all sorts of forces and factors, to spend time in commerce with people whom we daily encounter. Life shows us that no two persons are alike, suggesting that individuals do not experience life the same way. Given multiple realities and the large number of factors that make all of us different, a person's perspective on life still largely depends on what the consciousness records. Depending on the nature of our conscious life, we inhabit or leave unused, for all sorts of reasons, mental states that could allow us certain possibilities. Several times, to help pay the family bills, I taught at a maximum-security prison in Angleton, Texas, and once I had a singular experience.

Consciously aware people know that the significance or import of almost everything that happens in life depends on response, on the ability to recognize, interpret, and articulate views or sensations. Whether in the city, the country, or wherever, the postmodern world engages attention precisely because it assaults the senses, and such experiences keep us linked or separated from other human beings, depending on how we respond or choose to react.

Much of life for consciously aware people is a matter of deciding what we would and can be conscious of, of choosing, where our work and talents permit, and how we will spend and use our waking hours. Even though the environments into which we are born tend to provide us with the main ingredients that determine the nature of our lives, we can also—if we are aware of the possibilities immanent in our consciousnesses—shape the places we would mentally inhabit, depending on our personal circumstances. This view should not surprise readers, but it can, in that where we mentally dwell is seen as the result of where we are physically and the places we have previously inhabited or to which we have a tie.

To some extent, consciousness is something that we can help to create, a state of mind that can be selectively altered and changed as people choose, if we but think about how our minds can take us where we would go. Although the consciousness of most individuals is shaped by society, religion, and a myriad number of things, I wish to contend that the worlds we choose to abide in are often different from the places where most of us spend our waking hours. And being where mentally we would rather be may not be as impossible as we might at first suspect.

Escapism offers what I seem to be proposing, but I am not talking about that. I am interested not in escaping or seeking refuge, although certainly that can be a healthy enough response to certain stimuli and worlds. Rather, I am suggesting that we can travel to worlds where we would mentally go by willing ourselves elsewhere. Since our consciousnesses are shaped both by external and internal forces and desires, there are, of course, some things that we cannot control or change. I cannot, for example, easily change my barrio or ghetto, should I live in such a world. One can change such an environment, but, as I suggest, one has to work at it, for most forces in real life work to maintain the status quo rather than to change things. That is why change is especially difficult. With some attention to the issue, though, we can control some of the external forces that shape our consciousnesses.

In this piece, I wish to focus attention on the results of a type of liberating thinking that I want to communicate. There is much, apparently, that we can do with our internal lives, for, if we can teach ourselves to learn to control our inner lives, it may be possible to create another state of consciousness—vague as this statement may sound. Once accomplished, that goal can prompt us to begin to change our environment, which in too many cases keeps minority people locked into believing there is no use in trying to improve things.

Several years ago, when I taught a literature course to maximum-security prisoners, the experience proved instructive. I have now forgotten the texts and the materials that I selected for the class, but I clearly remember an exchange I had with one of the prisoners; it introduced me to what he called "autoprojection." That was the first time I had heard such a word used, and I have since searched the dictionaries. The closest word I have found is autosuggestion. Autosuggestion, however, is "the influencing of one's own attitudes, behavior, or physical condition by mental processes other than conscious thought." The word is then defined as "self-hypnosis," and although there is a certain degree of self-hypnosis in autoprojection, as I understand the term, this word suggests maintaining a conscious state of mind that allows the person willfully to project himself or herself wherever the person wants to go while asleep. This, at any rate, is how my prisoner student described autoprojection to me during several conversations we had during our class breaks. In the British West Indies, in Trinidad, more specifically, *soucouyants,* spirits, reportedly leave their skins and fly about in some form at night. The incident I am about to describe is something comparable. These are events told to me by a Mexican American student about the out-of-body experiences that he had while he was confined in the maximum-security prison where I taught.

The prisoner told me that he used autoprojection to "escape" from the prison. By employing autoprojection, he would see and feel himself clearing the walls of the place where he had been confined for a good number of years. Autoprojection, he told me, is the ability to envision, right before falling asleep, where he mentally desires to go after he falls asleep. The idea is to imagine oneself out of the physical place a person happens to be in order mentally to visit another place. It is, I have since decided, the transforming of a deep desire into the claimed ability—short of being there bodily—of going where one would, in mind, spirit, and, what I consider important, consciousness. Because the experience can be powerful, the prisoner claimed that when he was asleep he sometimes felt as if his body has actually been transported elsewhere.

I believe that such a feeling or experience is a measure of a person's desire for relief, of escaping the unnerving detention that prisoners suffer day after day, year after year. The best part about this mental experience, he claimed, is that no drugs or mind-altering substances are needed, which suggested that in prison there is recourse to such materials, too. The only vehicle needed for autoprojection is the power of the mind, and I confess that the prisoner's emphasis on that made an impression on me. Initially I thought he was putting me on, as people say, but the fact that he was a prisoner without a foreseeable parole in his future, suggested he was serious enough. He believed that one simply has to learn how to engage some of the potential that the mind has, a potential that has not often enough been harnessed for personal, therapeutic benefit.

How did he employ autoprojection, as I understood it? According to him, one has to employ autoprojection immediately before going to sleep.

I have since learned that one can also use that knowledge, to better purpose, when one is awake. But, let me first describe how he tried to harness what he called the power to project himself to where he desired to be. Before going to sleep, he said, a person has to decide where he or she wants very badly to go. One then concentrates all conscious attention on the place that one wishes to visit in spirit, for one needs to know, so as not to delude oneself, that only the mind's eye will do the traveling and the visiting. The endeavor, he informed me, requires utmost concentration and an immense amount of intense consciousness. The person then deliberately focuses attention on the goal. He went on to say that when the attempt has worked for him—for he is not always successful—as soon as he falls asleep he can see and feel his spirit, for want of a better word, slowly rise out of his body. Then he experiences himself moving past the iron bars and rising, clearing the prison walls. One time, for instance, he told me he decided, before falling asleep, on visiting his home, on seeing his friends. Although he has seen them and felt very happy because he has been near them, these friends and relatives have either been asleep, or they have gone about their business without noticing his presence. He said that while he visits, he feels himself hovering over, watching, and seeing them. His main business, he informed me, was to store up visual images of everyone and everything he sees in order to savor, to reflect on, and to enjoy these pictures and scenes later. On returning to the prison, he said that he has seen his own body as it sleeps in his cell, and that the whole experience usually exhilarates him. When the attempt works, he feels an immense satisfaction and comfort.

One can, of course, see how a prisoner would feel heartened by such an experience, and, when I consider the huge number of prisoners in our country's jails, one feels the necessary waste. At this point I am concerned with the idea that one can use the same type of mental faculties to visit or to return to a place where one has been. To do so when one is about to fall asleep, it seems to me, would require a sustained self-programming effort like the one the inmate suggested. To autoproject oneself when fully awake, I think, can initially be a little less rewarding and less exhilarating, but a successful experience, no doubt, should be satisfying and rewarding.

Before proceeding to describe how one might consciously use autoprojection, let me say that I have employed autoprojection, as described by the prisoner, successfully twice in my life.

In the first instance, I told myself when I was already in bed and shortly before going to sleep that I was going to visit my mother's home while I slept. I then did as the prisoner had explained, that is, I started thinking about my mother and where she lives, and the rooms where she spends most of her hours, and the people and things that daily surround her. When I fell asleep, I did not feel myself slowly rising from my body, as the prisoner had, but I did find myself traveling or feeling mentally transported toward her. I suddenly found myself there, and I clearly remember saying to myself, you have done it! You are here, just as you wished! I also remember hovering about, looking at the rooms of her house, and feeling that I was actually there. When I woke up, I felt much as if I had shaped and directed my own dream, and I felt very good because I had accomplished what I endeavored to do while I slept. I felt so good, in fact, that I called Mom to ask about her and to tell her that my own family members were doing well, as I usually tell her when I call.

Autoprojection requires that we move out of where we are to what we would see, that we leave our habitation for another environment or locale. In such a case, one is not mentally where one is physically, and this can be achieved by consciously working on establishing a frame of mind that will project us elsewhere.

Looking back now at what I have written, I see that my prisoner student's dream and my own experience with autoprojection essentially consist of the old dream of flying. That is the mystical, half-articulated medieval idea that a person could and would fly, if only the subject learns to concentrate on the task long enough. Several nights ago I tried projecting myself out to the scene of my childhood, and I also wonderfully succeeded.

This evening it is so humid that I virtually feel the grass growing outside our shaded home. Inside it is agreeable, sitting on my comfortable green leather sofa in the living room. I rarely sit in this room, and yet it is among the quietest, nicest rooms in the house. There is so much that needs doing, and I could start or continue anew with almost anything around me. I prefer, however, to think about going into the den, into any of the bedrooms, the kitchen, the bathrooms and there would be enough in any one of these rooms to occupy me the rest of the day. There is even the fourth bedroom, which is full of things that someday we will sell in the garage sale that we have now postponed for three years. But sitting here simply talking in this vein is infinitely preferable just now. These are the things of my consciousness, the issues of which I am conscious this Saturday morning. Outside, both near and farther off, I hear the shrill sounds of the lawnmowers, making, of course, the quiet inside the house all the more delicious. For I have been a lawn cutter for many weekends, until recently, when I decided to hire several Latinos to help them with some needed extra work. On such a day as this I sometimes think of how the world would be if social justice prevailed and all people treated others fairly.

I could and would visit any number of places where I have been and that I told myself I would someday return. Chicago, Europe, Buffalo, Oakland-Berkeley, New York, to name a few. I do not have the money to return, but I took such good mental note of the places to which I have traveled that by conjuring them up I can revisit them when I will. I find it strange that no one I know has addressed himself or herself to this type of carefree intellectual mental travel. In retrospect, for instance, I did not realize when I left South Texas for Chicago and later for Buffalo, that my friends and I were also already hurling through space toward the future. In effect, the moment we started on the road we were already moving toward the end of the century when Latinos and concerns about the place of Latinos within the United States would become a pervading question in America's future. Indeed, we were among the first to venture out of our *vecindarios,* our neighborhoods, with the capacity to record the nature of our experience. And, although change was central to our experience, everything seem so static, so unchangeable, and, indeed, so resistant to the changes that we dreamed being part of and that we Latinos have sought in so many different places of the United States.

Are we so myopic that we need to experience the travails of physical travel to an actual place in order to be there? Sometimes, indeed, people can become so worn out by the effort of getting somewhere that when they arrive they do not have enough time and energy left to appreciate fully the places to which they have journeyed. So, they return, feeling that the whole trip was somehow too unreal, too evanescent—were we actually there? What did I bring back from the experience of going to Austria, for example, the farthest point east to which I have traveled, or to Milan or Barcelona, where I once spent several days apiece? Can we mentally conjure up and recapture the experiences that we have had, and, more important, what was the significance of all of that hectic motion to and from?

But a closing note. There is a happy sense hovering about everything that I see this late summer morning. Life seldom fails to provide a new perspective when we truly need one. Fall is two weeks away. Summer has started to fade. The days are cooler and delightful, and one can only hope that there are places where a soul, short of heaven, can also access some wonderful weather.

19

Evoking Rimsky-Korsakov on the Eve of a Move

In the World Book Encyclopedia, which Dad bought for the consider-able sum of about $350 in the early 1960s, and which my brother Eddie still keeps in his home in Houston, there is a picture of Rimsky-Korsakov. He is the self-taught composer of *Capriccio Español,* the *Sheherazade,* and a symphony for the Arabian *A Thousand and One Nights.* Other than perhaps on the Internet, where else can a picture of the musician be secured today? One glimpse and we can see why Rimsky-Korsakov would have spent his Sunday afternoons looking at paintings at an exhibition that Mussorgsky imagined elsewhere. In that faraway fantasy place, pictures and portraits mysteriously morph and continue to change according to the seasons, adorn-ing the walls of an art gallery for an indifferent populace. In that quiet, in-ner space with high ceilings, visitors will meander everlastingly over the light-green hills and dales seen through the windows, wandering occasion-ally into the museum on Sunday afternoons when little else presents a dis-traction. The men in coattails, top hats, and white gloves stroll with ladies holding ubiquitous parasols, eyes coyly peering from beneath them, look-ing, looking, always looking. A *parasol,* the umbrella that stops (*para*) the sun (*el sol*) blocks out the imagined brightness of the day, enmeshed in the chiaroscuros of the gray Russian world. What more was left to poor, pretty women living in worlds where looks determine everything?

There is no visible sun in this spiritless Russian reverie, but no matter. Rimsky-Korsakov's world was bleak, making it delectably romantic. In the chimera of his mind, music offered glimpses of the sun, a handful of Pari-sian moments captured in fitful visions parlayed into a haunting, unforget-table music. The ladies sauntered, parasols in hand; would it rain this afternoon? And when they stopped in their flounces and heels, the men tipped and touched their hats, their coattails central to the pompadour. Where to go, where to, after all of the orchestrated scenarios? What to do, what to see, where to turn the eyes and what expression to wear? Forever the same questions. The music always asking questions, but where is the consolation of an answer? The museum, that center of centers where people wend their way at one time or another, always there. Here tea remains available, and, later, at some pleasant, warm place, conversations are possible.

He taught music at the St. Petersburg Conservatory. Before that he was a naval student, also in St. Petersburg, the article says. He would have taught at a conservatory, hoping, always, to conserve what he had yet to invent, creating nonetheless music out of a longing, out of his yearning for a different world away from the one he knew so well. What else could he have dreamed up for the Rimsky-Korsakov that he sought to fashion? Small anxieties must have seemed like major catastrophes, lapses actually, slights intended or not, the minutiae of daily life, hearts and souls broken and left unrepaired, unaddressed, unfulfilled because his peers had other priorities, other concerns on which they spent themselves, time ticking off. The word exhibition was high on his consciousness, coming, as it did through Mussorgsky. That tonal genius, unalterably associated with the Parisian and Viennese art galleries of Russia, appropriately named Modest. Ravel, music historians tell us, resurrected and finished Mussorgsky's famous notes for touring the picture halls, Rimsky-Korsakov finishing Mussorgsky's *Khovantchina* in 1883. But who ever heard the music he wrote? His melodies were hummed by the dreamy ladies that came and went with the parasols, the day working its way through the circumambulating minds that did not allow themselves fatigue, taking in the great halls of that endless picture place.

Rimsky-Korsakov was a youthful twenty-seven when he was pronounced professor of orchestration and composition at the Conservatory. Did he sense the long composing life before him? Oh, for the leisure and the years of such uninterrupted life, he said, little knowing it awaited him. That was like yearning for the prospect of moving to the altogether different place that actually awaited him!

Tone-deaf students materialized, which only drove him more and more into his work. These were the sons and daughters of patrons who partially paid the bills, but he held back on the truth. He did what he could; if the students had only started to hear the actual notes earlier. He turned his energies to the composition of fifteen operas, three symphonies, several works for choral groups, and a book on instrumentation. That one could read Russian; that we could all hear the notes he imagined, which approximate the ones he wrote.

Why consider the life of a frustrated nineteenth-century Russian musician? To decompress from the frustrations of not being able to make the world budge one whit, to appropriate an altogether different life, another way of apprehending and appreciating a different world. Living in a foreign country, in another time, that is periodically tempting to some, particularly people who hope the exercise will oddly help to reconstitute the world's realities, all in the effort to change the coordinates of our generation. So people suspect that Latinos, especially Mexican Americans can vicariously visit and imagine other lives, other than the constrictive worlds shaped and left at their doors?

As the passing years collected within him, at some point Rimsky-Korsakov sat at two thirty in the morning in his kitchen, too, spirit ablaze, with some of the possible notes dancing in his head. He also must have wondered where his composition ought to go, given what he lived through, what he knew about the constraints of his time and place and how he would rather create the world, given a chance. Spinning out conceit after conceit was attractive to him, but did the young musician notice the zigzag between the lace and top-hat world he offered the Russian masses? Did some people hear some of the actual music he was after, the music notes caught in spurts here and there in his compositions, suggesting a possible new sun, a cherished better day?

Occasionally a few notes of a new sound seem audible. But that music seldom lasts. Reality keeps tugging at the soul, keeping the new at bay, outside the door, outside the window, looking in when it can, as in that sun poem by John Donne. Such music, he soon learned, cannot be sustained, especially when the willingness to suspend reality is simply not possible. The new notes rise and ebb, dying the second reality intervenes, becoming a memory as soon as recognized, forcing repeated choices again and again until musician and audience are estranged. That is why the composer returned to the ordinary, to the familiar, to the quiet halls that filled the rest of the music season and the years, the years, the years.

Only excerpts from his operas are occasionally played today, on radio stations given to celebrating the classics. Tomorrow, early, before the world is up, I will place a for-sale sign on the front lawn, closing a wonderful decade of our family's life in the Gulf Coast area, quietly slipping off to begin a new life, anew, further inland, a hundred miles from Houston. Tomorrow, tomorrow and *mañana*. Disillusionment happened once before, when we left Berkeley, and it can always happen once again. That is life. It is a matter of always being ready to begin with a new sun whenever it rises.

How did he teach himself to compose, being from aristocratic parents and having endured lessons from the local St. Petersburg masters? That is a telling turn-of-the-corner statement about him that lingers. Yet, and likely due in part to that strange fact, he reached a professional standing accorded to few other music teachers. He exhibited a love for the notes, even when at times he saw the emptiness that the subject elicited. His music confesses what he saw, what he felt and sought to communicate, men in top hats and ladies with parasols on a Sunday afternoon. Ho-hum, the poor Victorians, even in that faraway Russian place. A stroll, the museum, tea, followed by all of their separate, private returns to the quotidian. One hears his understanding in the music, in the notes of his lone soul. Later, he taught Igor, too, leaving him to walk the exhibition halls in his place, to see what the prized pupil would find for the next generation. And Stravinsky found more life, better notes, as true artists will. But despite their efforts, in both cases the world went down other paths, as often it does. The Russian Revolution shook the quiet monastery walls of the museums. Michael T. Florinsky wrote that story best, in beautiful, enviable words! No more exhibitions, no more white gloves and lovely ladies looking, looking, looking. Royal blood dimmed the shine of those great reflecting marble floors.

At two thirty in the morning, Rimsky-Korsakov wrote feverishly, for a yawning audience, leading him to accept his path, requiring him to work quietly, steadily. His white gloves in his dresser drawer, useful for the convocation ceremonies of the students advanced by the Conservatory, in time found a home there. But, one night after he finished one of his better pieces, he clipped his moustaches and his beard for the pictures he had promised to take. One ended up in the encyclopedia. Which cravat should I choose, he asked himself. A carefully chosen one or did he distractedly pull out a tie at the last moment? How many ties did he own? He wasn't too concerned, as long as the notes of his melodies allowed promenading about in top hats; that was the business of the times.

What did his students actually know? Was he driven, angry, pleasant, engaged, disaffected? He was all of these, at different times. One could find out, of course, if the matter mattered. One can find out all sorts of things, when the need and the desire combine. But the music that he heard in snatches in his head is the important thing, especially when he was not taking students through their paces. Taking students through the notes was tough, but it kept him honed, difficult as he found it to admit that truth to colleagues and critics who followed his progress with their left eye.

He became famous for his colorful and brilliant orchestration. He knew he needed to write a text on instrumentation to make his knowledge about orchestras better known. So he did. Somewhere on earth, a poor music student knows that book well. Is it outmoded, the student has been told, but it was never in vogue. This late night strange evocation suggests another life, elsewhere. One contemplates many lives, a business that yields the pleasures of the endeavor, offering an appreciative audience the luxury of contemplating different music. Writing late into the night inevitably brings the dawn's rising sun.

20

Leaving the NASA Johnson
Space Center Neighbors

The Houston-Galveston area constitutes the hub of the upper Gulf of Mexico. When a for-sale sign appeared on the front lawn of our home in Taylor Lake Village one summer, our family had mixed feelings. Everyone marks time differently. When we left Berkeley in 1979 and arrived in the Clear Lake area in our 1975 russet-red yuppie Volvo station wagon, now more than two decades ago, my wife and I spent a good three days looking for the house where we knew we would raise our son and daughter. We called a real estate agent and told her that we were interested in a home in Clear Lake Forest, one of the original subdivisions populated by the people who worked at the NASA Johnson Space Center. Rita and I described for the agent the type of home we could afford, and she responded with a statement that, in retrospect, every person engaged in a move loves to hear: I have just the house for you. But this agent did. We saw several homes, and came back and bought the one on Willow Hill Drive.

When we rented and moved to Harlingen in 1986, our ten-year-old daughter said that she wanted to pick up our Clear Lake Forest home and move it to our new place in the Sierra Apartments off the Sunshine Strip in Harlingen. For the money we had available, we simply could not find a nice, comfortable house that felt right for the family, and feeling at home is absolutely essential. Our Clear Lake home had three bedrooms, one of the largest dens around with a large fireplace, an attractive living room, and a dining room that I used as my home office because our son turned the study into his bedroom. There was also a detached garage with a driveway that had a slight drive-up curve, instead of the regular Texas B-line affair, which came off a quiet residential street lined with pin-oaks facing a cul-de-sac. We had wonderful neighbors to our right and left, and great ones several houses over in a variety of directions, but especially in the semicircle fronting our home. If possible, we believe we would buy that place anew, for one always wonders when selling a home that one has loved whether another house as comfortable will ever provide the family with similar great times.

House particulars are important because they decree the nature of the experience. Outside we had thirty-seven pin-oak trees; twenty-four in the front yard, and the rest in the back. During the summer, the shade provided by the trees made our home one of the coolest in the Clear Lake Gulf of Mexico Bay Area. Except for the driveway side, where hurricane fears had forced us to cut the oldest oak that once extended three-quarters of the way across house, we were surrounded by tall, majestic-looking pin-oaks that stood like leafy sentinels straight up forty to fifty feet high. Although people do not think of cold weather in the Texas Gulf Coast, several winters were quite cold, and the oak trees always provided enough wood to burn in the great fireplace through the January and February cold spells. Some of the wood I was finally forced to give away because the July and August humidity in Houston generally ended by eating into the wood left out in the shade behind the garage.

On one occasion, I cut and stacked five pin-oaks in the backyard against the garage, because, unlike the front lawn, which was thickly covered with St. Augustine grass, the trees shaded the backyard so densely around the detached garage that little grass grew there. More sun was needed in the yard in the back to encourage the growth of the grass, a lawn man had told me soon after we arrived. So, like the young Abe Lincoln, immediately after the first cool crisp November northern moved in, I cut the first of several trees that I was to bring down during our stay in that house. It was cold enough, so as soon as I finished cutting the trees I rushed inside to drink my wife's hot chocolate with the kids. Nothing brings a family together like drinking hot chocolate on a cold November day, especially when the children are already thinking about what Santa Claus will bring them for Christmas.

One year, despite my efforts to prevent it, one of the trees fell across my back neighbor's fence. It knocked two six-inch slats off his six-foot fence, and he came out, saying that he thought he had heard something. The top of the tree lay partially across his garage roof, the trunk astride the broken slats of his fence. I offered to pay for the repairs, but he was a generous neighbor and said he had some extra pieces left when the fence was finished. I offered to do the work, but he wouldn't have it; he repaired the fence a few days later, with no damage to our relations. By the time we left, our back yard was nicely tufted with St. Augustine; so nicely, in fact, that between late February and Halloween, I knew the new owner would have to cut the lawn at least once a week. Let me buy a house with less grass next time, I remember saying. But, of course, we ended building as nice a home as we could stretch toward, and on a corner lot! That is where we still reside in south central Texas, a little over three hours inland from the coast. We don't have the trees, and in winter it is colder. But, as in the song, the stars at night from the backyard are just marvelous, summer, fall, winter, and spring.

21

Rio Grande Valley Meditation

I first left the Rio Grande Valley in 1968, and two years later the 1970 U.S. Census reported the population of Texas at 11,196,730 inhabitants. Thirty years later, the 2000 Census counted 20,851,820 people in Texas, breaking out the ethnicity of Texans into 11.6 percent African Americans, 53.1 percent Anglos, 32 percent Hispanic, and 3.3 percent other. Since the 1990 Census, the two large lower Rio Grande Valley counties, which primarily attracted Latinos, have continued to grow considerably: 176,128 new Hispanics for Hidalgo, which has a total population of 590,285 citizens, 88.3 percent of whom are Latinos. That is my home county. The other large Valley county is Cameron, which recorded a total population of 344,782, of which 84.3 percent are Latinos, including 69,741 new citizens. This kind of substantial Latino growth, duplicated also in the state's fastest growing counties, such as Harris (474,816), Dallas (347,099), Bexar (167,853), Tarrant (145,411), El Paso (120,035), and Travis (107,359), is simultaneously heartening and enervating. Heartening because such growth raises questions that have not been addressed for many years, and enervating because one can only hope that this significant demographic change will not create undue resentment for the many Latinos who are pursuing the American Dream.

Finding a new place in a world one left more than thirty years before can be disorienting. Everywhere one looks the new has been superimposed on the old, covering the recognized signs, summoning up memories of Rip Van Winkle. Flying from Houston to McAllen requires leaving the higher anxieties of the big city, which are simply more in number, resulting from the larger volume of people, for a less cluttered life. Still, the daily concerns tend to be surprisingly similar: running to work, running to the store to buy bread or a gallon of milk for the children, paying the bills on time, keeping appointments that cannot be avoided. The Valley is a place where a good number of people move less hastily because, even though the number of people has substantially increased, life in the neighborhoods has not provided any more options to keep people engaged on proving and improving themselves.

Seeing the Valley anew after many years from the air-conditioned cool-ness of a rented car presents a quiet thrill. The hot weather outside reminds me of the inescapable heat from which there used to be no relief. Driving on U.S. 83, the backbone freeway connecting the Rio Grande Valley cities, is invigorating because I remember the towns statically, fixed, unchanged. They have changed. The highway overpass that now links McAllen, Edinburg, and Pharr has shrunk the Valley, making it a sprawled-out urban center surrounded by the agricultural fields that traditionally have provided inhabitants with livelihoods in one way or another.

In the early 1960s, around the time that John F. Kennedy was shot, my dad was in the habit of taking an entire day to drive his forest green 1951 Chevrolet pickup through all the little Valley towns, from Edinburg to Brownsville to visit the Brownsville Savings and Loans, returning that same evening. Now the trip to Brownsville takes half a day and perhaps even less, in a fast car. He never said anything to me about why he always kept a few thousand dollars on deposit at the southernmost tip of South Texas, sev-eral blocks from the Mexican border. He became an American citizen about two years before his death on December 7, 1969, Pearl Harbor Day. And he did so only because he learned that his wife, my mother, would not re-ceive Social Security checks from the federal government if he should die a Mexican citizen. He had been paying into the Social Security system since it began in the 1930s during the Roosevelt years. He had always expected that Mom would be provided with a monthly check after his death. When he found out that his Social Security deductions would not help her with her needs, he was not pleased. He had no option but to become an Ameri-can citizen.

Today, many of the illegal immigrant workers who find jobs with fake Social Security cards secured somehow are in much the same situation. These workers pay into the Social Security system with every check they receive from their employer. They work years and years in the United States, but because they are not American citizens with the proper legal creden-tials, they are never able to claim benefits for themselves or their families following their deaths. This means that a sizeable amount of money will never be claimed; it will become part of the Social Security fund. Eventu-ally it will be used to pay other retired Americans, making this matter an issue that ethically requires attention.

The other reason why I now surmise Dad kept money in Brownsville is that I do not think he ever really felt comfortable in the United States, what with the Border Patrol and the things that he never mentioned but that he must have experienced in Texas between the 1920s and 1969. As far as I have been able to discern, I believe he felt that he had made his home and raised his family in another country, in the United States, where, even though he was a law-abiding, self-respecting immigrant who paid his taxes and gave everyone his or her right due, he might at any moment, for whatever reason, possibly lose everything. I think he felt better keeping some of his money in Brownsville, where, should occasion arise, he could access his resources in several hours, and either drive into Mexico or go elsewhere.

The only other country he ever visited, to be sure, was Costa Rica. My mother's family there absolutely loved him, no exaggeration. In Costa Rica my father was a different person. Among Costa Rican Latinos he was the embodiment of the successful Spanish-speaking businessman. From their angle, he had worked a business miracle, for he was the half-owner of a grocery store. More importantly, he had raised a wonderful family, and we were the happy evidence. He only showed us off three times in his life, when he accompanied us, every four years, to Costa Rica, the Switzerland of the Americas. Each trip we had a grand time, but finally, I find his story sad and difficult to explain to people not familiar with the politics, the 1950s and 60s, and the goings-on in the Valley. Not that things have changed much, despite the enormous population growth, nearly forty years later. The new Valley rests more visibly atop the old one, but the cultural, uneasy social separations among the people still exist. I can see that when I return to the streets or when I talk to the residents, Mexican Americans and Anglos.

The Internet and telephone directories do not list Dad's savings and loan association anymore, suggesting it is now defunct, or that another bank or corporation may have bought it. The new Valley freeway is like Highway 99 in California, which connects most of the cities that border the eastern side of the famous San Joaquin Valley. Together these two agricultural regions provide employment for a large number of Hispanic field workers who pick cotton and citrus fruits in Texas and beets, carrots, grapes, and a number of other vegetables in California, all foods that grace and nourish members of American households.

Brownsville, Harlingen, and McAllen are the Valley's three largest cities; the question confronting us was whether we should rent or buy. The dream of living within walking distance of work has always been attractive to me. The ideal would be to wake, shower, shave, dress, take a cup of *café con leche,* two slices of toast, and walk to work every morning for the rest of my life until death or retirement, whichever arrives first. That is a fantasy that makes my quiet life enjoyable, like a good number of the other pleasant experiences I describe for fellow Americans, as LBJ used to say. Nothing to play up or to howl about, though. We have more than enough hype these days, and most of it turns out overdone and unwarranted. To walk home leisurely the same way, stopping where one chooses to observe any part of the day, every afternoon after a good day's work would be reward enough. There are many ways to live, of course, but, as a teacher and writer, I have become used to a low-key lifestyle that allows me to study how education and the media together shape and affect Latino people. These two cultural arenas are big enough subjects to study. Clearly, some people will say, my imagination is limited, but I would be content with making a difference in how these two parts of a socially constructed vise impact Latinos.

Since I have not had the luxury of living within walking distance of a Catholic parish since I left the Valley, locating near a church would also be a great gift for me. Not all Latinos think as I do regarding religion. Indeed, more Latinas attend regular services, certainly more than the men. Although some educated Mexican Americans tend to move away from the church as they grow and develop, I have been through that, and I now realize that the Roman Catholic Church, despite its failings, is nonetheless part of my Latino heritage, the church founded by Christ Himself. Once, when I was young and full of myself, I believed I could see through the teachings of the church and the priests, and I concluded that I was better, that the Church could not hoodwink me. For a number of years, I went about thinking that I could not be fooled, that my intelligence discerned the truth and that the Christian teachings of the Church actually hurt Latinos. Thankfully, I have learned that no one has ever developed a better way of living than Christ, and today I rest easy with that belief.

I now personally work at following the teachings of the Church as best I can, and I possess a healthy respect for all religions, and especially for the admirable men and women who choose the religious life. Priests and nuns have difficult lives, and, as in all areas of life, there are great priests and others who work on doing the best they can. Whether religious or not, in short, life has shown me that people need to be guided by good moral, religious scruples, for everything depends, first, on loving God, which is difficult, since, unlike Thomas, we have never seen Him, and second, on respecting all of life. Not abusing or imposing our controlling wills on others is what I think we should all seek to practice, for many people are relatively defenseless. Many do not even know how to pursue their own interests, which some people may find difficult to believe.

Returning to the Valley raised the question of what would help Latinos most. I would say great teachers in well-endowed schools would greatly enhance Latino lives. Not good enough schools, which is what people have sought, but very good schools that can provide quality educations for the young. For the Latino contribution to American society largely depends on the kind of schooling that Spanish-speaking children receive today. If we cannot educate Latino children usefully to improve their prospects, their lives will only continue to replicate the dismal past. A future without quality schools ushers in all the undesirable things that no American wants, like drugs, crime, illiteracy, poverty, and barrio hopelessness.

Educating youngsters to prepare them for whatever they encounter is the only way that Latinos can successfully cope with tomorrow. This goal, although simply stated, is very difficult to implement, mainly because so many other agendas revolve around power and privilege issues that counter and interfere with the welfare of Latino and other minority children. Children should never be overwhelmed and defeated by the obstacles they encounter in life. Learning to adjust to changes and staying abreast of developments is an essential requirement for success. For that reason, I would provide children with all of the good things that most people profess to believe in, but which we adults simply do not make time to give them.

Many of us, indeed, would rather spend our time cynically depreciating, deriding, or being skeptical when confronted with the claim that we are today ignoring and leaving for the young the same kind of world that we experienced ourselves. Let youngsters figure things out for themselves, we are, in effect, saying. But that will not do. Look at our world. Were we left to figure things out when the post–World War II baby boomers rebelled in the 1960s? Money was a part of the world before, but life was not all about money as it is now.

Everything, I believe, should cater to educating and training the young so that they properly appreciate options and understand their responsibilities. When this principle is not observed, we tend to see some nasty consequences. We should take our stand in helping the younger generations to figure out what they can do, instead of allowing them to make too many unnecessary errors with their lives. There are many ways to spend time, such as helping humankind in any number of ways. We have to make a connection between helping other human beings and making a good, respectable living. The money, the achievement, and the accomplishment have not yet been placed in working out such connections. But if we start thinking about the needs of the young, someday someone will connect a good, respectable livelihood with the funds necessary for all people to live decently and more happily.

Our family has lived in three homes and one apartment, and it seems that we are always in the process of looking for a new house, a new home for the family. From several previous visits to the Valley, I discovered that it is not easy to find as nice a home as the one we now have—one, at any rate, that is within our budget. Real estate prices in the Valley have surprised us, for houses are considerably more expensive there than we had anticipated. Nonetheless, it is important to bring children back to the birthplace of the parents, if possible, so they will know their family roots, so they will see for themselves where their dad and mom spent their formative years. Although there have been many changes, the old Valley is recognizable. It is there, as soon as one turns off the newer streets and the latest residential developments. In less than five minutes, I am right across the cotton fields of my youth, parked in the car looking back once more at the rows of cotton. The fields still offer the spectator the neat rows, exactly like the ones I used to pick in the early 1960s.

The first day I stooped down to pick cotton, I remember smiling and saying to myself, here I am, just like all the other Mexican Americans who have gone before me, including my father, uncles, and family. Not that I had to pick cotton then. Dad had thankfully provided a nice middle-class life for us, as I previously said. But that day I gathered eighty-seven pounds into my new fifteen-foot cotton sack that I was embarrassed about because it was so new and not good and dirty, like the ones my friends and all of the other workers had. Two days later, though, it was as dirty, and on its way to reaching the tea-colored tint that the sack permanently kept by the time the 1961 season ended. The following year, I joined the noontime canal-swimming group, which my mother's injunctions had kept me from enjoying the year before. I had asthma between five and fifteen or thereabouts, and mom was absolutely terrified when I walked barefooted or when I did what she called a *desarreglo,* took a health risk. But, even then, the day arrived when I rebelled and jumped into the canal, after much soul-searching about whether I should obey or disobey. An hour later, the sun was so hot that it had miraculously completely dried our clothes, and, since I did not suffer an asthma attack, I never had to report the news to my parents that I had taken to swimming in the canals that bordered and watered the cotton fields we picked.

The story that I have had to look into, because we were never informed about our own local history, is that sometime in the late 1920s and early 1930s, the lower Rio Grande Valley was dug up and outfitted with an irrigation system. As I understand it, water from Falcon Dam on the western side of the Valley between Laredo and Rio Grande City was channeled by canals throughout the Valley to irrigate the crops. Unless people are involved in agriculture, this vast system of pipes that provided turnkey water locks for almost every agricultural field is one of the best-kept secrets in the Valley. Water, indeed, is the Valley's life-blood, for during long droughts, its irrigation system has saved many crops, providing much needed moisture for cotton, sorghum, citrus fruits, alfalfa, tomatoes, carrots, melons, watermelons, and other crops that form the agricultural goods produced by Valley farmers year after year.

While I sit here on the aisle seat, writing as the jet flies toward McAllen, the face of a baby girl, a Chicanita, just popped up three empty rows in front of me. She is a beautiful child with little earrings, dark hair, and jet black eyes. Do other people see beauty in this four-year-old Mexican American girl, or will they treat her as Claudia and Pecola were treated in Toni Morrison's *The Bluest Eye* (1970)? Will she someday be selected for the cover of a magazine, an example of Mexican American beauty and the promise of tomorrow? And will all of the adults in her life, including, of course, her teachers, spend their days helping her to achieve her full potential? These are the questions that need to be addressed today.

Sometimes I wish our people were more involved, engaged in empowering activities, bent on making more of ourselves instead of accepting the fact that we have been historically marginalized. But how is this to happen when we continue to be largely discouraged and left to flounder, unconnected to the rest of American society that is bent on working up productive networks that will advance citizens? Since we have been taught, in effect, not to be engaged by much in American society, we feel there is nothing wrong with figuring things out as best we can. But there is. Most U.S. Latinos are disengaged because we respond that way to the many signals that are daily sent to us and to which we react. With little guidance and attention, we do what we can, all the while observing how others who are seen as natural inheritors of American culture are provided with opportunities and the materials to make more of themselves.

The mother of the little girl I mentioned, I have learned from comments she has made to her neighbor, is returning home to the Valley from a visit to see sick relatives in Houston. Again, where will this little girl be in ten or twelve years? How will she see the prospects for her own future? How can her future not be contained by the limited education she is receiving today, by what the people around her believe and tell her, in what is placed day by day in her head? In this business of working to change how people see themselves and how they respond to others, I am always happy to discuss my views whenever invited. That, indeed, is why I am on this trip.

But, we have arrived! Cloudy, 59 degrees; it is a nice, brisk-looking late October day. Hellooo, Rio Grande Valley! Hello, McAllen! *¡Aajjuaaa!!! Ya llegamos a Penjamo, de nuevo!*

22

Showdown across the Border in Reynosa

A number of people are understandably reluctant to travel in countries where their language skills fall short. Since Spanish is my first language, friends and acquaintances may find the following experience difficult to believe, but it is the kind of incident that warrants an analysis that I want to leave to readers who may be familiar with similar events.

I had been working since December 8, the feast of the Immaculate Conception, without missing one day. It was the day before my very reliable secretary, who had organized our smoothly running office, was to leave to work for the Bishop of the Brownsville Diocese. I had accumulated one day per month of sick leave for nineteen months running, and would lose my sick leave when I also would leave my administrative position in five weeks. My family had been putting off a trip to Matamoros or Reynosa for more than a month, and because it would be more difficult to take a day off after my secretary left, I decided to do what I had never done. I called in sick.

We chose to cross over into Mexico at Reynosa, which is located about ten miles south of McAllen, Texas, on the Rio Grande. On the way there in the station wagon with my wife Rita and our two children, I alternately felt both good and bad about having taken the day. I felt good because I had been working straight from seven thirty to past five thirty pretty consistently for over a year and a half, and I had been giving my job my best energies. Even though one should not feel as I was, I felt that I was due something, given that I often stayed in the office until seven in the evening, taking care of business that I could not get to during the busy days. And I felt bad because no matter how I turned it, I disliked calling in sick, regardless of how well I felt I could use the time with my family. I am, I said to myself, a Chicano with a puritan guilt conscience, a product of my upbringing and U.S. education.

The day was beautiful. It was warm, a bit on the muggy side, but in the air-conditioned ten-year-old Volvo station wagon, the heat did not bother much. The fifty-minute ride from Harlingen, where we lived, to McAllen and Hidalgo and across the bridge to Reynosa was taken up discussing our upcoming return to the Houston–Clear Lake area. We felt that we had profited immensely from our year-and-a-half stay in the Valley. Although I grew up there, when we lived in California, where our children were born, and later in Clear Lake, I had always lamented the fact that we could not afford to take our children to live or to visit my hometown area for any length of time. I always felt that if they did not live for a time in the Valley, they would not know about my background, they would not know what it is like to be a Chicano or Mexican American from South Texas. Because I had been fortunate enough to secure the arts and sciences deanship at the Valley's only community college, I felt that I had been able to provide Rita, who is from Puerto Rico, and the children with the opportunity to see how my people in South Texas live. For this opportunity, Rita and I were very pleased and thankful, for there was nothing I could have said or written that would have given my children the type of experience that only South Texas, in its own unique way, can provide while one still lives in the United States.

Although I had taken the family to Matamoros several times before, on occasions when Rita's Puerto Rican parents from Buffalo had visited us, today I was going to take the family to Reynosa. Reynosa is the border town that I had occasionally visited with my parents and later with teenage friends before I went off to central Texas to study in Austin. Rita had gone with a friend the previous week, and both women had come back saying they thoroughly enjoyed shopping in Reynosa because it was cleaner and less congested than Matamoros. I was pleased that she wanted to go back to buy some other items that we wanted to take with us to Houston.

We arrived at ten forty-five in the morning and parked immediately after we crossed the bridge to the Mexican side of the border. I wanted to drive into downtown Reynosa and park closer to the *mercado,* the marketplace, but Rita said that she and her friend had parked safely where we did and that the attendants had taken good care of the car while they shopped. An attendant came over and asked me for one dollar, the set fee. This was a change, for how much one used to give the attendants, I recalled, had been up to the person.

We walked toward the church, which faces *la plaza,* the town square, as churches do everywhere in Mexico. We paid a short visit. Back on the street everything indeed looked cleaner than I remembered Reynosa, and I was encouraged. I recalled having heard on a Spanish radio station that a new mayor had been voted in on the promise of cleaning up the city. He was going to root out corruption, promote tourism, do what he could to bring in direly needed money for Reynosa, a northern Mexico city of over 500,000 people.

The Mexican border cities along the Rio Grande Valley generally have large populations because many people from the interior of Mexico who want or hope to find work in the United States tend to go to Reynosa and Matamoros. From there, they somehow hope to work their way over to the American side where wages are considerably higher. The Mexican economy, as far as I can remember, has always been very difficult on the average Mexican citizen. The poorest of the poor in Mexico, having next to nothing at home, make tremendous sacrifices to cross over into the United States to see how they can make a living for themselves and maybe have something left that they can send back to relatives at home. When one crosses the border, one sees many of the poor, the destitute ones from the Mexican interior, asking for money to help their loved ones. The sight has always made me feel bad, although I have heard it said that the people who ask for alms do well enough from it. I have never believed this, so I usually give them what money I can spare because I simply cannot be convinced that their lives are not tough. Picture a mother dressed in rags with a baby in her arms, and three or four other children around her selling gum to passersby for a livelihood, and you will see anywhere from twelve to fifteen similar cases at any one time on the Mexican side of the bridge.

We proceeded, holding hands and walking through the people-filled sidewalks, to the mercado. After comparing prices in three or four jewelry shops, we bought our son a watch and baby clothes for our goddaughter whom we would see in August in Tucson, Arizona. Our daughter then espied a Yamaha recorder in a glass showcase, and realizing that Japanese products are also in Mexico, we bought the recorder for $2.85.

On the way back to the car, we stopped in a liquor store and bought two liters of Chivas Regal, one for us and another for a gift. It was then about ten minutes before one and Rita remarked that she felt it was hotter in Mexico than it had been across the border on the U.S. side in Harlingen. Since people and their frustrations are crowded together, propped as it were, up against the northern border of Mexico, up against the southern rim of the Rio Grande Valley, everything appears more congested in the larger Mexican border cities.

The car was especially hot. We opened the windows to let the hot air out. Because there was a line of cars waiting to cross the bridge toward the American side, I did not turn on the air conditioner. We left the windows opened, but there was not the slightest breeze.

On the way out of the parking lot, I had to turn left, and stay in the left lane of a two lane one-way road in order to head toward the bridge. A policewoman, though, a new sight in Mexico for me, stopped traffic and motioned me and the cars behind me to go to the right on the congested tow lane road going toward the bridge. I needed to stay in the left lane, which I could see led directly to the bridge. But she insisted that I move to the right lane, and seeing that a car at the top of the line on the right lane nonetheless turned left, I entered the right lane as she bid. As soon as I did I knew I had made an error, for the policeman up ahead was routing right lane traffic away from the bridge.

I told the next *guardia civil,* the Mexican official directing traffic, that I needed to turn left because I was returning to the U.S. side. But he motioned me to continue going directly ahead. I told him that I was coming from Reynosa and that I sought to cross over to the American side, where I had just come from that morning. He said that I had to go straight, that if I did not go on as directed he was going to give me a citation or take me in. He was sweating like everyone else. It was very hot, and the intense midday sun, the dusty streets, and the engines of the cars did not help matters. I held back, unwilling to go straight, for I saw the long lines and I knew that it would take us a good while to get back to the spot where we were in order to cross. He was sending me to the back of the line. In the heat, and with the family on board, and not having eaten since our early morning breakfast, I did not want to go back. But the policeman was insistent. He looked at me for the third or fourth time and told me to move on. I was obstructing traffic. Miffed, I did as he said, and after I turned away from the bridge, I went one, two, three, four, five blocks into, I felt at the time, deep Mexico. The long line of cars continued to snake around the streets. At every block we could see cars stalled two or three blocks in every direction.

The traffic congestion apparently consisted of the regular Mexican traffic and cars lined up to cross the border. Upset at the traffic problems I had been forced into, I took several turns, once I came to a clearing and drove up to a line that I felt was the best I could do at that point. We waited and waited while the traffic inched forward. Everyone in our car was sweating by now and feeling very uncomfortable, sticky, and hungry. The car lines, however, had stalled. We sat; my son opened the car door to see if some breeze from somewhere would happily blow in. We waited and waited.

A car was parked crosswise on the street, forcing oncoming cars to do what they could to move forward. Another policeman at this juncture in the traffic snarl was also stopping these cars, and drivers were showing him what I supposed were their drivers' licenses. The car crawl was that; the policeman continued to delay traffic. He was looking at what now appeared to be white tickets, and in another case, a blue card, with large numbers written on it. I must be in some kind of after-game traffic jam, I told my family. An impatient driver pulled up next to Rita's side and she overheard him ask another man who stepped out of the car behind us to talk to the policeman to see if he would take five dollars. The man didn't answer. He wiped his forehead with a towel. It was too hot. I didn't like that.

When I was nineteen, I had once offered a Mexican policeman a *mordida,* literally a bite, that is, a bribe, to release a friend of mine that they had just decided to pick up. That policeman had given me a backhanded slap that dropped me to the ground in complete surprise. In my brash youthfulness, I got up ready to fight, but he went for his gun, and I smartly dropped my fists. Two other officers suddenly appeared and before I knew it one had twisted my arms behind me and the other one handcuffed me.

I had offered the bribe because I had heard that this was the practice in Mexico. Policemen in Mexico were expected to supplement their small salaries with money made by working out arrangements with people. On that particular occasion, I had asked why the policeman who hit me was arresting my friend who had not done anything. (This friend, by the way, is now a successful, practicing lawyer in South Texas.) When he ignored my question twice, I asked him if he wanted a mordida, which, thinking back on that, was not the word I should have used. My friend and I were then both taken to jail in Reynosa, and that had been my most unsavory experience. We were freed the following day, when another friend of ours posted bail, but only after we had spent the night among people brought in for all sorts of reasons.

The thought of that awful experience had never left me and it now loomed threateningly anew before me while I waited in line. I had told Rita about my night in jail in Mexico, and I brought out again that I just could not trust the Mexican police, for I have never been able to predict how they will act or respond in any given situation. My own father, who was born in Mexico, would have nothing to do with the police, and, primarily for that reason, he tried to avoid going to Mexico when he could, and he especially stayed away at night. He did, of course, take us as a family, as I was now taking my family, but only during the day and he was always concerned, and I understood why.

We inched our way to the officer checking cars, and when he came to my side of the car, I asked him what was holding up the line ahead. He disregarded my question and asked me to show him my *boleto,* my ticket. I asked what ticket. He said the one you got earlier. I told him that I had not been given a ticket or anything else when I crossed the border that morning; I had simply been waved through. The other policeman who had forced me to go directly ahead when I needed to turn came up and told the policeman who was asking me about the ticket that he had told me earlier that I had to go to the end of the line. I told both of them that I had been stalled in line for the last fifty minutes in the heat like everyone else, and that I had to cross the bridge, that we had not eaten.

They asked for my ticket again, and I told them that I did not know what ticket they were talking about, that this was the first time I had heard anything about a ticket. They told me I had to go back to the station to get a ticket. I asked what station, and they said the police station. I found the whole scene baffling, incomprehensible. They told me to pull over to the side. I hesitated and didn't. I got by the car that I now saw had been parked across the street apparently to slow down the traffic, and proceeded thirty or forty paces to the car up ahead.

There the traffic stopped again. The policeman, the friend who had sent me around to the back of the line, walked up and told me to turn again to the right, that is, away from the line leading across the bridge to the U.S. side. I did not budge. I told him that I needed to cross the bridge, that I did not understand what they were asking me to do by securing a ticket. I had never heard of tickets to cross, that I did not know Reynosa and could not have secured a ticket, even if I wanted to. They told me that without a ticket I could not cross. Frustrated, I again asked them to allow me to go ahead, that I had my family, as they could plainly see. If I was alone, I added, I would have gone to get the ticket they needed. All the time I kept thinking that maybe this was a ruse to fluster me and that what they really wanted was a mordida, but, of course, I was not about to venture that and possibly insult them and perhaps wind up in jail twenty years after that other time.

So I did not. And I did not budge. And it was my turn to cross the street and thus proceed on to the border area where I would report what I had bought, pay my liquor fee, and drive home.

But the policeman was there, standing in front of my car. He was a big man, and he was bidding me to turn right, now, thus to turn back to Reynosa. A pretty picture, indeed, I remember telling myself. My one vacation day and look what happens.

He told me that I was forcing him, that he would give me a citation, and that he would arrest me if I did not turn to the right. I closed my window and asked Rita and the children to close theirs. The children complained about the heat, but did so reluctantly. I insanely felt like going on, through the policeman. I could not believe that I had taken a day off from work to show Reynosa to my family, and that we had all immensely enjoyed our trip until this moment. Now this policeman was standing before my car and telling me to turn back into Mexico because I did not have a ticket. And I did not have a way of finding out what it was that they were requiring of me.

The whole scene and series of events since we had returned to the car was absurd, this showdown in Reynosa. No one would believe this story, I told Rita. She said that she would not believe it either if she had not seen it herself. She could not figure out their behavior. What has he to gain by antagonizing visitors, she kept asking. What is in it for him or for Mexico that policemen are allowed to harass tourists?

I was not turning. I felt like gunning my car and charging forth, but I kept my place. My children were telling me to turn and so was Rita. They did not want to see their dad hauled off to jail. I looked at the policeman from behind my windshield. He moved his feet back and forth in front of the car and kept motioning me to turn. I stayed like that for at least a minute, possibly longer. Under such circumstances, a minute is too long.

I looked at him, trying to understand, and I was suddenly aware that there was no way I could understand him. He was just following his orders, or what he saw as being right. I was clearly in the wrong. After all, I did not have a ticket. He would as soon have taken me to jail for disobeying his order as motion the next car, which might have been driven by a pretty girl, through. He was as Mexican as I was Mexican American, and this, I believe, was the crux of the matter.

I did not understand him, had never really even bothered to understand him, even though I had lived across the river from Mexico for twenty years, I confess, and he clearly did not like what he saw. What he saw was somebody who looked very much like any other Mexican citizen, but this cocky guy had a Volvo station wagon with U.S. license plates. There was also a pretty wife and two children, asking to be allowed to return to the United States. But this Chicano guy was too confident, and he was not following directions, and he did not have a ticket that he should have gotten at *la jefatura,* the police station. Given that, he must have thought, I am not about to let one of those Chicanos from across come over here and tell me how to run my business.

I eyed him, as I said, from behind the windshield of my Volvo, but when I realized that there was nothing else I could do, I turned right as he said and went down the street back toward Reynosa.

The next policeman had seen the standoff, and he was more conciliatory. He told me that I had to go to the police station. If I waited there, the new chief would come in later on in the afternoon. Likely he would help me out. I told him that I did not know where the station was. He looked at me with both exasperation and commiseration; he was also perspiring under the two thirty sun and the hot engines on the streets. He gave me directions, and, although I listened, I lost him after the fourth street corner where I had to turn. I was thinking about the Mexican cop and me, about our little point-less altercation that nonetheless brought into relief all sorts of things—many of which I could write about for some time. When he finished, I thanked him and headed off in the direction of the end of the line. I went to yet a third officer down the traffic line, and asked him how we could get to Progreso or Matamoros, the other two border cities.

He told me and within minutes I was out of the traffic jam, headed south-east along the Mexico side of the river toward Matamoros. At three fifteen or so, a russet-red 1978 Volvo crossed to the American side of the Rio Grande at Progreso.

We were the only car crossing at that moment, and the event was such a relief that, while I paid my duties for the items we had bought, I even exchanged pleasantries with both the Mexican and the American customs officials.

To this day, I suspect that the large Mexican policeman who would not let me cross because I did not have a ticket must have been baffled by the disappearance of that red station wagon with the Chicano who glared at him.

Sol Radiante:
Public Policy Issues

23

On Seeing Giant, *after Avoiding the Film Many Years*

Now that I am more than half a century old, I am somewhat embarrassed to admit I rented the video film *Giant* the other day, the one directed by George Stevens in 1956, for the first time in my life. I had been purposely avoiding this film, missed seeing it on three or four separate occasions in Austin, Buffalo, and in Berkeley over the years, because I simply rejected how George Stevens's film represents Mexican Americans. When the mainstream representation of Latinos is scarce, why patronize films and programs that misrepresent us? But, having successfully avoided the four-hour-long motion picture for many years, one weekend I gave up. My wife and I rented the video and went home to see it.

I knew the film had spawned *Dallas,* the television series that much of the world became addicted to in the 1970s and 80s. The connection between *Giant* and *Dallas,* I understand, is partly underscored by the J. R. initials used by the character that James Dean played in the film. That is the type of fact film scholars and buffs focus on, ignoring how the film really harms Latinos. Having now seen *Giant,* I fully understand, again, how and why Mexican people, who had already lived in Texas for roughly four generations before Stephen F. Austin brought in white people as colonizers to Tejas in 1821, have been so completely undone before the eyes of the rest of the world. But even at this late point, if we are going to improve relations between people, we need to begin with films like this one. We need to recognize the hurt, the psychological damage, and the dastardly treatment historically inflicted both in real life and by the media on Mexican Americans. Only then can we educate Americans about how the people who control our media world ought to represent Mexican people to advance the common public good.

Since I was born in Texas, the fact that I had consciously avoided *Giant* and other films that purposely miscast Mexican people has been with me since memory serves. For that reason, *Giant* has always seemed the embodiment of what media moguls need to avoid. Except for my graduate education in Buffalo, and the five years that I taught at the University of California-Berkeley, I have lived in the Lone Star state most of my life. But it was not until I saw *Giant* that I was successfully able to understand the pernicious extent to which Latinos and Anglos have been fed false pictures that misconstrue the lives of Mexicans and Mexican Americans in Texas. Can education begin to undo how the film and television industry in particular have cast Latinos? We have to hope so.

I want to explain what I mean. For, if racial relations in Texas and across our otherwise great country are to improve, readers have to understand how Latinos have been consciously and purposefully devalued for many years in the United States.

For the forty-year anniversary video reissue of *Giant* the accompanying advertising blurb on the video describes the film as a "Hollywood classic from Edna Ferber's novel about a rich Yankee girl who marries a Texas rancher & the dim-witted ranch hand who strikes oil. With Carroll Baker and Dennis Hopper as the kids. [James] Dean died shortly after filming on 9/30/55 and was posthumously nominated for Best Actor." Actually the girl played by Elizabeth Taylor is not a Yankee but a southern woman from Virginia, which is quite different. I had not wanted to see this movie before because, to my way of interpreting the first few scenes that I had previously caught, the film was not about the Texas that I grew up in, or about the larger Texas that I learned about when I left the Valley. It was about Rock Hudson and Elizabeth Taylor and Hollywood's sense of Texas.

And, I was correct, though there were some interesting turns and, surprisingly, a true commentary throughout, emphasized at the end of the film. Until I viewed the film, I had not cared to pay too much attention to the celluloid renditions of Texas history, especially films cast along the lines of grandiose reproductions like *Gone With the Wind, Ben Hur,* and *The Ten Commandments.* My Puerto Rican wife Rita, who left that wonderful island at age eight when her family moved to New York to work, clarified something for me. While we watched and disagreed with how the film was portraying Spanish speakers, she informed me that virtually everybody outside of Texas sees Mexicans and Mexican Americans as *Giant* portrays them. That hurt, to be sure, for I then realized that all along I had wanted to resist seeing that view, the terribleness to which Hollywood subjects Latinos.

Giant dramatizes, for anyone who wants to see, just how the Spanish-speaking population of Texas has been maligned. These are not strong words, as some people may think; they are the sad truth. Both in the world of the film, and because films pervasively shape the psychological realities that people believe, not only are Mexican Americans automatically expected to be subservient, but we are also seen as living and principally existing to serve and to make the world continually more comfortable for Anglo-Americans. Latinos were not subjected to slavery, as African Americans were in the South. But the Spanish-speaking characters in the movies nonetheless are represented as the servant class, much as blacks were forced to live if they desired to stay in the United States after Lincoln freed the slaves in 1863.

In the scene where Elizabeth Taylor returns to her home estate in Virginia, a black butler is shown catering to her Virginia parents, in contrast to the white community cast of *Giant* where Lupe and Polo and their families live and exist to serve as their Texas catering counterparts. The message is very clear: when Mexican Americans and blacks are allowed or permitted in Hollywood and other media, they are present mainly to do the bidding of the ruling whites. When Mexican and African American characters are not around, it is because the whites can do without them, which occurs during most of the movie. Some readers may take offense at my bald interpretation of Hollywood's celluloid reality, but, unfortunately, that is the reality that every person who sees this film, young or old, is invited to absorb.

Students of the movie have pointed out many other insights about *Giant,* but the greatest injustice is that an entire people is represented as playing up to the values of the dominant class. That fact is downright shameful, and no great people can or ought to take real pleasure in basking in a glory fabricated by thoroughly soiling the reputation of others who have traditionally enjoyed fewer advantages. I want to end this essay by focusing attention on just how terrible and insidious the film is. Mainly I want to say that, as in the case of Margaret Mitchell's *Gone With the Wind,* almost everything that the white overlords and bosses do is seen by the dominant culture as natural and inevitable, as if what happens is divine destiny. That exactly is where the real hurt and the harm has been done to Mexican Americans and blacks, the two minority populations who have been largely left without decent educations. Indeed, this deficiency is so pronounced that we have been historically unable to defend ourselves against cultural encroachments such as the one manufactured by this country's film industry. How the minority characters are portrayed in this film calls into question everything else in the movie, though, of course, that is not the focus or the reason for focusing attention on the Mexican-Anglo relations at all.

Giant tries to portray gender differences between the Texas male culture and the female world. But, although that comparison palpably works to a point, the real story is in the fact that Elizabeth Taylor the Virginian cannot understand why the Mexican population is treated so inhumanely in Texas. That is the way that Edna Ferber apparently felt, for she reportedly followed the founder of the American G.I. Forum, Dr. Hector Perez Garcia, for three days when she was writing her novel to see how Mexican Americans lived. At one point in the film, the white ranchers of the area are meeting in the living room of the home to which Rock Hudson has brought his new southern bride. The men are clearly engaged in making important business decisions. Their wives, patronizingly engaged in more gossipy conversation in the back part of the same large living room, are surprised when Elizabeth Taylor moves toward the men, causing sparks to fly between Taylor and Hudson. But the sparks die when it becomes clear that the males are only more concerned with how they can continue to exert control on the lives around them, including farm properties that they have shadily amassed. Their whole indefensible way of life nevertheless has been severely questioned by Elizabeth Taylor's words and presence.

I want to pass up the opportunity to talk about all of the separate unsettling scenes in *Giant* in order to make one final point. In the last scene of the movie, director George Stevens prepares a camera close-up of two boys who are each about two years old. One is a Mexican American child and the other is an Anglo, though the film reverses that order. Both children have been cinematically placed in the same symbolic baby crib, both are standing, holding firmly to the railing of the crib, and both were filmed looking directly into the lens of the camera. The Anglo child has clear blue eyes, and the other one has dark brown eyes. Both are the grandsons of Mr. Benedict, the cattle magnate, played by the towering Rock Hudson, the white landowner and boss of the Texas ranch.

Mr. Benedict's daughter followed social expectations and married an Anglo man, whereas his headstrong son rebelled and married a Mexican American woman. *Giant* in many ways is about the nature of the social problems that intermarriage between Anglos and Mexicans can cause in a world where races are not supposed to and are not encouraged to mix. We could discuss such issues presented in this classic film at length. But, I will settle for considering the final scene, the one where the camera first focuses attention on the attractive confident blue eyes of the Anglo youngster, followed by the image of the uncertain brown eyes of the Mexican boy. But perhaps I only imagine that the blue eyes of the Anglo are attractive, and that the Mexican American boy's eyes are uncertain? Who is to say where the power of the media ends and how films shape the realities that we actually see?

Ending such a high-powered movie with this particular contrast, it seems to me, said that in the middle of the twentieth century, during the Eisenhower years, Texas and, indeed, the citizens of the United States were already wondering what the future would bring. This is half a century before the current demographic changes, long before the sizeable growth in the U.S. Latino population. In light of the nature of the racial relations since the United States signed the Treaty of Guadalupe Hidalgo in 1848, the unasked question a hundred plus years later, though, remains: what will happen when and if the races are mixed? Stevens's film asks viewers to consider what we have experienced by watching this motion picture about Texas culture. The question he clearly wants us to dwell on is: are we Americans ready for a new relationship between the races, or do we want to continue living as we have? Nearly fifty years after *Giant,* it is clear that we have not yet sufficiently considered the issue, largely because we have not felt comfortable enough talking about the cultural differences and the expectations. We have not known how to talk about socially discombobulating realities that call into question the type of Texas braggadocio that image-conscious Texans like to display.

So, *cuándo,* when are we going to begin to address the question of how Latinos and other Americans will relate? When are we going to talk about how Spanish-speaking people from the United States *and* from countries south of the Rio Grande are going to be worked into American society? And how ought we to treat one another in the meantime? Ironically, regular everyday life has continued to shape the ways that we live, and the ways that we relate to one another, often solidifying the old prejudices without ever acknowledging or even pointing them out. In *Giant,* Rock Hudson tells Elizabeth Taylor something like, "Honey, you don't have to talk to them [the Mexican American help]." There are class and racial distinctions here, and we have not yet had the extended conversation on the subject that our society needs because people have not felt the need to talk. The conversation about how Mexican Americans relate to other Americans, as this film shows, is long overdue, one that Texans and all Americans courageously need to address within our families, our churches, and in the schools. We should constructively build, once and for all, a communal foundation that will benefit all Americans, Latino or not, one that will unite us and not separate us further.

24

Words for Better Lives

When we try to discern our personal responsibilities within the communal constructs in place, indistinctness and ambiguity are disturbing. Very real problems and unclear relations usually mix with our imagined anxieties, creating difficulties. As Spanish-speaking U.S. residents part of our challenge is to shape and to mold different, better futures not only individually for ourselves, but also for the people who live around us. How exactly we do that is in the hands of every person in the country. In light of the history of U.S. Latinos, it is not an easy task to establish better relations with non-Hispanics, but that is exactly the nature of the challenge. Unlike other groups, we Latinos cannot afford to promote only ourselves and our friends. We need to persuade ourselves that no one has the right to think for us and to represent us, especially since we are often overlooked or miscast by people who do not have our best interests before them. Lacking the necessary education and networking connections from which other groups derive advantages, we have often sat on the sidelines where we have been relegated.

The test for twenty-first-century America and the world is to see how responsive we can be to the needs and concerns of people who are different. Personal, local, regional, and national accommodations and adjustments are required. If we do not allow space for the interests of others, ethnicity, difference, and skin color can be destructive. But if we do, these same characteristics can be wonderfully appealing and instructive. The best way to navigate toward a better life is to invest time and energy in helping people who need to build and to sustain the future that the people of the United States and the world require. Short of that, the lives of people without the resources and wherewithal will not improve.

There are always so many people with more serious needs than our own. At a certain point helping them requires us to stop thinking primarily about ourselves, and generously to think of and to work for others, too. By creating spaces and places for all people, one day our generation's legacy will be that we extended the American Dream to everyone. Personally, I am hoping that the generation of baby-boomers to which I belong will choose to leave behind a better world than the one we received, good and selfless as the sacrifices of our mothers and fathers were during World War II and the years after. The alternative is more of the kind of individual and corporate selfishness that we already know too well, what we often witness in news reports. Does anyone have a better idea for a legacy that serves the interests of a younger, rising Latino generation? Now, how about an afternoon *taza de café* at a restaurant where we can discuss a progressively better life, resulting from public policy changes and community action on issues like the following ones?

25

Reinventing Ourselves

S hortly after *El Diez y Seis de Septiembre,* I was asked to make a presen-
tation to open a series of community activities in celebration of Hispanic Heritage Month, which yearly takes place between September 16 and
October 15. Many Latinos in the United States, especially Americans of Mexican ancestry, commemorate El Diez y Seis de Septiembre. On September 16,
1810, in the town of Dolores Hidalgo, a native mestizo priest named Father
Miguel Hidalgo y Costilla raised *El Grito de Dolores* by ringing the bell of
his church and calling upon the Mexican people to rebel against the Spanish occupation. This event is comparable to the famous midnight ride of
Paul Revere, which also celebrates the desire for freedom.

The American Revolution of 1776 and the late-eighteenth-century writings that eventually led to the French Revolution of 1848 served to provide
the Mexican people with the sense that they too might be able to revolt
against the hated Spanish government. For nearly three hundred years, Spain
had kept Mexican mestizos and Mexican Indians in poverty and ignorance,
making these populations serve the economic and cultural interests of the royal
Spanish government. Father Hidalgo's motley group of revolutionaries armed
themselves with knives, axes, and clubs, gaining followers as they marched
across the streets of Guanajuato and Guadalajara. Because the dissatisfaction was so deep and pervasive, the revolution spread through most of the
regions of what was then New Spain. Aroused and then propelled to defend themselves by *El Grito de Dolores,* the peasant revolutionaries soon controlled most of Mexico. Spanish troops, however, captured and executed
Father Hidalgo the year after he sounded that famous alarm. Jose Maria
Morelos y Pavon, another priest, then organized and trained an army that
subsequently won many battles, including the recapture of Acapulco in 1813,
using guns confiscated from the Spanish. That same year, Morelos declared
Mexico independent, but battles continued, and the Mexican War of Independence was not actually secured until eight years later, at the end of 1821.

I suspect this synopsis is about as much as most Spanish-speaking Americans have ever learned about El Diez y Seis de Septiembre, since Mexican

history is not ordinarily taught in U.S. schools. Indeed, I believe it is time to state that I have never had one single lesson in a U.S. school where I was taught ONE fact about Mexico or Mexican history. Although a downright shameful admission that I feel compelled to make, I suspect this is the case with most other Americans. We should make it our business to learn something about Mexico, since Mexico and/or Mexican history has not been part of our regular schooling and education. Certainly, since Mexico buys more products from the United States than does France, Germany, Spain, and Italy combined there is no excuse for not remedying this outrageous cultural and economic lacuna in U.S. schools.

On the day in 1810 when Father Hidalgo rang the bells of his church, the oppression under which Mexicans lived was so overwhelming that for a priest openly to call upon the people to rebel against the Spanish authorities was an act of desperation. Taking this step required courage, for the outcome of such a public alarm was as unpredictable in the social changes it would unleash as Father Hidalgo's execution was predictable. At that point in their history, the Mexican people forgot caution and set out on the road to reinvent themselves.

When I talk during Hispanic Heritage Month, I feel compelled to recall the event to encourage Latinos here in the United States also to reinvent ourselves according to our needs. Of course, the times and the circumstances are vastly different. I am not calling for revolution, for there is no greater form of known government than what we have in the United States. But my sense is that too many Latinos today feel frustrated and dissatisfied with many things that have been in place for generations. And, although taking up arms to roam the streets, like Father's Hidalgo's forces, is out of the question, I do encourage people to think about how we should peacefully remake and recreate ourselves as the new needs of American society require.

How can one better express the idea? It seems to me that, to end Hispanic Heritage Month in ways that provide people with useful guidance, I need to show *how* we Latinos can "reinvent ourselves," and that is what we need to consider.

The mind is a wonderful instrument, and today we have to change the world, not with knives, axes, clubs, and guns, but by putting our minds to work. Through thinking and through the creative use of our experiences and knowledge, we can change the world so that we, too, can make a better place for ourselves among other Americans. If we are to make real progress in the United States, we have to learn how to capitalize on what we already know. The idea is to appropriate everything that will help us become more successful Americans, including the use of English, college, and constantly reading and retooling ourselves for better job opportunities.

Before addressing the *how*, though, *why* would it be advisable to "reinvent ourselves"? Are we dissatisfied with what we are? Are we unhappy with our educations, with the ways in which we were brought up, with the world in general?

We all have, of course, different answers to such tough, intrusive questions. I believe we constantly need to build on our pasts, improving ourselves as needs decree. I make this statement because many Latinos feel that once in the United States they ought to strive to become as Americanized as they can, leaving behind their Spanish-speaking customs and ways. Traditionally, American society has supported this inclination. But I disagree. As Mexican Americans, I think we should consider embracing the changes and the understanding that we want to generate, for every generation is challenged to recreate itself from the materials provided by hard-working parents. Our current responsibility, as I see it, is to shape and to create the world we want to live in, for soon we will be in the position of handing over what we have accomplished to our own sons and daughters. That is why the earlier we start to transform and improve the world that we have inherited, the sooner we will be in a position to articulate and then to accomplish the goals we desire. Collectively and individually I believe we have little choice but to reinvent ourselves. Otherwise, in America, the Internet and the rest of the world will continue to portray us as such forces see fit, leaving us behind to take care of ourselves as we best can.

I believe America is a wonderful country, but the problem for most Latinos is that the majority do not yet know how success works in the United States. So, how do people succeed in America?

In America most people are not expected to work at a particular kind of position for too long. Generally speaking, people are expected to work at a post for something like one, two, or three years. After a certain time, most workers are either promoted, demoted, or they move elsewhere or go into something else, into some other kind of business. Places and positions are like musical chairs. Someone is always in a desired chair, in a place that other people would like to have. When that is the case, people simply either have to be willing to wait, or they can choose to leave to try to secure a comparable or a better place elsewhere. That is the beauty about work opportunities in America. People can always move; they can always choose to go off to start life anew elsewhere, though, of course, sacrifices are required when this option is exercised. The important point to realize is that we can always bring with us everything we have learned to another job or the same kind of job.

To meet our changing needs, we have to consider how we need to reinvent ourselves, sharpening up and improving different sides of our personalities in order to continue succeeding in America. I am not saying that we have to be so flexible that we are chameleon-like, that is, changing only with the times in every which way. What I am saying is that we have to seek out people actively, that we have to use our minds to prepare and to package ourselves in ways that are spiritually and culturally satisfying, while also meeting the needs of potential employers. That is what our résumé should do: tell people about our employment strengths, and our talents and skills; what we can do, given an opportunity.

If we continue working on improving ourselves, before we know it, we will be where we want to be in three, five, seven, or ten years. The idea is to envision where it is we want to be in three, five, seven, or ten years. Then study the steps we need to take to achieve that goal. This is why school and our continuing education are so important in our goal to transform ourselves for success in the United States. For the schools and the courses we take either prepare us to succeed or they do not. And, if the schools fail us, then, of course, whether we succeed or not will depend upon how well we make use of what we have gone through to reinvent ourselves.

26

Race Should Not Matter

B ut it does. Race still separates Americans long after the Civil Rights Act of 1964, and it should not. Most adults today believe that race should be ignored. After all the altercations, the violence, and the disillusioning disappointments, the consensus sadly appears to be that if left alone, race relations will somehow improve of their own accord. For this reason, some federal courts have embraced color-blindness, and we are being encouraged to be race neutral in our thinking and hiring, yet unhappiness abounds. Central to this legal approach is the requirement that everyone has to pretend that race, skin color, and ethnicity are not real, that they are illusions. And, yes, they are superficial characteristics that should not be issues, but realities like racial profiling and other kinds of discrimination tell us otherwise. My sense is that Americans are tired of pretense. We want to change reality, not only on television where the lives of game show contestants are sometimes changed, but also in the arenas where our lives are so much less than they could be. I believe we have arrived at the juncture where we need to accept one another, as we are. We need to learn respect, something unfortunately not taught in the schools. If we can respect one another, perhaps we can learn to appreciate what each one of us can contribute to American society.

Some search committees ignore race; others follow Affirmative Action. To ignore only race, skin color, or ethnicity, and not to disregard any other human quality is to say that something is wrong with these traits, or, with us. The First Amendment allows full and opened expression in keeping with all of our innate makeup and identity. Why are some of our human qualities an anathema to some people? People naturally want respect for the whole person. Who can do without respect?

After a racial incident, a person has the choice of reacting or not. Should racial slurs or insults be overlooked? Should an individual pretend that nothing has happened? What if another racial incident occurs followed by another and then another? And what about the person who refuses to be upset? Is that how people are expected to react? Don't create a commotion or a fuss. Get over it. Are people of color expected to ignore racial incidents, to avoid escalating encounters, regardless of provocation? Should everything be situational when we consider race?

If a racial event assaults the constitutional rights of one individual, everyone is implicated. Most victims know they can resort to the courts to end harassment, intentional insult, or physical, psychological, and spiritual hurt caused by others. But what about the rest of society? What is the role of the community when one person is taken advantage of?

Why not encourage people to feel as confident as possible, not by disregarding race and skin color, but by embracing and accepting all of our human attributes and qualities? Americans work hard to feel good and confident about themselves—race, skin color, and ethnic origin included. Why beleaguer or taunt another person over skin color or race? This elementary lesson, taught in most schools, needs social reinforcement. No citizen should allow another American afflicted by a race incident to suffer and endure such pain.

That is why victims of race incidents find little relief in color-blind and race-neutral laws. How can race and skin color not matter? Everyone knows that job and college admission applications are the exact junctures when long-standing social and economic inequities can either be changed or continued. Try as people do to erase race and skin color, these characteristics remain. They are innate, part of the individual person. The judicial charge is not to prefer one group of people over another. It is to dispense justice equally, to individuals and also to groups of people previously ignored and bypassed. To ignore skin color and race and ethnicity is to disregard a significant component of a person that no one person can control. Who chooses his or her race and skin color?

People need to recognize that race and skin color affect the nature of our experiences. Historically, race divided people. Race now needs to unite us. Instead of legally asserting that race is illusory, we ought to embrace our human qualities and traits, excluding only what harms others.

Ignoring parts of ourselves heightens tensions and distresses. It might appear polite not to consider race and skin color, but excluding race has oddly made us more indifferent, callous to everyone else, except our own personal interests. Americans are not selfish or insensitive people. Not to acknowledge or to respect a person's race is to ask citizens to try to see others as they are not. That is unrealistic, immature, and it will not help race relations in the United States or anywhere else in the world. That, indeed, is essentially why the Supreme Court, in a five to four vote, decided on June 23, 2003, in *Grutter* that race can be considered in college admissions.

27

Affirmative Action

Still the Best Idea

So, even though Affirmative Action policies are not being uniformly enforced, why do I think that Affirmative Action is still the best idea that we have devised to try to equalize the playing field for applicants of different races? Because Affirmative Action was initially intended to affirm the practice of seriously considering minority people for positions previously off-limits to African Americans, Latinos, Asian Americans, women, Native Americans, and other discriminated-against groups and persons. That democratic need has not disappeared simply because the majority of Americans now seem to believe that Affirmative Action is reverse discrimination. Reverse discrimination is the view that white applicants for college admissions or working positions are being discriminated against because Affirmative Action policies and regulations require that minority applicants also be considered. People who claim reverse discrimination believe that Affirmative Action favors and prefers minorities, excluding or crowding out whites, but that is hardly the case. What has happened is that minorities have usually been found to be less qualified and less prepared because, of course, they have not received the quality education that more whites have, from kindergarten through college.

Government and demographic data amply support this view. Where minorities have gained a few college slots or positions, reverse discrimination adherents have claimed that these posts have been "given" to them, calling the competence of minorities into question. The claim has made some minority citizens want to disassociate themselves from Affirmative Action policies, basically to show that they know they could have achieved their positions by dint of hard work themselves without any help from Affirmative Action. They want to demonstrate that they are perfectly capable of competing without any benefits that Affirmative Action might give them. The result is that Affirmative Action, though well intended, has ironically made some minority people question the nature of their achievements, thereby becoming one of the most contentious issues of American society. Only abortion today is as hotly debated.

Although the intention to hire more minorities has been advisable, some people have also wondered how minorities, who have not generally benefited from the better educational and training opportunities available, can seriously be considered for positions alongside better-prepared candidates. Since 1965, when federal Affirmative Action became effective, hiring has been influenced by recognition and consideration of this basic inequity. But the extent to which government-recommended guidelines have actually affected hiring practices has remained problematic, and supposed Affirmative Action hirings are more exaggerated and talked about than real. In some companies and higher education institutions, the fair and more balanced hiring of minorities has partially materialized, but, from what I have seen, in most other cases that goal has not even been approached. Today, minorities are still considerably underrepresented just about anywhere we look. If there are questions, look at the hard numbers, at the data.

In the thirty-five years since Affirmative Action has been in place, we have seen both travesties and honest hires shaped by the policy. Honesty and a fairer evaluation of candidates is what the idea calls for, but since the practices of the marketplace are so varied throughout the country, federal and state regulations intended to assure the integrity of hiring practices have tended to yield more failed Affirmative Action searches than successful ones. Not, however, that Affirmative Action has ever been whole-heartedly liked, accepted, or embraced either by whites, who have seen themselves as losing to minority people, or by some minorities and women, who have understandably seen such a process as tainting their professional credibility. No, Affirmative Action has never been a panacea or even a satisfactory solution to the problem of hiring minority candidates. This is precisely why so many people, both majority and minority, have been so ready to bypass Affirmative Action guidelines.

Many people, also, have never really understood that minority people do not usually receive the same kinds of opportunities and encouragement and support that other mainstream Americans tend to enjoy. In a tough, competitive world, whites work, and very hard, to achieve what they have; so, why should minority applicants (even theoretically) receive more favorable attention and consideration when applying for a job? An available opening is an opportunity and in such cases, the thinking goes, honest competition should prevail, and no candidate should be given any preference based on race or ethnicity. To be sure, honest competition usually does prevail; that is why whites tend to beat out minority candidates. Preferences are what being born, going to certain schools, growing up with certain comforts, and choosing a productive lifestyle are all about. How can preferences not be the name of the game in the United States, where everything is about living and doing better than the Joneses across the street?

The federal rule of hiring and college admissions selection since the Civil Rights Act of 1964 has sought to act out of the knowledge, provided by the study of history, that competition for employment and education has not treated minority people fairly. The known view has been that minorities usually begin life in disadvantaged ways, and that, except for some cases disproportionately showcased by people objecting to Affirmative Action, the majority of minorities continue to remain disadvantaged through most of their lives. We have only to notice how the different races of people of Anytown, U.S.A., live in order to see and to understand who wields the power and influence in our communities, who is afforded the amenities of life, and who holds the less desirable jobs.

Minority people who have been "affirmed" by being hired through Affirmative Action guidelines have always paid the price of being more scrutinized than employees who have not. Are they as good as whites, people have always wondered. Would a white person in that position do a better job? These and other similar questions have progressively given rise to more objections against Affirmative Action, and these issues have been raised since the program's inception. Following the 1978 *Bakke* case at the University of California-Davis, where Alan Bakke's lawyers successfully argued that their client had been denied admission to medical school in favor of admitting a less qualified minority applicant, such views have been increasingly vocalized until they have become the screamed objections of the 1990s. Most people understand the view that some people feel more comfortable living and working among people who look and think like them. That is exactly what Affirmative Action has sought to change, since ethically equal opportunities ought to be afforded individually to the entire diverse population of the United States. But conservative voices have arisen to conserve practices as they have traditionally existed in the United States.

Due to the rather recent outcry against Affirmative Action, today the courts and the very government is wondering why minority citizens were ever recruited aggressively due to their race, and why they should be preferred in a hiring process. Certainly in a democratic country like the United States no one individual or group of people should be given advantages, since the Constitution clearly says that everyone should be considered for employment on equal terms.

But equal terms are hard to see when hiring begins, largely because the lives of white and minority Americans are so noticeably unequal from birth, through school, at work, and in death. In the trajectory of life, if we were to compare, say, the average Mexican American, African American, or another minority applicant to the *average* white citizen, can people honestly say that the minority person has had the same opportunities as his or her white counterpart? Consider where the average minority and the average white person would be in kindergarten, the third grade, the seventh grade, the ninth grade, and as seniors in high school (supposing both graduate), or as juniors in college (same assumption). Occasionally, yes, the minority person may even stand out as having had better life quality experiences, but how often is that the case? Try to point to more than one or two such instances where we see such a case operating. In every such case, I believe we would be looking at the exceptions, at the exceptional cases, not the average minority life experience.

This is why I remain convinced that for all of its well-known shortcomings and mixed results, Affirmative Action is still the best system devised by government representatives to provide candidates of all races with a fairer evaluation. Given what I have personally experienced and seen, I am not persuaded that without Affirmative Action minority candidates will receive a fair look. The reverse discrimination theory now assumes that minority candidates are just not as competitive as whites, keeping minorities from receiving serious consideration, and giving preference to candidates who have usually been the beneficiaries of life-long, more sustained preferences and amenities.

How Affirmative Action works in every single case, of course, depends on the integrity of the people chosen to enact a search process. Affirmative Action guidelines, like any other set of human suggestions promising and seeking to shape responsible, professional behavior, can only be as good and as effective as the people charged with the self-regulating task of making them work. Not, of course, that a better system might not yet be devised or worked out some day. In fact, I would love to see a plan that would work better than Affirmative Action. But dreaming up a different way to insure the equal treatment of all Americans has proven extremely difficult, suggesting the challenge might be next to impossible, since no one, as far as I know, has written up a better plan. Most people, though, now seem to be convinced that we need something better, and I would be the first to agree. I am waiting, indeed, to see what our leaders propose next. In the meantime, judges, I do not think we ought to throw out Affirmative Action since we do not yet have a better plan to put in its troubled place. To leave minority candidates without the nominal protection that Affirmative Action at least theoretically provides, would be to disregard America's history and to be irresponsible in applying the constitutional needs that might still insure and safeguard fair and serious consideration for minorities.

28

Diversity Is Natural

Diversity is the true offspring of the civil rights movement and Affirmative Action. Diversity means difference, and it is natural for human beings to want to be different, to show others that life can be imagined, conceived, and lived differently. If campuses and organizations have traditionally undertaken special efforts to advance their own images, now that the demographics of society have changed, schools and social institutions also have an obligation to make the same kind of special effort to advance difference and diversity. This effort requires proactive programs, because diversifying companies and campuses calls not only for a different rhetoric but also for some necessary high-level decision making.

Given the goals articulated and pursued, and the alumni spirit of camaraderie that is needed to accomplish the strategic plans of an organization, schools, and most forms of institutional life understandably advertise views and attitudes that encourage homogeneity instead of difference. Agreeing with a proven, tried philosophy, in turn, is valued precisely because embracing and practicing such values and outlooks promotes a desired future, supposedly moving schools forward.

But the problem with prizing and insisting on homogeneity is that visible difference is then made to stand out, and when difference stands out, often some kind of response is prompted or invited. In such cases, difference is sometimes encouraged; but most of the time it is worked on, and even cajoled into falling in line with the homogenous view. When their presence is noticed or even slightly called into question, visibly different persons tend to grow ambivalent and may feel ousted, or only nominally included.

The public relations people of schools and organizations often downplay people who are seen as being less representative of an institution, preferring, instead, to underscore common values and attitudes. Constantly expressing embraced values and practices is interpreted as actively creating and promoting multiple bonding opportunities that allow organization members, or students, faculty, administrators, and patrons to develop and to sustain commitment, assuring long-term, energized supporters. Once a coalescing unity is achieved, loyalty, discipline, and appealing to the interests of an organization or a school advance the name and the interests of an entity. Changing a successful formula is difficult, but since the emphasis on diversity is a relatively new concept in organizations and on campuses historically known for their exclusivity, that is exactly what the challenge of making room for diversity requires.

I believe that universities and business organizations, like the armed forces, have to establish climates that embrace visibly different people. Mature cultures rightly respect all the attributes of all individuals, whether people choose difference or homogeneity. Respect, as I see it, is conscious, so it is conscientiously and forthrightly accorded; running roughshod over difference simply cannot be accepted, encouraged, or allowed anymore.

The tendency in most schools and organizations is toward thinking and behaving alike, and that occurs because most activities are expedited by mutual cooperation. Difference, on the other hand, implicitly seeks to be asked; it likes to be invited, and then persuaded. Difference wants to be taken seriously, it wants to be included; it wants to belong, to be a part of an organization or of an institution with which it is associated. Difference, though, also requires to be convinced, convinced that benefits will follow from accepting or rejecting the will of the majority.

Diverse viewpoints for that reason can serve as correctives. Diverse considerations check facile, dominant views. Diversity offers alternative paths and possibilities, singling out options not regularly or usually considered by homogeneous thinking. Alternative approaches thus ought to elicit appreciation, because they offer different, new ideas, and the possibility of change can even refashion life. Diversity means seriously considering another view.

A university endeavors to be a smaller version of the universe, which means that diversity is central to what the definition of a university is. Indeed, a homogeneous university seems a contradiction in terms, especially since students and faculty constantly consider ideas they question, and that may even lead them to counter and to reshape society's beliefs in new, needed ways.

Diversity is visibly different or it dares to be different. Most people recognize the distinction. Daring to be different is sometimes interpreted as an affront or a challenge to the status quo, as it may well be. Does that mean that pride in casting oneself as different, wanting to embody something else, should be shunned, ignored, drummed out, or otherwise disposed of at schools that are ambivalent about the degree to which diverse opinions ought and need to be tolerated? Shouldn't we celebrate diversity, instead? Healthy intellectual environments require inclusiveness, not exclusion. If homogeneity is the *arroz* of universities, diversity is the *frijoles;* they are *yin-yang* partners. Together they constitute smaller versions of the universe that universities pursue when they endeavor to construct diverse, challenging environments capable of expanding the minds of students formed by the world's many, and very diverse, cultures.

29

On the Theory of Bilingual Education

What do Latinos and Mexican Americans, middle class or not, think about contentious issues such as bilingual education and Affirmative Action? Like the majority of Americans, we too have opinions that range across the political spectrum, some of which have been expressed and others that have not. Since most U.S. Latino Americans continue to speak Spanish, or some *Español,* or feel that Spanish is part of our heritage and cultural background, there is a sense that speaking both English and Spanish is a natural enough activity. Bilingual education for this reason is also perceived as a sensible, natural approach to education, since words for the two languages are part of our communication repertoire. Differences generally begin to arise when Spanish-speaking Latino Americans are asked about bilingual education as a school discipline and as an area of study that might be taught throughout the schools and or perhaps even at the university level. At that point, some Latinos express the belief that actually learning Spanish, or better Spanish, in the schools may "hold back" their youngsters. This point of view sometimes prevails because most English-speaking Americans appear to believe that in the United States assimilation occurs *because* one goes to school to learn English or better English speaking and writing skills. Learning English, however, should not necessarily be taken to mean that Spanish and all other languages by extension are not as good as English, relegating other languages to being seen as inferior or less acceptable ways of communication. Indeed, anthropologists have shown that every language enriches the possessor of that language, offering an individual a different way of apprehending and understanding the rest of the world. Pope John Paul II reportedly speaks twelve or more languages. Isn't that grand?

Everyone should agree that languages empower people, and the ability to speak two or more languages makes a person considerably more impressive and more competitive throughout the world. Having two or more languages also helps people appreciate the beauties and the intricacies of the verbal skills and knowledge required of a person who can think and who can speak in another or in other languages. The best way to learn how a person's main language works and how a person learns is to require that person to consider how a word or a certain expression is actually said correctly in another tongue. When people ask how something is said in Spanish or in English, French, German, Chinese, or Russian, people are saying that they wish they could speak that language so they can communicate their needs, views, or beliefs.

If languages are important, and if most people agree that the more languages a person speaks the more impressive such a person is, why is bilingual education, or the study of two languages, such a hotly debated issue in the United States? Why does bilingual education raise such strong feelings in people who interface with almost all world cultures? This is an issue that I have never understood. Shouldn't the schools be training our students to communicate with people from other cultures? I suspect that moving in this direction would require students to begin to pay attention to the ways that we actually talk. On this score, I think Americans have shown, in a variety of ways, that we do not particularly care for grammar rules and conventions, especially if we have not grown up constrained by such practices. In the United States, in other words, we are free to speak and to communicate however we wish, in keeping with the First Amendment, so long as we do not transgress on the rights of others. English is the currency of the realm, and most of us speak and express ourselves as we choose. Which is to say that paying attention to how we should speak to make sense to non-English speaking people is not an activity that most of us now cherish.

So where does that leave us regarding bilingual education? I think we need to reconsider other languages both for their value and for what they would add to our culture. First, though, I am convinced that we need to understand, in particular, why bilingual education is so divisive in a country that believes the best way to create unity is to speak not many languages but only English. English is the language of commerce throughout the world. But we need to understand that the best way to comprehend the difficulty of learning English is to make the effort to learn other languages.

Given this position, I now wish to defend the *theory* of bilingual education, mainly because it is very difficult to defend how bilingual education has actually been approached and taught in the United States since the mid-1960s. Always suspect and unduly politicized, teaching students in two languages or bilingually today has been so severely maligned by people who do not want to speak more than one language that one cannot easily explain the advantages of bilingual education without raising more negative static. Opposition to bilingual education is often based on emotions, on the feeling that two or more languages will separate Americans instead of uniting them and allowing better communication. That sentiment, though, has been so exaggerated in the United States that it ought to lose credibility almost as soon as it is examined. We need only to look at how Switzerland, on the one hand, has long educated students successfully in French, English, German, and in Italian to see how socially supported, pedagogically sound language programs can produce excellent students and first-rate language learning results. In the United States, on the other hand, we have always approached bilingual education suspiciously, which means that we have been reluctant to provide full support, preferring to hold back believing in its efficacy. As a result, we tend to experience, when we reluctantly implement such programs, mixed and uncertain results.

Several years ago in California voters approved the passage of the Unz initiative, or Proposition 227, which shut down bilingual education. The pedagogical approach that can work best for students whose first language is not English then moved to the courts. Bilingual education will continue to be debated, but it is important to know why bilingual education has not been as successful as it might be. California Latino voters surprised everyone. Polls taken before the election predicted that as many as 80 percent of Latinos favored Proposition 227. But the actual vote count tells us that 63 percent voted against Proposition 227, and that only 37 percent of Latino voters supported the initiative to stop bilingual education. How can pollsters be so wrong? What Hispanic voters did they poll?

Here and there, where well-prepared teachers believe in teaching two languages, good bilingual programs exist, mainly because dedicated instructors and some school systems have had the true learning interests and welfare of their students at heart. But most bilingual programs throughout the United States now have records of five, ten, twenty, or more years of lackluster performances. Why? Because state legislatures, school administrators, and the general public have not deemed bilingual programs important enough to provide the necessary social and financial support. As in the case of the Vietnam War, the United States did not win, essentially, because we held back, because the Johnson administration sent conflicting signals to the soldiers doing the fighting across the ocean. Historians are now in agreement on this interpretation. In the case of bilingual education, universities and colleges, too, have not sufficiently known how to train and how to educate teachers well enough so that they can competently instruct students bilingually, that is, successfully in two languages.

Teaching bilingual education, it should by now be very clear, is a demanding proposition. It requires skill, very good training, commitment, and competence in speaking two languages easily and comfortably or without hesitancy. What can we think when we encounter bilingual teachers who do not fluently use one of the two languages that they are supposed to be teaching? When bilingual education is approached ambivalently, with minds and hearts that do not really understand and that do not believe how one language can be used to help a student learn another one, the results are not going to impress anyone. And that is what we should HEAR from bilingually taught students: two well-spoken and written languages.

In schools where bilingual education has improved the learning of students, the success can be attributed to the support of the education system and to the hard work of courageous teachers. Such educators have refused to give up on children who need to be taught both in English and in their native language. Seeing bilingual education rescinded by voters who do not understand that bilingual education has failed because the necessary financial resources and higher education pedagogy have not materialized makes for a very sorry education story. That should not be the case with education in the United States, where we have more pedagogical resources than in most countries of the world. This is the case despite the fact that our leaders have chosen to fight a war in Iraq, and are now contemplating going to the moon again and beyond, leaving behind the needs of education.

Will politics continue to be intertwined with everything attempted in the classrooms of America? When the issue concerns the place of other languages in American culture, the forces that believe English supreme tend to ignore students who have no recourse but to use their first language to learn English better. Without proper bilingual education, such students will continue to be abandoned in school systems that discourage them. That is why we have low graduation numbers and even lower college admission enrollments, particularly from first-generation Americans who are not sufficiently prepared for higher and professional education. English-as-a-second-language students want and also deserve to be successful American citizens. Such students have long been ignored, and public school systems that continue to disable students whose first language is not English, in effect, are engaged in the business of creating untold problems for all Americans in the twenty-first century.

Without high school graduation and useful college preparation, students whose first language is not English are not likely to provide well for themselves and their families. They will become burdens to taxpayers or earn so little that they will create problems for everyone, negatively impacting the American economy. Better-off Americans will continue to inquire, "why can't those people learn to take care of themselves; why must the government use our tax money to help them?"

How can they, we should ask, if we voters allow our schools to undercut the bilingual education approach that could be as successful as the teaching of languages in other countries has been. In voting not to teach students by sympathetically using their first languages, we are, again, relegating such students to sink today, disabling them from swimming in American culture tomorrow. Enough students have already sunk over the years. That is why bilingual education should not be outlawed, disowned, or abandoned. In the United States, we have not approached bilingual education correctly, with the right and necessary attitudes. The courts should reinstate bilingual education, and it should be properly embraced, championed by enlightened state legislators, and supported by the American people. With the correct approach and support, bilingual education can be made to work for many youngsters who now are victims of a less sensitive, less effective, roughshod way of teaching them English.

30

Latin America and the United States and Mexico

In the United States, we hear and know more about developments in Europe than in Mexico and/or Latin America. Mexican president Vicente Fox is fond of saying that, following NAFTA, the North American Free Trade Agreement, Mexico buys more from the United States than France, Germany, Italy, and Spain combined. This fact surprises most Americans. Such a reality often leads Latinos to ask why Mexico and Latin America are not extended more favorable commercial agreements and treated with greater thoughtfulness. One would never guess that Mexico ranks higher in buying American goods than Europe, since the Euro and everything east of us appears to have a more prominent position in the American consciousness. But, although the east/west commercial ties will remain, the north/south axis is increasingly becoming more significant as we move into the new century.

Since many Latinos are convinced that the United States needs to know more about the countries in our hemisphere, an effort to educate Americans to realities in Central and South America should be part of the U.S. Latino agenda. People should know, for example, that my family, like other Latino families, listens to the Spanish radio and television stations because they report not only the news about Latin America but also about other salient events that occur in the United States, Europe, Asia, and Africa sometimes not covered by U.S. news. In the United States, only a newspaper like the *San Diego Union-Tribune* seems to have made a serious effort to find out what goes on south of the Rio Grande. Other newspapers, including those in the large cities of the Southwest, where one would think there should be some interest, appear to be focused mainly northward. Even the larger urban dailies in the north, which ought to be aware that their economies and lifestyles directly connect with the Spanish-speaking countries to the south, perfunctorily cover the kind of stories suggesting that Latin America is a poor, unhappy place to live. Aren't we glad we live in the United

States, the stories all seem to say. Cultural influences by themselves should not sufficiently explain the fact that we are told little about Latin America's daily life, especially since so many people from Spanish-speaking countries arrive in the United States not only in search of a better life but to spend tourist money.

When Latin America is broached or considered, unattractiveness tends to enter the minds of most busy Americans. Disreputable and corrupt governments do not help, but neither does an unskilled American press that is not sufficiently interested in understanding how the Latin American economies and realities directly influence our own way of life. Now that Vicente Fox Quesada is president of Mexico, breaking the seventy-one-year grip of the PRI party, realities may begin to change. The fact that Fox has shown that a democratic revolution can take place at the ballot box is significant. For the moment, Mexico has gotten the attention of the United States, ameliorating mindsets that believe when developments or plans "go south" things have turned bad, an expression epitomizing Anglo attitudes toward Latin America. If we did not have common economic ties to unify the United States and Latin America, I believe the connections between the people of the northern and southern hemispheres would be weaker than they are. I suspect that bias exists because there is a felt but unexpressed sense in the media that little of consequence happens in the Spanish-speaking countries that interests the people of the United States. For a reputed world power, this way of thinking is sadly myopic and detrimental to the relationships with Latin American countries that should be developed and nurtured.

But one does not have to point to Latin America to show how much our media fails to cover. One has only to go to the border region between the United States and Mexico to see the type of economic, social, and cultural activity that we seldom hear about, unless the news is associated with drug problems, home security issues, or other predictable troubles. According to the U.S. Census, the border area between the United States and Mexico had a population of 10.6 million people in 1995. That year, the United States had 5,851,052 people and Mexico had 4,759,428 people living on each side of the border from Brownsville, Texas, to the Tijuana, Mexico, metropolis south of San Diego. The projection is that if the current growth rates continue, the border region will double its population in the next twenty-five years (<http://www.infomexus.org.mx/eng/total.gif>). The border is a world of its own, created by political, economic, and social forces that the people who live there daily negotiate. Borders are where the undulating ripple effects of laws, policies, and human desires that emanate in the capitals of Latin America and in Washington D.C. cause great anxieties as well as opportunities. No description of attributes or qualities will satisfactorily summarize the heterogeneity of the people and the conditions that one encounters in the border regions, and that unpredictability is what keeps the area remaking itself.

Woe, however, to the immigrant. When times and the economy are good, residents take them for granted. When times are bad, the residents invariably turn upon the poor immigrants, blaming them for working for less pay, and for living among them in ways that lower the quality of life. Yet, in America it is the immigrants who continually revitalize the economy and keep it humming. The residents, therefore, should work to educate the immigrants so that the latter can continue to develop in ways that allow them also to nourish and contribute to American society. As a country of immigrants who displaced the indigenous people, we Americans should not claim that we do not want or need other immigrants, for we certainly use the ones who show up looking for work in our cities and towns.

Were one to visit any foreign country, as journalists and business people do, one would see that most people are concerned with meeting their daily needs. The greatest amount of human energy is expended on taking care of matters and issues that cannot be avoided and simply must be addressed. Other things that require attention, including work and recreational activities, tend to be next in priority, even though the general supposition is that work is first. When one has lived in a place a long time, private and personal matters generally take precedence in life, and other activities and interests follow or accrue around the desires and wants that people develop. There are excellent reasons to provide Americans with some of the leading developments in the Spanish-speaking countries to our south, since the future of the United States will be closely related to the border and Latin America. *¿Hablas Español? ¿Cuándo vamos a aprender?*

31

Heat, Undocumented Workers,
and the Border Patrol

W here should one start regarding two reported incidents — a mid-July, 1998, news story that appeared in the *Austin American-Statesman,* and an April 14, 1999, "World Briefs" piece disseminated by the *Bryan–College Station Eagle,* the fastest-growing newspaper in Texas? Both news items showed up as wire reports in the daily papers across the nation, but, given the fact that there are seldom follow-up stories to what the journalists call newspaper fillers, incidents like these indicate, at least to me, that they do not matter much. Indeed, together the two items oddly remind me of Guy de Maupassant's short story masterpiece, "Love." In that story, a newspaper account of a failed love affair prompts the memory of the writer's persona to think about the coldest hunting trip he ever took, making him recall a moving experience that no summary can adequately capture.

The first news story states that up to mid-July of 1998, "At least 30 immigrant deaths believed to be related to exhaustion and exposure to harsh weather have been recorded along the Texas-Mexico border this year, prompting officials to worry that they are seeing the beginning of an unprecedented death toll, according to a published report." The Associated Press report goes on to state that seven deaths have been recorded in the Del Rio (Texas) sector, that eight bodies have been found in Kennedy and Brooks counties, and that eleven more bodies have been discovered, dead from dehydration, in Laredo. The Border Patrol, which monitors such deaths for the U.S. Immigration and Naturalization Service, reports that only one death due to heat has been confirmed in Arizona and New Mexico. For readers familiar with the desert country south of Arizona, New Mexico, and Texas, this is a difficult claim to believe. One has only to read the stories of Miguel Méndez, a leading Chicano writer who until recently taught at the University of Arizona in Tucson, to know otherwise. In "Ambrosio Ceniza," which I translated in 1980, Méndez vividly describes crossing the vast expanses of the southwestern terrain, where there is little water, during the hottest days of the summer. That people nowadays suffer from the sun's intense heat when walking endless miles without water and without relief because they are scared of approaching a gas station, a house, or some other shelter for fear of being reported to the Border Patrol is downright barbaric. Some generous Christian people, I understand from media reports, have started to organize water and food patrols to help immigrants who become victims of the intense heat. Still, the terrible prospect of having to risk death to immigrate should be outlawed. As the new century begins, a country that prides itself on being compassionate and sensitive to human rights through-out the world, needs to understand that what motivates Mexicans to cross the border into the United States is not the drug trade, as some people claim, but hunger. What American would not go five hundred miles or several thou-sand to put food in the mouths of his or her starving family?

The Kennedy County sheriff, who is a veteran with more than thirty years of law-enforcement experience, says "he's never seen so many bodies so early in the year." He adds, "We had four just last week. We buried [an unknown boy this week] and we still have one at the morgue." The sheriff stated that, "the county spends up to $3,000 on investigations, autopsies and burials for every body found." In 1996, twenty bodies were found, and eighteen in Kennedy County in 1997. "I know there's a bunch of them we haven't found out there somewhere, anywhere between the strips of land next to the ma-jor U.S. Highways 77, 281, 35 and the other smaller state roads." Officials claim that, "There's water along the way in places, but you have to know where it is." Then, of course, people have to be willing to be seen, recog-nized, and picked up by the Border Patrol. The agency has now developed what the newspapers call Operation Lifesaver, that is, a program that trains agents to provide emergency medical relief. This initiative has been making videos that are sent to the Mexican radio and television stations all along the two-thousand-mile border warning immigrants of the dangers of cross-ing illegally into the United States. The message conveyed is, "Stay away, stay alive." We just hope the word goes out in Spanish, indicates one official; but, do undocumented workers watch television and listen to the radio?

"One hardly has time for anything," one middle-aged man who has crossed the border many times to work in the United States told me in Brownsville a few months ago. He has been caught a number of times, he confided, but the pay in Mexico just does not compare, and the need is so great in his family that when he has been caught and returned to Mexico often he has turned right around and tried it again. Most of the time he crosses successfully, and ends up working for several months out of the year in Houston, Dallas, and even as far north as Kansas and Iowa. As we talked, I noticed he occasionally looked at the Buffalo Bills cap I was wearing to ward off the strong South Texas sun. When we finished talking, I thanked him, and, on an impulse, I gave him my cap. His eyes lit up and he smiled. Then he thanked me and said that the cap would help him. I have since thought of that hard-working man, who paints houses for a living, wearing my Bills cap. He had to make his careful way in a country that needs him badly enough to hire him cheaply. Nonetheless he can be nabbed at any moment and returned empty-handed to his native Mexico.

The second story, from Mexico City, informs us that Mexico's Immigration Under-Secretary, Fernando Solis Camara, made the following statement to four southern California mayors: "The number of Mexicans who died while trying to cross illegally into the United States quadrupled last year as a result of tougher surveillance by the U.S. Border Patrol." According to this official, "The Mexican government estimates more than 350 people died trying to enter the United States in 1998." The Border Patrol, I learned, counts only bodies found in the underbrush across the common border between the United States and Mexico. The estimate of the Mexican government, on the other hand, may be more than the actual number of deaths. The truth likely lies somewhere in between, which, looked at from any angle, is nevertheless substantial. One such death, under such circumstances ought to be one too many. To put this outrageous yearly massacre into perspective, let us be clear, can anyone envision even one Canadian citizen dying, without legal and human rights consequences, from attempting to cross illegally into the United States?

Amalia, whose three children were born in the United States, once told my wife and me how she crossed the border. Her children attend local schools in central Texas and they did well in their studies in the elementary grades. But now that the teenagers are in middle school and in the early years of high school, different problems are presenting themselves. One has joined a gang, and the two others are slacking off in their courses. They feel they don't have attractive clothes and they don't believe they have a good chance of graduating and going on to college. The young girl now has a boyfriend, three years older than she, and we expect to hear any day that she is pregnant and will be dropping out of school. Another one of their friends has gotten pregnant, and this is the way such youngsters choose to escape a school environment that does not sufficiently nourish them. At that age, all young people badly need attention, and they deserve to be encouraged.

But I started this story to relate how it took Amalia nine days, she said, of going up and down and all around the mountains of El Paso, looking for water to drink. Wherever she found it, she said, it was only because God led her to it. Otherwise, she grimaces, she would have died. What she remembers most vividly was sleeping out under the stars at night, after being utterly exhausted by the day's heat, in the cold open air of the mountains after the sun went down. Often she did not know where she was. She secured her bearings daily by making use of the fact that she knew the sun rose to the east and settled to the west. She kept out of sight of all cars, but she was always within view of a highway, going north by the sun, seldom knowing how far she had already traveled and not knowing how much more land there was ahead of her before she was actually in the United States. Throughout her ordeal she constantly prayed for help and guidance from la Virgen de Guadalupe, Jesus, and God. Experiencing headaches, dry mouth, cracking lips, and feeling weak, she ate what she could find, what she was willing to eat. At some indefinite point in her story, she stopped telling us what she went through, believing that it was painful for us to hear, and then she smiled, saying, "but God is good and I made it and that was when I was younger, about twelve years ago. Now my children are in school, and, though my husband occasionally drinks and sometimes gets in trouble with the law, I am happy, for I can work, *gracias a Dios,* thank God, for we are all in His hands, always, whether we realize it or not." There is no stronger or more spirited woman. What more can I do but to try to suggest a few of the difficulties that she went through, without endangering any one?

In light of this widespread U.S. bureaucratically imposed suffering aimed at Mexican citizens, how should American citizens respond to a Saturday, May 29, 1999, article in the *Bryan–College Station Eagle,* which is owned by the *Dallas Morning News,* that ran on the day before the U.S. Border Patrol celebrated its seventy-fifth anniversary? According to the "McAllen Sector Assistant Chief Patrol Agent Harry Beall, who delivered remarks at the outdoor ceremony," we are told that, "The Border Patrol has a very long and distinguished history. Its officers have always displayed a singular loyalty to 'The Patrol' and an esprit de corps that is matched by very few." He continued, "We respond to any call to duty, no matter what it is."

The Border Patrol is divided into twenty-two sectors found along the northern and southern borders of the United States and the island of Puerto Rico. The Patrol was created by an act of Congress on May 28, 1924, and,

"The first group [of agents] was chosen from the civil service registers from railway postal clerks and immigrant inspectors. The organization was charged with preventing people from entering the country illegally and combating immigrant smuggling. During the first few months, the small band of officers had no uniforms and had only their badges to identify them as border agents, so they were easy to ignore." By December of that same year, however, they had an official uniform and the rest is history.

In 1993, there were more than two thousand agents spread across the Mexican and the Canadian borders. During the last seven years of President Bill Clinton's two terms, though, largely as a result of heavy lobbying by senators and representatives from the southwestern border states, significant federal money was set aside to increase the number of agents to more than eight thousand. As a consequence, 92 percent of the agents are now stationed along the Mexico–United States border while only 8 percent patrol the three-thousand-mile Canadian border. That fact alone tells us where the federal government believes the main business of the Border Patrol is, but this discrepancy does not explain why the state senators and the representatives of all the states that border Mexico constantly besiege the government for even more agents and resources. The argument of these powerful politicians is that more agents are needed to stem the very profitable drug trade that they associate with illegal immigration from Mexico and Latin America. But everyone knows that the drug people have so many resources and are so sophisticated that they are not likely to attempt passing contraband where the regular Border Patrol agents are stationed. It is the Mexican workers who are also trying to cross the border to work for minimum U.S. wages who are being detained. Indeed, even though drug shipments are periodically stopped by Border Patrol agents at border crossings, the majority of drug shipments appear to make it into the United States and Canada by ship and plane, according to media reports. Illegal workers on the other hand have to try alternative routes, and that is why their bodies are daily being discovered dead in the desert.

Friday, May 16, 2003, and another horror story is that more undocumented immigrants have been found dead in a failed smuggling attempt that carried about one hundred people, including children, in the back of a semi-trailer so hot that nineteen suffocated. How many more similar incidents will be recorded before some kind of workable system sensibly allows Mexican workers to help our industries legally? What would be a sensible plan? Let us say that farmer X in California, business Y in Illinois, and industry Z in New Jersey or Alabama need a certain number of workers for a specified number of months or years. These employers ought to be able to submit requests for Mexican or Latin American workers willing to work under set conditions and pay that the Border Patrol could monitor. These would be jobs that would not compete with or eliminate U.S. workers. Such a change in policy would help both American employers and Latino workers, benefiting the economies of both hemispheres. Where this idea becomes unworkable is when people become greedy and want to set up terms to benefit themselves, abusing others.

The last relevant part of our current inhuman public policy is that the Border Patrol today offers one of the highest entry-level salaries and pay scales. "In many cities on the U.S.–Mexico border, they are the largest law enforcement presence and routinely help local police." Local police, given the considerably higher salaries paid by the Border Patrol soon learn to aspire to become Border Patrol agents, if they are interested in increasing their take-home pay. Is there, indeed, a clearer instance where prejudice and traditional discrimination against Mexican citizens has misguidedly been transformed into governmental public policies that end creating social realities of which we should be ashamed? Surely there is a better and more humane way to legally admit immigrants who are interested in working in the United States; there is a dire need for their services here.

32

Luis Alfonso Torres,
the Mexican Rodney King

I t happened again today, but only a few of the newspapers, mainly in the
Houston area, covered the incident. I checked the east coast papers and
the west coast media, but I didn't see that they reported or followed this
developing story. Relatives of a man dialed 911 to ask for help, in keeping
with the commercials they had seen on television and the announcements
posted on billboards around the Houston area. When three Baytown police officers arrived, they found "that an incoherent man was walking in the
street," reported Cindy Horwell in "4th Officer in Torres Case off Patrol,"
an article in the March 23, 2002, issue of the *Houston Chronicle.*

When the three officers asked the man to wait, the police video, taped by
a camera mounted in the patrol car of the only officer wearing a microphone,
shows the man, Luis Alfonso Torres, trying, instead, to walk away. "The
officers can be seen and heard talking with Torres for a few minutes," on
"Main Street shortly after midnight." Then, when he begins to back away
from them, another officer, Aldred, "is seen sticking out a leg [behind him]
and tripping Torres so the officers can subdue him and determine whether
he is a danger to himself or someone else."

I suspect most people would have tried to move away, even from the police. Torres did not speak English and the officers apparently knew no Spanish. But explanatory details like these are not included in the story, and we can
only hope that such realities are brought up and addressed when the case goes
to court for a resolution of this and other misunderstandings that occurred
during this incident. Language is always an issue, often the main issue, but
too often whether a person speaks Spanish or not is seen as insignificant and
irrelevant. Yet it is an increasingly necessary professional competency issue in
the United States. Indeed, the story does not suggest or indicate that language
difficulties on both sides may have caused Mr. Torres's death.

How else can the following events be explained? "After an intense struggle
in which the officers roll in the street with Torres and one of them punches

him five times, they manage to handcuff him." Officer "Evans arrives near the end of the struggle and Billeaud arrives after Torres has been handcuffed." Events were a little unclear in the first video, but in "a version that was enhanced by the FBI," the lawyers and observers can now see the night "images[,] and the audio are more clear." We are not told what words Mr. Torres said from the beginning of this whole incident to the end, and we should learn what he was trying to tell the policemen.

In this particular case, unlike several others that I have read about, or that I have heard discussed with understandable emotion by Latino members in the community over the years, we learn the following unreal detail: "At one point, Dillow can be seen with at least one knee on Torres' shoulders near his neck." Then, a little after that, "Billeaud later can be seen stooping beside Torres with a knee on his back as Torres lies face-down with his hands cuffed behind him." Still, "A short time later, Dillow is heard saying, 'Hey, is he all right? He's starting to turn colors. Take the cuffs off.'"

Imagine being able to see that a man who is already handcuffed and who is face down on an asphalt pavement in a darkly lit midnight street is already beginning to turn colors? Next readers are laconically informed that, "Police and ambulance personnel then begin trying to resuscitate Torres. He was pronounced dead soon afterward at a hospital." Given the video, and an earlier claim that Mr. Torres had something that seemed to "shine" in the darkly lit street, which did not prove to be a gun, as the police stated, everybody now knows that this case is headed straight to the courts.

Earlier in the article we learned that, "Harris County Medical Examiner Dr. Joye [*sic*] Carter ruled the death a homicide, saying that Torres, 45, had died of mechanical asphyxiation—meaning that his airways had been constricted so that he couldn't breathe."

Who was Mr. Torres? "Torres, a Mexican national who had a visa allowing him to work in this country, died January 20 after struggling with officers on a Baytown street. They had been called to find him after he fled from an ambulance crew called by Torres' relatives, who said he suffered from hypertension and was behaving strangely."

What can any spectator humanely surmise? That Mr. Torres seems to have been ill. That he had papers that legally allowed him to work in the United States, and that he died trying to avoid being questioned by three policemen one cold night in January in a language that he did not fully understand. Rodney King at least understood the words hurled at him by police officers, and, though severely beaten, he did live to sensibly ask, "Why can't we all just live together?"

I wonder what Mr. Torres would have told America, if America were to listen to what he might say, had he been provided with the opportunity? President George W. Bush recently visited Monterrey, Mexico, to talk to Mexican president Vicente Fox and other Latin American leaders. In another story in the newspaper, President Bush is saying, great, we are making "'good and steady progress' on speeding up the process of issuing immigrant visas. Legislation is pending in the Senate, and Bush said he hopes it will pass soon because 'migrants make a valuable contribution to America' and the families back in Mexico who rely on them financially."

Yes, it is refreshing to see our leaders attempting to lead. But, if people at the local level, like the police officers involved in this case, have not been properly educated to respect and to help foreign workers, what is the benefit of working out better relations at the level of the presidents? American citizens often do not understand that many American businesses depend on Mexican and other Latin American workers. Deaths such as Mr. Torres's have occurred for many decades in this country. Hardly a year goes by without several similar instances happening, invariably because of some language misunderstanding. I hope that this time people will notice. The death of Mr. Luis Alfonso Torres cannot be just another unfortunate case, one more unbelievable, outrageous story. But after September 11th, are we capable of being shocked by the specifics of one migrant worker's death in Texas?

The last word that I have heard on this case is that the lawsuit regarding the unprovoked death of Mr. Torres was settled out of court, a fact that I do not think the media noticed. What kind of justice is this?

33

NAFTA and the Maquiladora Babies

We know about Domingo Gonzalez who lives at the extreme end of South Texas from reporter John Quiñones, and we know about the babies also from another videotape that aired nationwide on the ABC *Prime Time Live* television program more than a decade ago, on June 1, 1992. By then, apparently, Mr. Gonzalez had been trying for some time to raise awareness about the chemical and other waste products that the American maquiladoras dump into the Rio Grande. But it was not until Quiñones brought the cameras into South Texas that people throughout the country had an opportunity to learn about Mr. Gonzalez's admirable struggle. The question now, though, is: do we still remember the issue, and, more important, has anything been done about it?

The word "maquiladora" appears to have been taken from the Spanish "maquina," which means a machine. Maquiladoras generically refer to the factories and plants established by over 2,600 American and Canadian companies and corporations along the Mexican border from Texas to California. In his television news report, Quiñones first introduces Domingo Gonzalez as a local resident "who has been driving across the river between Brownsville and Matamoros for several years," like many inhabitants of the area. Mr. Gonzalez, Quiñones informs us, is convinced that the chemical and production plants have been endangering the health of Mexican Americans in South Texas and of northern Mexico residents during the last decade. But being only a concerned Mexican American citizen, we learn that he has not been able to garner the type of national attention that this life-threatening problem deserves. After struggling for media attention for a number of years, we see that in less than a week John Quiñones has remedied that fact, for he has arrived, interviewed Mr. Gonzalez, and brought out this information to all Americans.

So why are more than 2,600 American and Canadian maquiladoras located on the common two-thousand-mile border that runs from Tijuana, south of San Diego, California, going east to Matamoros, Tamaulipas, Mexico, which is next door to Brownsville, Texas? Although an unspecified number of maquiladoras moved from the United States and Canada to Mexico well before the North American Free Trade Agreement went into effect on January 1, 1994, this agreement legalized the practice and increased North American corporate activity in Mexico. As early as 1989, the United States and Canada had agreed to remove trade restrictions between the two countries, but bringing in Mexico was not as easy. The NAFTA accord, signed during President Bill Clinton's first administration, has since encouraged businesses associated with motor vehicles, automotive parts, computers, textiles, and agriculture products to consider relocating their operations or part of their production facilities along the border with Mexico. Here, cheaper labor costs trim costs, significantly improving stockholder profits. Under the sponsorship of the Murdough Center for Engineering Professionalism at Texas Tech University in Lubbock, representatives met at a NAFTA Forum in Puerto Vallarta, Mexico, in January 28, 1995, to draw up the "Principles of Ethical Conduct in Engineering Practice under the North American Free Trade Agreement." This international arrangement between corporate officials specifies minimum wages, working conditions, and environmental protection practices, promoting the continued globalization of the world's economies. But, in this pact, protecting the environment was largely left to the goodwill of the companies themselves.

Quiñones's investigative report focuses attention on one horrendous fact: over fifty Mexican, Mexican American, and American babies whose parents live within two miles of the Rio Grande have been born, within a five to six year period, either without brains or with partial brains. It happens that the American plants started to move into the river area during the 1980s when Ronald Reagan was president. The other fact that is still not widely known is that babies with this kind of serious birth defect allegedly had not previously been reported by the medical community. The assumption is that these babies began to appear after the maquiladoras arrived. *Prime Time* makes an effort to connect the cause with the effect. The question, then, is: who has jurisdiction on the border as well as the necessary political will to rein in the health-threatening abuses of maquiladora owners who are making more money for shareholders than they did when they paid union wages in the United States?

In 1988, I was commuting daily between Harlingen and Brownsville. At the time, I served as Dean of Arts and Sciences at Texas Southmost College, a community college with 5,200 students that is now part of the University of Texas at Brownsville. The college is so close to the Rio Grande that I would periodically walk the three or four blocks across the U.S. Customs bridge for lunch in Mexico. I would pay the nominal fee of twenty-five cents or so, cross the international bridge that facilitates daily commerce between Mexico and the United States, and return to my office, all within an hour.

On several occasions I remember stopping on the span of the bridge to peer down at the slow-flowing river, my attention attracted by the fact that children on the Mexican side were bathing and playing both in the water and by the river's edge. Along the shore, I usually found cows, a goat or two, and some chickens feeding from whatever they could find in the vicinity. Once, when I crossed over into Matamoros, which was a city of roughly 650,000 people, radio reports said, I encountered a rather large pig that crossed the street in front of the restaurant where I was headed. On two occasions, I leaned over the railing of the bridge and happened to see two totally nude men crossing the river to the American side at high noon. They held their clothes as high as they could above their heads, while they partly walked and partly waded across one of the narrower places in the river. When they arrived on the American side, it was clear from their movements that they were in the habit of darting into the nearby clumps of tall bushes. There, without drying themselves, they quickly dressed and sat in the bushes, waiting their chance to jump over the fence and wire barriers set up by American Border Patrol officials.

On such occasions, one cannot help but wonder what factors and forces had placed me on the bridge to witness these scenes and why those particular young individuals were there, struggling below the bridge, trying to find something, anything by the river that they could sell so they could eat. What unseen but felt geopolitical realities kept each of us where we were? We saw each other, they asking for alms in a paper cup tied loosely with a string to a long wooden pole extended to passers-by on the bridge, me, giving them my pocket change and a spare dollar apiece that went into their two cups. At one end of the bridge, the U.S. customs officials carried on with the business of stopping cars to ask if all passengers were American citizens; on the other, the Mexican customs officials waving vehicles through into Mexico, aware that much of the Mexican border economy depends on American tourism. Life on the bridges between the United States and Mexico has gone on like this ever since I can remember, for the international bridges along the border have always served as the lifelines of the regional economies of both countries.

When I returned to Brownsville as dean, I remember in particular the story of one company, the students and families of whom I knew at the college. This company, I learned, terminated all of its union-member workers in New

York State in about 1985, and bought the houses of two hundred or so of its top management officials. The company then paid the relocation expenses of all of the managers it needed and moved them and their families and households to Brownsville. When they arrived, these company officers and their families proceeded to build brand new attractive houses in Brownsville, South Padre Island, and in the surrounding towns and neighborhoods. They became the newly arrived golfers and fishers who joined the "snowbirds," older citizens who vacation in South Texas during the winter months. These winter northern tourists, as I previously mentioned, normally start arriving around September to Mission, McAllen, Edinburg, Pharr, San Juan, Weslaco, Mercedes, Harlingen, Brownsville, and South Padre, and then stay throughout the winter into April and May. At that point, they start returning home, largely to the colder Midwestern states of Iowa, Nebraska, Minnesota, Wisconsin, and others. At any rate, the new company money clearly improved the economy of the Valley, but, since the Environmental Protection Agency (EPA), does not monitor the waste products eliminated by the maquiladora plants, the health of the local inhabitants is being impaired, according to environmental watch groups.

The anencephalic babies that Mr. Gonzalez and John Quiñones brought to the attention of the nation usually die within months of birth, but the very high rate of babies born with anencephaly has raised a number of social, ethical, and disciplinary questions. At one point, Quiñones makes the claim that there is "a strange invisible killer that is sweeping through the Rio Grande Valley," a hyperbole that does not appear exaggerated. According to Quiñones's report, Carmen Rockwell, a Mexican American medical doctor in Brownsville, was apparently the first professional health official to take note of the babies. She noticed that a considerable number of babies had been born within the last five or six years with "significant parts of their heads missing." Quiñones's video focuses the camera's eye on a map where Dr. Rockwell has been placing little red flags that pinpoint the residences of parents who have given birth to anencephalic babies. These births, we are told, constitute "the largest group of cases of anencephaly ever known" anywhere in the world. At the time of the 1992 news report, Dr. Rockwell's map showed nineteen red flags on both sides of the river. Quiñones says that the "rash" of such births "seems like an epidemic," and the young mothers, interviewed by Quiñones, have been asking themselves "are we jinxed?" raising images of *brujería*, witchcraft and other superstitions for which there is a propensity there.

Quiñones's video asserts that this part of the world is experiencing something like an "industrial revolution." All of this commercial activity has been the result of talks advanced by Presidents George Bush, Sr. and Carlos Salinas of Mexico. The business idea is that American firms will not have to pay the high labor costs and wages that living in the United States requires, and that by opening these new areas for economic development, the Mexican government will also be able to provide more jobs for Mexican workers. Most of these assembly-line jobs pay Mexican workers a reported average of forty dollars per week, or, eight dollars a day, as opposed to the eleven to seventeen dollar an hour salaries plus benefits that American companies previously paid to union workers in the United States. The difference in the profits goes to the shareholders of these large corporations and to the CEOs for finding cheaper ways to produce their products. In Mexico, it turns out, American corporations do not meet the same stringent health and safety regulations that the U.S. government and state agencies require.

Domingo Gonzalez takes Quiñones and his open-lens camera crew to see the landfills where the maquiladoras dump their refuse. Since the laws of Mexico are not enforced, something that Mexican president Vicente Fox wants to change, the maquiladora companies can virtually do what they want. What we are shown is that the refuse has not been filled and is pretty much exposed to the open air. At this point, Mr. Gonzalez inserts a shovel where he says that one of the companies dumps waste, virtually in his backyard, and John Quiñones physically backs away from the strong odor. The shovelful is dark, sooty. Four Mexican boys from around eight to ten years old, attracted by the cameras, stand around looking. It is clear that this is the playground where they regularly play. In another of several similar scenes, Quiñones says that chemical waste burned in the open air in Mexico is taken by the Gulf winds across the river and into the United States. These "highly toxic fumes" are carried by the wind northward; nothing, though, is said about the same fumes that the Mexican people have to breathe every time the wind turns. One hour of breathing that air, Quiñones informs us, made members of his camera crew sick for four days.

The American EPA director in Brownsville hedges when Quiñones asks questions. "Do people have a right to know [whether the EPA is inspecting and monitoring emissions from these plants]?" Quiñones asks. "I don't know," the director responds, "that's an interesting question." It becomes clear that he is not in a position to answer questions comfortably, for he will likely be dismissed if he cooperates. "We can't just build a wall," he adds uneasily, and "we do not have legal jurisdiction in Mexico," suggesting that things might be different, if Mexico were a part of the United States, as some Americans desired following Polk's war with Mexico, 1846 to 1848.

"Legal jurisdiction." Will the people of the Valley and from Mexico understand these words from the Americanos? The underlying supposition from the American businessmen is that Valley people should be thankful that the Americans have left their northern homes and moved to the Rio Grande to help out Mexico with jobs. That is the prevalent thinking in the language used by the politicians, businesses, and the editorial pieces in the regional newspapers and media. It is clear that when the powers that be want something, most of the wheels begin to turn in the desired direction. That is the rhetoric that shapes the reality being created, and the words of the elected leaders are the words that count. Domingo Gonzalez, on the other hand, spends much of his time talking to others like himself. Without investigative reporters like John Quiñones, Americans are not likely to know much about what is going on with the maquiladoras, for the stories we likely see in the media are all about success and more employment and economic advances.

To make sure that they are not making more out of what one company's CEO dismisses as "mistaken test results," from his executive offices south of Chicago, Quiñones and Mr. Gonzalez sent landfill and local water samples to an EPA-approved testing laboratory in Boston. Yes, the sample was highly toxic, the report concludes: there is xylene, benzene, mercury, and other toxic chemicals in the area, they aver. The very land where the children play and where the people who do not have running water facilities and electricity dwell is contaminated. Indeed, that is what I thought about when I looked down from the Matamoros international bridge to see the children playing next to the Rio Grande that slowly makes its way to Boca Chica and to the Gulf of Mexico.

Quiñones's crew next filmed Domingo Gonzalez leading a group of people as they approached SEGUE, the Mexican government's counterpart of the EPA. The people in this part of the report are Mexican citizens, one man and seven to eight older women. They have scheduled a meeting with the director of SEGUE. The director did not know anything about the industrial waste materials, he says. He will need time to gather information. Come back in three days. When the group returns three days later, John Quiñones and the camera crew are not allowed inside the building to film the meeting. The camera group patiently waits outside the door. The women come out drying their tears. They have been told, we discover, that they are communist infiltrators, and that they will be under surveillance for their activities!

What constitutes this text, this highly dramatic tableau of life, as it is daily being played out on the Rio Grande? Who is at the center of this tragedy, if not the people and the children? Would we have known about Domingo Gonzalez's efforts if John Quiñones and reporters like him had not brought ABC's *Prime Time Live* to the Valley?

Who decides which issues warrant the attention of the American public? When I asked this question of my students, the immediate response was "the media." Sad that we are so conditioned to think that an issue is important only if and when the media makes a matter an issue. No wonder most of our Mexican American Domingo Gonzalezes fail to become Cesar Chavezes. Our people just aren't camera-seeking types, and our educations simply have not equipped the majority of us with the public-speaking skills and the language necessary to make an impact on the American consciousness. But a good education can fix that, *¡raza!*

Here is Domingo Gonzalez taking time from his life to call people's attention to a devastating health issue. One would think the authorities would have responded, but he has been eminently unsuccessful in securing attention. Even after ABC's John Quiñones unfolds the grisly economical and political relationship that joins the interests of Mexico and the United States it is doubtful that anything will happen. The politicians are too busy elsewhere. So, caught between certain poverty and the need to improve social and employment conditions, the poor on both sides of the border have little choice but to work for the maquiladoras to improve their livelihoods. They cannot, of course, do much against the companies that offer them poor wages, but that is better than the well-known alternative of no wages at all.

This tragic situation reminds me of the simple equation that I found in *I, Rigoberta Menchú: An Indian Woman in Guatemala* (1983). Rigoberta Menchú is the recipient of the 1992 Nobel Peace Prize. Although Menchú's book has been called into question for including events that did not specifically happened to Menchú herself, her text does capture transgressions endured by the indigenous people of Guatemala from right and left armed forces who have taken advantage of the population over the years. Rigoberta Menchú formulated what I think is one of the most profound observations that I have ever heard or read anywhere: "Poverty *is* Violence." Is there a sadder truth? To be poor, indeed, is to be in a position where violations of all kinds are endured from all quarters with little or no recourse.

What we have here by the Rio Grande is violence against the lives of the people of the region. It is a violence from which the people of South Texas and northern Mexico cannot well protect themselves. They cannot escape, and since most of the population does not sufficiently know to what extent they are the victims of information withheld, of options that are not available, who is to know better? They cannot control their environment.

What do you think, reader, one needs to ask directly at this point? I say this deplorable set of conditions could be addressed *and* solved, if the will existed, both from the American and the Mexican governments, to correct the human tragedy that has been allowed to unfold here. But businesses clearly are more interested in making money than on helping the defenseless poor.

What is all too clear is that there is not enough willingness to solve the problems of birth defects and other health issues, pollution, poverty, and lack of education. The exploitation of people is currently working too well, and not interfering with the accounts of stockholders. Those lifestyles are well sustained by the violence that daily afflicts the ethnic people of the South Texas area. What do wealthy stockholders in the United States, Hawaii, or likely in other recreation resorts care about sacrificing a few babies?

34

A Realization and a Memory
in Southmost Texas

Some days my experiences seem like exasperating pieces of a life I hardly recognize as part of the American tapestry. Issues that I think important for the Latino community do not receive so much as a passing mention anywhere that I can see. Latino matters do not register much on the Geiger counters of the politicians and the elected leaders, since they continue to receive pap or poppycock, as Richard Nixon used to say, in one form or another, again and again. Today we are living through leadership bonds and friendships formed throughout Texas and the rest of the United States thirty, forty, and fifty years ago, when it was perfectly acceptable not to pay attention to the Mexicans. People in power then did not care to distinguish between Mexicans and Mexican Americans, a practice that continues. Although leaders like Hector P. Garcia, the founder of the American G.I. Forum, and later José Angel Gutiérrez and Cesar Chavez, agitated for change, between their resistance and our inertia only a few Latino lives improve every generation. Today the children of the people who resisted change before are now in leading positions throughout the country everywhere. They are continuing to create, to shape, and to justify laws and public policies in the government at the national, state, and local levels primarily for their benefit. They are leading the corporations of America, the major companies, the banks, the universities, and they are at the helm wherever power and social control can be visibly exerted. That is my analysis today as I look at South Texas, my way of trying to explain why change is so difficult, why changing the status quo sometimes appears insuperable. We cannot improve the social infrastructure of the United States to provide better educations and job opportunities for Latinos, blacks, and other minorities until attitudes change. Our leaders have to be convinced that they also stand to gain from opening up real opportunities to all.

The real problem, though, is that because we lack the proactive support of sympathetic leaders, American society is not doing anything noticeable to educate and to change the thinking of the leaders or their sons and daughters. This new crop of teenagers, and the twenty- and thirty-something cohort is also going through the best schools, receiving better educations, being coddled (like their parents and, perhaps, even like their grandparents), made to feel, in short, that they are entitled in America. As I see it, they have been the beneficiaries of most privileges, amenities, and preferences in a social system that has been set up to encourage the best and brightest. But what has been grossly unfair for many generations is that Latinos and other minorities have not been allowed to become the best and brightest. We have not been treated as equals, and, worse, our children are still not being provided with the same opportunities, despite all of our efforts and entreaties. The moment we raise issues like Affirmative Action and scholarship inequities, the very people who have traditionally enjoyed most of society's advantages immediately ask: why should minority people receive preferences? The argument they raise is that opportunities should be based on earned merit, but they conveniently forget that they have earned merit because they have had advantages that most minorities have not enjoyed, since minorities generally receive less education, less attention, and usually less of everything.

Minorities, though, are beginning to see how such people manipulate the social systems that have been put in place behind the scenes to maintain power and control. It is clear that they have been taught and have learned to use their influential positions to benefit themselves and their friends at the expense of others who have been less fortunate and who have less access to virtually everything. I think the Enron, Arthur Anderson, WorldCom, Adelphia, Tyco, ImClone Systems, and other similar business disasters have amply demonstrated the insidiousness of some corporate leaders. Although they profess to work in the service of the general public, such people have proven that they are interested in shaping the world mainly to function for their own benefit and convenience. Shareholders and innocent people trusted these leaders. Such events explain why there is no "trickle down" economy or benefit, as Ronald Reagan coined it, for the masses, since almost everything is under their control. But Americans are now recognizing that the same worn-out platitudes that have been heard throughout the twentieth century will not sustain minority people for long in the twenty-first. Latinos, whether Democrats or Republicans, realize that promises of education, jobs, health benefits, and social programs have never materialized for Spanish-speaking Americans. Our needs and desires are not heeded because they counter the prevailing tastes and attitudes that were set up many years ago to give preference and to benefit the people who run America and their corporate, private, or public interests.

That is why I can write equally well at the Winthrop House, The Houghton, or at my brother's house in Houston, as I have recently done. Sometimes even the great library collections of the past do not help Latinos construct the future that society needs. Where one works is almost immaterial these days. I continue to read extensively and to write a little in this cool, clean, recently built, people-filled townhome on the outskirts of Brownsville. At the southernmost tip of the United States, I am actually where the transnational commerce daily occurs. That is where the international bridges are located. In places, there are no discernible borders in the area, since the river carries little water, and the fences have fallen or they have been pulled down. I feel symbolically at the center of two great cultures, but that rhetoric is academic and even political these days, which, unfortunately, is to say it is quite useless. Who pays attention to the writings of a Mexican American in the United States of America?

And, if I were to move to Mexico or somewhere in Latin America, would being a foreign writer or correspondent help? Perhaps, but I don't see that as a successful alternative, as providing the type of forum that might help Latinos realize that we seem to be on our own and are not receiving much help from anyone. I am not suggesting separation, only that we realize why life has, again and again, shown us that we should not expect much from the powers that are in place, that we need to create our own strong bonds to benefit ourselves and our children. Otherwise, we will continue being left behind or elbowed out across the board wherever we show that we want to become better Americans. Yes, it is difficult to say no to a handful of Latinos who have succeeded, despite the odds. But most of the other Latinos, for one reason or another, still find the road toward the American Dream stressful, for helping hands are usually not available when needed.

Mexico has a different grandeur from that which people in the United States appear willing to recognize. One can discover the beauties and the attractions of Mexico and the Mexican people by visiting cities such as Mexico City, Puebla, Xalapa, Palenque, Oaxaca, Querétaro, or resort centers like Acapulco, Cancún, Puerto Vallarta, and others. That world is so varied and diverse that it defies description or summary. The best word here, to all Americans and Latinos, is simply to visit the country and discover what exists. I have had to do this whenever I have been able to, because as an adult I have always been short of resources, as most Latinos are in this country. I spent most of my growing up years, as indicated earlier in *Sol Naciente,* in South Texas. When we were teenagers we partied out by the ocean, on the Texas Gulf Coast. Even then, beer, *la música Norteña,* and the lyrical compositions of José Alfredo Jiménez and the songs of Pedro Infante mixed nicely with Freddy Fender and the Dick Clark rock and roll era. We talked about the nice-looking girls we knew, the sunsets, and what we were going to do when we grew up, all of which helped us while away the hours of our youth.

As in most things in life, returning to a certain area occurs for different reasons at different times. In this locale I am reluctantly reminded of the time I assumed a new administrative position at the local college more than fifteen years ago. My wife and I had removed to the Valley, as I previously said, primarily to provide our children with an opportunity to improve their Spanish and to live in the area where I grew up. The faculty at my campus had also selected another person for an administrative post for which I had applied. I had been waiting for that position for seven years, and, although I had never expressed the desire to anyone, my colleagues knew of my interest. By letter, I protested to the appropriate administrators that the search had been unfair because the person appointed had been intimately involved in setting up the search criteria, and other irregularities now inconsequential.

Doing something, however, would have required going to court. When I went to see the top administrator, he told me, "It looks as if you are going to have to get bloodied." He then caught himself and actually said, no, I didn't say that; disregard what I just said. I must be one dumb *pendejo* Chicano in his eyes, I said to myself. At the time I remember thinking that I wish I had the opportunity to bring out this and other similar behaviors by colleagues and administrators before a group of twelve people. But two lawyers whom I consulted were too expensive. It always turns out to be a matter of money. What was that quip between Hemingway and Fitzgerald? Fitzgerald saying that the rich are different, and Hemingway cutting him short with something, like, yes, they have more money. At any rate, it was clear that these lawyers did not work to help minorities, even though they claimed to have gone to law school for that purpose. Why did their advertisements still say they specialized in Affirmative Action cases, I asked my wife.

The first lawyer charged me $187 for an hour, and told me I had a good case. His services, however, "would cost me, and quite a bit," he added. After two months and not hearing anything—clearly letting me know I had to initiate further action—I went by his office, and retrieved the papers his secretary had filed. The second lawyer wanted $250 for the initial hour, and a down payment of $3,000 for his services. I could not afford that, so I thanked his office manager and guardian of the purse, and said, like John Wayne in the movies, that I would let it ride. (I have to use John Wayne, because few readers would understand if I said, like Luis Aguilar in his younger days.) I would have liked, though, the opportunity to show twelve jurists, what Lord Acton (1834–1902), the British historian, must have meant when he said, "It is bad to be oppressed by a minority, but it is worse to be oppressed by a majority."

So I left without further complaint. The worse part of the affair is that, when one is a Latino, one assumes one has friends among the Anglo professionals with whom one works. But the moment there is a position available, I have since discovered, I may as well forget about applying. Affirmative Action has never made any difference, except when the people in charge want it to work. Otherwise, the rest of the people in a company or firm will select a person with whom they feel comfortable. That, it turns out, is the bottom-line criterion: their comfort. And, of course, even though I had been among them seven years, and had proven myself a good colleague, as a Latino, I still represented discomfort, or not as much comfort as the friend they were allowed to select. Nothing that I have experienced since—and I have applied for countless administrative and faculty positions—has *shown* me that a minority candidate among a group of people who are physically different will be selected. People may think this a hard assessment, but it is the truth. One is okay so long as the white script is followed, but, when people learn that a Latino is capable of possibly making some changes, then a minority person faces an altogether different ball game. At that point, one applies, and one's colleagues do the rest. That is why I have turned to writing, to inform other Americans about the Latino situation so that people can ask whether their experience appears to match with what I am saying. Throughout all of these years, my summer outings in the company of my family along the Texas Gulf Coast have proven the greatest relief, thankfully.

My trip down to the Valley to find employment among other Mexican Americans was of a different order. I had gone uncertain of how I would be received. With the exception of a fellow Mexican American faculty member who approached me because, he said, I looked like someone he knew, the rest was business. There was an uneasy air: since my curriculum vitae showed that I had accomplished more than my colleagues in the Valley, what was I trying to achieve by applying for an administrative position with them? Clearly I had an "agenda," as one person actually said. So this is how the next generation of Mexican Americans has been raised, I said, to myself. Well, it is the new order, the new world, and we just have to hope that certain forces and factors come together to make it better. At this point, we have to wait, which I am very good at, to see where *la raza* community thinks it wants to go. What are we willing to do—not only for the ones who have succeeded in achieving some power through their positions, but also for our more unfortunate members who are seldom helped generation after generation?

What do I mean? Although I have been mulling over my own situation (like the Anglo-American writers I taught for many years in Buffalo, Berkeley, and Houston—writers like Emerson, Melville, Hawthorne, Thoreau, that whole introspective northeastern gang so far removed from Latino America), I cannot avoid mentioning problems within our own Latino community. There are very real Latino problems not far from here, as I will shortly show, and we also need to consider how we go about creating and encouraging change within the Latino community. This is a complex and difficult problem to address, but I broach it here to open up the issue, and to invite Latino professionals to talk openly about what the Latino community actually needs and how its goals can best be reached. Personally, I think we have had more stasis than is healthy, and if we do not opt for change I do not see that progress is likely to be made. Why should it? Other than César Chávez and José Angel Gutiérrez, have U.S. Latinos ever publicly asked for change? We are used to simply taking the world as it is, and then saying, *pues así son las cosas,* that's the way things are. That is what a number of Latino leaders and administrators have unbelievably told me!

While I have been brooding over the significance and implicit futility of my desire for change, I am reminded of Cameron Park, which is situated at the southern tip of Cameron County, outside of the city limits of Brownsville proper. A Sunday, June 9, 2002, story in the *Houston Chronicle* subtitled "Residents along the border endure 'Third World' living conditions," for example, is what everybody associates with Latinos. But the *colonias* are only a small part of the growing Latino world, and our whole *mundo* needs attention.

Cameron Park, Texas, Lynn Brezosky of the Associated Press tells us, has the "dead last" lowest per capita income in the United States. Its 1,209 households live on a yearly average income of, hold your breath, $4,103, gasp! That is less than what most Americans earn per month. The national median household income for 1999 was $41,994, according to the 2000 Census. This kind of poverty is unbelievable today. It is what people used to subsist on in the neighborhoods I knew when I was growing up in Edinburg in the 1950s! And this is fifty years later. Brezosky says that in colonias like Cameron Park, as well as in 1,800 other similar *barrio colonias* that exist along the two-thousand-mile border with Mexico, "Gunshots no longer erupt with the sunset and pavement means children can walk to the bus on rainy days without wrapping garbage bags over their shoes. Television [now, following some recent improvements] runs on electric lines rather than car batteries. There are stoves and refrigerators—some even indoors." Poverty of this magnitude is shameful and inhuman. "Educational attainment in Cameron Park also is among the state's worst, with only 19.3 percent of people age 25 or older having a high school diploma or better. The state average is 72.1 percent." This kind of reality, indeed, is what Americans and other Mexican Americans, who have been residents living for several generations in the United States, need to notice, and to stamp out by change.

Most resident Mexican Americans are doing considerably better than their destitute *primos* who live in the colonias, but, even then, the majority still remain in America's lower middle class, with fewer in America's solid middle class. Such living conditions may suggest why most Latinos do not define themselves by the pursuit of money or through class position, largely because employment opportunities that can change lives are not readily available to most U.S. Spanish speakers. That may also explain why many of us have learned to settle for life's other offerings. But, I do not want readers to think that we are altogether happy and satisfied with where we are, that our world is a Pollyanna la-la land. For the record, it is not.

Still, the pleasures that our family lives provide are centrally important. Preparing good food—like cooking *arroz y frijoles* for dinner, a great casserole, a good, healthy salad, or a hearty breakfast, or organizing a backyard cookout, enjoyed with relatives, friends, and neighbors, all depending on the amount of food available—offers incomparable family pleasure. But so do the hundreds of other activities that cannot be itemized. Attending religious services, playing *la loteria,* or Monopoly, chess, or dominoes are wonderfully salutary activities, countering the destructive stories of killings, knifings, shootouts, drugs, and other similar abuses that we read about in the newspapers. What needs to be said regarding the bad Latino stereotype is that the overwhelming majority of Latinos are law-abiding citizens, since most of us have a healthy respect for order, process, justice, and fairness.

But the question, given our many-sided and tumultuous Spanish-speaking world, is: will we, nevertheless, help improve the colonias, and thus ourselves? Or, will the majority of Americans as well as successful Latinos remain focused mainly on continuing to help themselves, leaving the less fortunate to work things out as they can? What will we do as a society, as the leading civilization since the end of World War II? Are we Latinos going to reinvent ourselves; and, if so, how, since so many of us live difficult lives that need to be considerably improved? The future is before us. As I see it, we can either make more positive statements about ourselves, or statements will continue to be made for us. What are our lives going to be like *¿gente nuestra?* And, on this score, I can only hope that we do not become distracted, as we have in the past, and begin to fight among ourselves on things such as what we ought to call ourselves. Invariably this issue, for one, has often kept us successfully separated and apart from one another. Personally, I believe that we are all Hispanics, all Latinos, and Chicanos, Mexican Americans, Puerto Ricans, Cuban Americans, and others; it is not prudent to insist on differences that separate us. We are all simply Spanish-speaking Latinos.

Such inane fights remind me of the sad joke about the police officer who stops three Spanish-speaking men and asks one, "Where are you from?" The man says, "I was born in Buenos Aires, Argentina, but I am a naturalized American citizen." The officer then asks the next man the same question, to which second answers, "I am a Mexican American. I was born in North Carolina, and I have lived in the United States all of my life." The third says, "I am from Puerto Rico, and I am an American citizen, because Puerto Rico is a commonwealth of the United States, as you know." "Just what I thought," retorts the officer, "You are all Mexicans!"

35

Latino Voting
and Election Promises

I heard the other day that the next elections are around the corner, since they regularly occur every two and four years. The question is to what extent will this or a subsequent election matter as far as Latinos are concerned? Every fourth November, Americans vote for a new president, punctuated by state and local primaries and elections every two years. Judging from the newspapers, political commentators and pundits have been in a dither lately, as they usually are when elections are approaching, wondering whether the Latino vote will make a difference in the next election turnouts. Everyone it seems is interested in predicting what issues are likely to land the Democrats or the Republicans in control of Congress, the White House, the state legislatures and the local posts. Indeed, regardless of the issues, elections for we Latinos are about making our voice count and gaining some control over the decisions that are made for us and our children. So, every election we ask, who is promising to provide us either with more or less opportunities, and who will help the community more and control us less?

For most Latinos, one party appears to be like the other. Still, the degree of traditional indifference is markedly decreasing, because the Latino population is increasingly expected to be in a position to vote in one party or the other. Traditional, because the little we have actually received from both parties in the past definitely ought to explain the apathy that Latinos have built up toward voting. It is difficult to convince Latinos, after more than 150 years of neglect, that suddenly our interests are going to be seriously considered. But that is politics. Politics does not like to dwell on the past; it prefers to focus on the future. It prefers to make promises about what the different parties intend to do for Latinos. But promising and actually delivering on promises, we have learned, invariably change after the elections.

There are Latinos seriously involved in creating a better future as Democrats, while others are working as Republicans. Some Hispanics are even involved in third parties, but, by and large, no party has yet delivered on any of the political rhetoric that the candidates regularly dole out when they visit the Latino communities. The twentieth century is now history. The results in that century for Latinos are in; the records are there, waiting to be studied, as historians will. Will people be surprised to see that Latinos did not factor significantly during any part of that entire twentieth century? Indeed, since the southwestern territories were annexed to the United States during President Polk's nineteenth-century administration, when have the views of Latinos made a difference in how the United States has been constructed? The twenty-first century definitely will be different, but who can say in what ways?

Since 1929, when LULAC, the League of United Latin American Citizens, was founded in Corpus Christi, Spanish-speaking Americans have endeavored to establish dialogues with other Americans. Initially mainstream Americans heard conciliatory approaches, but after years of continued discrimination, the talk from the community became angry and rough, led by Chicano activists such as Cesar Chavez, Dolores Huerta, Reyes Tijerina, José Angel Gutiérrez, Willie Velasquez, Mario Compean, and others. But Anglos did not like that approach, and most of the Latino citizens were not sure of where that method of creating change would lead. But that has been our history, and one cannot easily refuse to recognize either reality. Activists who became too strident ended up being written off. And over the years, some conservatives have periodically continued to blame Hispanics for not pulling hard enough on our own bootstraps to reach the American Dream. But what can people do when the policies in place have been stacked against them and when the actions of the people in control keep communicating, in one way or another, a continued reluctance to help? If Latinos cannot find the type of employment that pays well enough, and if we cannot secure good employment because we have not received quality educations, then a better, quality education is clearly the place to start. With quality educations, Latinos ought to be able to begin to find better employment, better pay, and perhaps create better public policies that also provide more opportunities for more people.

Today we have an increasing number of Latinos who are beginning to vote conservative. Often I have wondered what exactly such voters are interested in conserving that we so badly want to keep. I mean, who is not interested in less taxes and in less government interference in our affairs? Not, to be sure, that the liberals do any more liberating for Latinos either. Indeed, between the promises of both parties, we remain perennially teased by the prospect of better educations, better jobs, better living and health conditions. But actually delivering on any of these promises, again, is forgotten, often even before the elections are over. At that point it is clear whom the candidates and the politicians, regardless of race or background, serve; and, it has not been the average Latino voter.

This is why the main agenda for Latinos has to be a quality education, though I know no one who would refuse political and social help in just about any area. The most pressing need, however, is for a good, high quality education, because we need to educate the young better than we ourselves were educated. How else are they going to be more successful, more competitive in the employment arena than our generation and the previous ones have been? The political parties have known about this need for sometime. That is why most Democratic and Republican candidates who visit the barrio communities always promise better educations. But politicians cannot actually deliver on that promise because most of them do not tend to understand the complexities of the education systems that have developed over the years. If we do not understand the education systems, which are designed to advance the norms and the values of society, Latinos will not be able to access local, state, and federal resources to provide the quality educations so desperately needed.

Long after the schools were legally required to welcome Spanish-speaking Americans following *Mendez v. Westminster* (1946) in California, and *Delgado v. Bastrop Independent School District* (1948) in Texas, Latinos have not fared too well. But the prospect continues to improve for the better. Unlike African Americans, we still have not yet developed a nationally recognized positive presence that everybody can point to with communal pride. Achievements tend to be individual triumphs, not the kind that include and raise a whole people. Other than the commonality of the Spanish language, Latinos are so different that we do not share a common culture, and most Latinos barely continue to survive in the big-city barrios and in rural America where they labor hard for very low wages. The years of neglect have essentially taught Latinos not to take the trouble to vote, and not to listen to the promises of politicians, which have not materialized in ways that can discernibly effect a difference. Like the Native American populations, Latinos often feel disenfranchised enough to stay home on Election Day, and that is the saddest comment one can make, given that Latinos are now the largest minority population.

Over the years, the more successful Latino politicians have shown us that we have had to learn how to fold our interests into larger interests and issues of American society. But doing so continues to make us invisible, or barely keeps us visible. Although I intensely dislike saying it, we remain America's field hands; custodial work, crop picking, and minimum-wage work are Hispanic mainstays. We work for white bosses, people will tell you. And when Latinos achieve success, they are seen as exceptions to the rule, as the models people understandably encourage the young to imitate. Affirmative Action should have provided us with more indoor, air-conditioned jobs, but, without proper education, forty years later, this always contentious, troubled federal program benefited some African Americans, and, after Nixon, mainly white women, leaving Latinos pretty much as outliers in American life and culture. To attempt to remind people of the nature of our lives, in the 1960s some Chicano activists, led primarily by César Chávez and Dolores Huerta in California, organized boycotts and marches. In Texas and the Southwest, La Raza Unida asked for social justice in the early 1970s. Immigration, NAFTA, and Henry Cisneros were part of the 1980s, and Victor Morales and Tony Sanchez more recently raised hopes again for Texas Latinos. Still, who will offer what Latinos need in order to contribute more to the United States?

For our votes, both parties are offering promises mixed with the usual platitudes. At what point will their words materialize into deeds? Hispanics badly want to believe that the candidates will actually do something good for Spanish-speakers every time there is an election. But Republican conservatives such as Linda Chávez, Richard Rodriguez, and Ward Connerly in California, and other Latinos who appear to want to disassociate themselves from the perceived problems that race, color, and ethnicities have given them in the past, continue believing that Affirmative Action cheapens the nature of their accomplishments. I do not believe that is the case. Like most minorities, a politician like Colin Powell supports Affirmative Action because he has seen that social change slows down considerably without it. The Democrats and the Republicans support education, but such "progress" has not substantially helped Latino students who continue to drop out of school in unacceptable rates.

Why should Latinos leave behind *lo propio,* that which has traditionally helped them to survive, in order to internalize values and social mores that have so widely failed to provide them with better housing, food, clothing, educations, and jobs? Republican principles of less government, tax cuts, and more privacy protections sharply contrast with Hispanic needs. But the Democrats do not offer anything that is substantially better. Despite talk to the contrary, I believe the fastest growing American minority population is still being bypassed. This fact continues to defy comprehension, since the way to raise America's standard of living is to provide better education and health coverage to the poor, and to provide it in ways that allow the poor to improve their lives.

Will "take care of your own, and let others do what they can" continue as the prevailing message and philosophy of the conventions again? In America, Spanish speakers, like African Americans, have to work twice as hard to be exceptions to the Latino norm; that is the way that some Latinos succeed. Otherwise laws, policies, and the social infrastructure can be reliably counted on to serve as obstacles that strangle Hispanic promise and hope. That is why most Latinos, young and old, are still being regularly turned off by the public schools, the media, and Anglo-American attitudes. But is anyone noticing and addressing these distressing realities? Too many Hispanics continue to live where their parents lived when the last No Mexicans Served signs quietly came down after World War II. No one wants to remember those disturbing placards. Yet, as a culture, we need to talk about a past that continues to shape Spanish-speaking Americans today, so that we can move forward, as the Latino sun rises over much of the United States.

President George W. Bush has repeatedly expressed an interest in increasing trade with Mexico, but that is also the mantra of Corporate America. How will such changes directly improve the lives of U.S. Latinos and Mexico? Shouldn't we all promote the types of education that will also upgrade how Latinos are universally seen? Who needs a two-prong Immigration and Naturalization Service when Mexican citizens should ethically have the same kind of relaxed borders that Canadians enjoy, despite the threats of terrorism? The question is: What can Bush or any future president do to help Latinos usher in a better future not only for the nearly 40 million Hispanics, but also, indeed, for all Americans? And when Mexico and Latin America were so clearly before us as part of our immediate future, why did we suddenly take a detour and go off to fight Iraq when the interests of the American people were in the western hemisphere? Who will give Latinos the special attention that is needed?

For special attention is exactly what Latinos require. Hispanics have lived elbowed out of American life since the United States defeated Mexico and took over the Spanish-speaking Southwest in 1848. That is more than 156 years of living, and constitutional fairness demands it. Will the Republicans and the Democrats address the real Latino situation? Today we need inclusion and provisioning. Nearly 40 million resident Latinos comprise too great a number of Americans to be disregarded any longer. There is no doubt that it is time for the political parties to offer Spanish-speaking citizens less rhetoric and more real opportunities. If Latinos do not participate in the political process, perhaps it is because candidates are still not offering anything that makes us want to go to the polls on Election Day.

36

Batos Locos

Batos Locos can have great fun, and occasionally I encourage Mexican Americans to act out such roles, especially when a break from routine can help establish some feel-good, therapeutic parameters when around those who don't grant Latinos much cultural space. Nonetheless, being a Bato Loco all the time, weekends, and five days a week, I found out pretty early in life, is a tremendously limiting experience. For playing such a role, that is, conjuring up and sustaining a proper Bato Loco persona, can keep young Latinos from developing and from working on many other personality matters that require encouragement. Latinos are as diverse and as multifaceted as any other group of people in the United States, yet by representing ourselves mainly as Batos Locos I think we consciously limit our potential and diminish our future prospects. By choosing to portray ourselves only in ways that establish rapport with other Batos Locos, we dispense with shaping and defining ourselves in the mature ways that will benefit our families and our younger generations.

I am bringing out an observation that I know is likely to upset some Mexican Americans, while others may applaud the effort. My objective, however, is not to alienate, not to separate Hispanics into factions, or to create problems or animosity for anyone. I wish to point out that being a Bato Loco or any other version of what some people may think is the archetypal or typical Chicano or Mexican American is only one way of being a Latino in the United States. Since we now have a population of well over 38.4 million Spanish-speaking people in the country, everyone knows that Latinos depict and represent themselves in a variety of ways, in keeping with First Amendment rights. Having made the point about Latino diversity yet again, though, I think we can leave the rest to the type of dialogue that I am hopeful will develop when people consider how Latinos can best represent themselves. Since sufficient Latino models are not abundant, and since the media have not helped by championing enough Latino figures to emulate, how we consciously shape and depict ourselves to others is an important issue warranting discussion.

I believe that we Latinos need to sort out how we should be encouraging our young people to present themselves. The goal, I believe, increasingly ought to be to become more comfortable with ourselves as we grow and develop in the United States. What do you think, reader?

37

El Día de los Muertos
in the United States

Most of us are unaware that commemorating the Day of the Dead, which is known as *El Día de los Muertos* in Mexico and in most Latin American countries, began to be observed more widely in the United States in the 1970s. Before that, Spanish-speaking Americans kept El Día de los Muertos more to themselves. The day follows the November 1 All Saints Day, which is a Catholic holy day of obligation. November 2 in Mexico and in most other Latin American countries has traditionally been set aside to visit and to maintain the family cemetery plots, spending the time in activities specifically designed to remember deceased family members. Families cook special foods, clean the cemetery tombs and headstones, and often prepare or redecorate home altars built to commemorate the memory of departed relatives and close friends. In Mexican society, as Octavio Paz and other writers have brought out, the responsibility of maintaining close kinship with departed family members, of course, rests with the living. The purpose of this commemoration, which is actually a celebration of life, is to remind everyone that death awaits all of us, that no one escapes it, regardless of position in life. El Día de los Muertos encourages people to reconcile themselves to that final inevitability.

Although no anthropologist or historian has been able to document conclusively where the commemoration of the dead began, it is believed that El Día de los Muertos originated with the Amerindian people. Likely it was the Aztecs or one of their predecessors, like the Toltecs or one of the many other indigenous tribes that inhabited Mexico and the Mesoamerican Yucatán region before Hernando Cortés arrived near present-day Veracruz, Mexico, with his Spanish soldiers of fortune in 1519. Since the Spanish conquerors characterized the practices of the indigenous people as pagan observances, the Catholic Church initially tried to wipe out most of the social, cultural, and religious rituals of the Aztec people and their surrounding neighbors. But when it became clear that the identity of the native people was intimately connected with the customs they observed and celebrated, the Church wisely recognized that people's beliefs could not be summarily changed, much less eradicated. What the Church did was to replace the native customs and practices with Christian religious festivities. Today El Día de los Muertos is both a Mexican holiday as well as a day set aside to remember the souls of the deceased.

Although November the second has been observed as the Day of the Dead by Catholic Latinos since the Southwest was a part of Spain and later Mexico, El Día de los Muertos, as now commemorated in most of the larger American cities, acquired a new significance during the 1970s. This reinvigoration of an old practice occurred because in the period following the Civil Rights Act of 1964, passed when Lyndon B. Johnson was president, Mexican Americans and other Latinos started looking for occasions and historical events that would allow us to identify ourselves better in the United States. Spanish-speaking Americans had been politically constructed by the signing of the Treaty of Guadalupe Hidalgo, which ended the two-year U.S. war with Mexico in 1848. But, even then, most Mexican Americans and Latinos residing in the United States were not seen as regular American citizens until World War II allowed Mexican Americans to show the world that they were also being decorated for bravely sacrificing their lives for the United States. That is, even though Spanish-speaking Americans have taken part in constructing and defending state and federal American sovereignty since before 1848, only now are U.S. Latinos beginning to enjoy full citizenship rights.

To help accord the nearly 40 million Latinos living in the United States a fuller measure of recognition and to celebrate one of the customs traditionally observed in Mexico and Latin America, Mexican Americans and other U.S. Latinos began to highlight El Día de los Muertos in the 1970s. I reiterate this watershed decade because in the 1950s and 60s, the two decades when I grew up, El Día de los Muertos as a public day for commemoration was not widely observed as a secular feast day by most American Latinos. Some families who consciously endeavored to maintain Mexican customs and practices, I remember, customarily went to mass on that day, and they visited the cemetery plots where relatives were buried, erecting, also, home altars to recall the lives of their dead. But, for the most part, November 2 would not have been widely recognized as El Día de los Muertos, as it is increasingly known today, according to a master's thesis completed in 1999 in the anthropology department at Texas A&M University by a friend, Hillary Standish.

El Cinco de Mayo and *El Diez y Seis de Septiembre* are the two other imported holidays that in the last twenty-five years Latinos have begun observing as a way to make ourselves more visible and better known in the United States. Part of the problem is that without these three days of celebration and observances in some U.S. Latino communities, Spanish-speaking Americans would not have any culturally significant day that would connect us to our roots. We do, of course, celebrate the Fourth of July and the other regular American holidays, but during the last quarter-century Latinos have felt we need some events and occasions that are distinctly Hispanic *también*. Irish Americans, for example, observe St. Patrick's Day, and as Americans we now commemorate the birthday of Martin Luther King, Jr. as a national holiday. So U.S. Latinos are now beginning to mull over the significance of these three Mexican feast days. If not for these days, what nationally known event or observance would remind the world of the large Latino presence in the United States?

El Día de los Muertos is useful in other ways, too, for we all owe debts for advantages daily enjoyed to the people who have gone before us. It is psychically good and honorable to set aside a special national day to remember relatives, friends, and other people who have helped us and who are no longer living to celebrate the progress that individually and communally we are making to shape a better life for ourselves and our progeny.

The United States is a country that has traditionally been sympathetic to the holidays of other countries, and, as the years pass, I hope more Americans will begin to see the wisdom of observing El Día de los Muertos. The indigenous people of Mesoamerica who consciously chose not to forget and to remain connected to the dearly departed started a great idea. Personally, I believe that a national day of mourning for family members and friends who helped us grow and develop would serve all Americans well. Setting aside at least one day of the year to honor and to remember significant people who helped us become what we are would show our maturity as a society and civilization.

38

Regarding a Mexican American Holiday

A friend and colleague stopped by my office the other day to continue what has become our life-long discussion regarding the stagnant state of Latino issues in the United States. We were to have a meeting with other Mexican American community leaders to discuss *El Cinco de Mayo* plans for downtown Bryan, Texas. Since my colleague is a historian, I asked him if we have a Mexican American holiday or feast day that could be celebrated regionally or nationally. We celebrate Cinco de Mayo, I explained, with fanfare and festivities to honor the brave military victory of the Mexican people against the French army in 1862 in the famous Battle of Puebla. We also observe El Diez y Seis de Septiembre, we reminded each other, the Mexican Independence Day, which Chicanos celebrate yearly to commemorate Padre Miguel Hidalgo y Costilla's *Grito de Dolores,* much as we celebrate the Fourth of July in the United States. With the Cry of the town of Dolores, Father Miguel Hidalgo demanded Mexico's independence from Spain in 1810, as previously stated. Also, aside from the day on which each city, town, and village in Mexico celebrates its patron saint, the two main religious holidays are *El Doce de Diciembre,* December the twelfth, when La Virgen de Guadalupe's 1531 appearance to Juan Diego is widely remembered, and El Día de los Muertos. All of these holidays, I summed up, are Mexican days of celebration that we respect and proudly honor. But, do we have one comparable Mexican American day, as other ethnic groups do in the United States?

Well, he said, I guess we don't, at least not days that we can properly call Mexican American feast days or holidays. The closest day we might have would be February the second, when the Treaty of Guadalupe Hidalgo was signed in that Mexican town by the same name outside of Mexico City. The 1848 Treaty of Guadalupe Hidalgo, as stated, is the agreement that ended the 1846 war with Mexico that President Polk started because he believed that the idea of Manifest Destiny gave him the right to secure the northwestern lands of Mexico for the United States. This treaty effectively created Americans citizens out of the Mexican people who lived in the southwestern states of New Mexico, Arizona, California, and the southern parts of Nevada, Utah, and Colorado. A year after the treaty was signed, the Mexican citizens who inhabited the 55 percent of the lands that Mexico was forced to cede over to the United States in 1848 for the sum of 15 million dollars became American citizens if they still resided on their now American lands.

Or, then again, I added, we might regionally celebrate March 6, the day the Alamo fell, since some Mexican Americans also fought in the Alamo against the Mexican troops of General Santa Anna. If this day were selected, such a Texas holiday could be celebrated with accompanying explanations. Indeed, our seldom articulated, little-known history would have to be explained to the world, for Mexican American history and culture need to be better understood, particularly in light of the fact that there are now more Latinos in the United States than the 31 plus million Canadians now residing in Canada.

This brief explanation ought to clarify why Mexican Americans are quite different from the citizens of Mexico, as well as why Mexican Americans are usually not seen as regular Americans and are often mistaken for being Mexicans by other American citizens. In the 1970s, Mexican Americans and other Latinos began to celebrate El Cinco de Mayo, El Diez y Seis de Septiembre, and El Día de los Muertos, Mexican holidays, because Mexican Americans and U.S. Latinos do not have any other known day that is celebrated. Again, we are proud of our Mexican and other Latino backgrounds and cultures, but as Spanish-speaking people living in the lands that became part of the United States after 1848, we do have a different history that is strangely absent from the consciousness of American society.

We could, of course, celebrate the birth of César Estrada Chávez, the leader of the farm workers, but then, when Chávez was alive, Mexican Americans and farm workers did not all embrace his views and practices. This is a fact that seems to have been forgotten: that even though Chávez was an inspiring leader for many Latinos, he actually had difficulty securing the full support of the farm workers themselves, particularly in states outside of California. According to Peter Matthiessen, who wrote *Sal Si Puedes: César Chávez and the New American Revolution* (1969), Chávez was born on March 31, 1927, on: "160 acres of sage and mesquite desert in the North Gila River Valley about twenty miles northeast of Yuma [Arizona], part of which he [his father] built carefully into a farm." The Chávezes lost their land about ten years later and the family moved to California where César Chávez eventually attracted national attention for courageously advancing the interests of the people who picked the crops in the agricultural fields. Today, The National Council of La Raza and other Hispanic groups have been moving toward requesting Congress to declare a national César Chávez holiday, just as the third Monday of January is now the official holiday that celebrates the birth and life of Dr. Martin Luther King, Jr. It turns out that, by coincidence, March 31 is also the day that Selena, the Mexican American Queen of Tejano music, died in 1995.

Rosa Parks is rightly credited for bravely refusing to give up her bus seat to a white male passenger in 1955. But do most Americans know that César Chávez and Helen Fabela, his future wife, "were arrested in Delano for sitting on the wrong side of the segregated movie theater and refusing to move" ten years before, in 1945? That event, like much of the rest of the history of Mexican Americans in the United States, has never received media attention, and, it is doubtful whether those records are still available. Indeed, all sorts of records exist that document other acts of courage as well as civil disobedience, but what would bringing out such facts prove? Mainly what we already know: the extent to which Mexican Americans have been left out of the American story.

So, we Mexican Americans observe the American holidays, too, some of us very patriotically, others less so, and still others not at all, I suspect, for reasons that people believe obvious. Following the Civil Rights Act of 1964, which, in effect, is an uncelebrated watershed date also for the Spanish-speaking people of the United States, we have progressively embraced Mexico's holidays primarily because they were observed by our parents, grandparents, and ancestors in the old country. Since we do not have a single Mexican American day that is commemorated by the rest of the country, how else can Mexican Americans nourish self-esteem to promote and encourage positive, future activities of young Latinos? But, is that true? We do not have *one* single day? Come on, there must be at least one day somewhere out of the 365 days of the year? My friend and I thought about it, but that was the way it looked, the last time we spoke. But we are always ready to hear what other people think.

What is certain is that people communally or individually choose to commemorate some days and not others. We remember Pearl Harbor, for instance, because that "Day of Infamy," as President Roosevelt called it, served to rally the United States against Japan during World War II. History has its uses, as some historians liked to point out. We can choose to remember some events, and we can choose to forget others. That much is clear.

39

War in Iraq

The war in Iraq reminds me of one of the three trees that we have in our backyard. When we were building the house in Bryan, our family would walk about five blocks from the home that we were renting to the site where we were building. For a year, we rented from an African American colleague who was away on a sabbatical at Harvard between 1991 and 1992. During a six or seven month period, we saw the corner property we bought transformed from a weedy lot covered here and there with hardy, wild berry vines over which the evening breeze blew to part of a residential area for newer residents like yours truly. Even today I still find roots of the wild, thornylike berry strands, mostly in the spring, mixed along with the roots of the St. Augustine grass, both having made their peace with each other, though lawn grass now covers most of the square footage of the home lot. Before the area was turned into a residential subdivision, I understand that neighbors used to walk over to pick some of the wild berries that grew in the area, but that community practice has now gone by the wayside since the bulldozers changed the land for residential living.

When the construction crew built our house, preparing the land to pour the concrete for the foundation and the landscape to insure proper drainage, like all new homeowners watching the progress of their abode, we saw our little corner of the world daily transformed into our home. Once construction begins, though, so many things happen at the same time in a very coordinated way, that it is difficult to pay attention to everything that different companies and workers contribute to building a new house. The plumbing, I learned, has to be prepared right after the land is leveled and certainly before the foundation is poured, after which a variety of carpenters show up to do their part, followed by the electricians, the sprinkling-setting team, the landscapers, and other workers.

In the well-coordinated activities with which workers carry out their tasks, it is difficult to watch all the particulars, so much is being done simultaneously. I make this observation because, although I tried to follow what different workers were engaged in, I now have to confess that I did not see the kind of decisions that, of course, one learns about only after one has lived in a home a few years. At any rate, I have written these rather long prefatory remarks to bring out that among the points I did not fully notice was the planting of three trees in the backyard behind the house. There, I asked that two elm trees be planted, and one afternoon, my wife and I went out about four in the afternoon and pointed to where we wanted the trees planted. About five years later, I planted a burr oak myself to the north of those elms and that constitutes the three trees planted in that place.

My reason for connecting these trees to the war in Iraq is philosophical. When the two elms were planted, I did not notice that one of them, the one in the middle of the three trees, was not planted by the workers sufficiently deep so that it could grow straight and tall like the other one. Indeed, after more than ten years, the tree that was not planted deeply enough is shorter, and, although I have since propped it up with three black hard rubber stakes, it still leans more than I like toward the house.

Now, when I began to notice that the tree's roots had not been planted deeply enough so that it would not lean toward the house, the tree was still young and short enough that I could have pulled it out and replanted it. But uncertain about how to proceed with that option, I dawdled. By the time I considered transplanting the tree to the northeast side of the back yard, at about eight feet tall the tree was already taller than me. Thinking that I could accomplish that task on a weekend, I took my shovel and my good intentions and set out to perform the job. It was a nice summer day, so I thought I would first dig out a new place of about four or five feet across and about four feet deep for the roots of the elm. Before doing so, I went to the elm and noticed that the tree had been planted shallow enough so that if I took the trunk with my right hand, I could move or wiggle the tree about half an inch back and forth. I had done so once before when I first noticed that the tree was not planted deeply enough, and, indeed, it was in so doing that I had encouraged myself to consider transplanting it. However, when I began to dig at the earth about five feet away from the trunk, although the surrounding sod was initially moist, I began to see the chore differently. It soon became clear that pulling out what I thought was a little tree and then replanting it at a better, more appropriate depth would amount to quite an undertaking.

I began to realize that I would have to dig out a circle of about ten feet all the way around the tree first. This meant I would have to dig another ten- to twelve-foot area where I intended to plant the elm. At this point it struck me that to do so I would have to dig about four or five feet into the ground to provide what I figured would be sufficient space for the roots. After digging a little and noticing that three or four inches into the earth the ground was suddenly harder than the soil at the top, I began to think differently about the whole operation. I soon saw that moving even the smaller elm tree would require a considerably larger effort than I had anticipated. I began to contemplate the idea of hiring a tree-removal company with the proper equipment, which would mean paying several experienced workers who would doubtlessly arrive with a well thought-out plan, all certainly requiring more time, effort, and money than I first believed. As I said, initially I had thought that I would devote the greater part of a weekend to digging a hole where I wanted the elm. Digging out the elm, and moving it (two distinctly different operations), with some help, perhaps from my son or a neighbor, would be the next step, before transplanting it securely in its new place. However, given my first rather slow attempts, it became clear that such an undertaking would be considerably more difficult than I thought. Certainly it would take more time than I was prepared to spend.

Today I have gradually resigned myself to looking at the leaning middle elm tree. It is now more than ten feet tall. I have rather reluctantly developed a healthy respect for the tree, since, even though I well know that it was not initially planted deep enough, it is nevertheless alive and continues to grow. Every spring, in fact, it brings out its leaves about a week sooner than the taller, well-planted elm. That little tree oddly reminds me of the war in Iraq, a country that, time is increasingly telling us, we might best have left alone. Things do not always turn out as we want them to. Still, we develop rationales for most things—until we learn or hear otherwise. Whenever we have strong winds brought on by the remnants of a Gulf hurricane or a northern that might bring some serious rain or even hail, I notice that the elm tree appears to lean a little more. But, having tried to remove it once, as we tried to correct Iraq during Desert Storm, I know that we cannot easily change the world to suit our tastes. Perhaps other natural forces may someday accomplish what my elm tree taught me to respect.

40

Thanksgiving Idyll

When the turkey, the capons, the stuffing, and the *camotes,* or sweet potatoes, are in the oven, when the proverbial abundance of food, undreamt of in the poorer third world countries, is ready, I go to the toaster about eleven in the morning and take two nice-sized chomps from the toast left over from the morning breakfast. The Thanksgiving dinner is part of the afternoon's festivities, but, by eleven, and with so much food around, I become so extraordinarily hungry that only a few big bites of the morning's left-over toast will temporarily ease that totally unexplainable hunger that on such festive days actually appears to eat at our spirit.

Then, five or six hours later, when I have finished eating and there is still too much food left in the house, I again choose only our daily bread. Doing so for some strange reason allows me to savor the dry, crumbling bread more than the dinner. On purpose, I avoid everything since breakfast at seven. By eleven or near noon, the two bites into a four-hour-old piece of simple wheat bread, *sans* butter, tastes superb. The practice underscores the primacy of bread, reminding me on this day of thanks of the fact that sometimes not enough of these morsels are available to the world's indigent. Tonight the ten o'clock news will offer glimpses of the homeless here and faraway people elsewhere who did not have what the rest of us lucky Americans had in abundance today. There is so much want and sadness, even in the United States. Still, Thanksgiving deserves to be widely choreographed as our well-earned, national day of thanks.

At the moment, I capture, photolike, our Thanksgiving scene. I try to record, in words, the happiness we are enjoying, amid the thought of people who feel particularly distressed on days like today. Happiness, properly mollified—that is Thanksgiving at home for me.

Thanksgiving postpones work for another day. The opportunity to stay home with family and friends has to be seized and thoroughly appreciated; it will not last forever. Good that society collectively prescribes such days.

Everyone can hypothetically do as he or she likes on this special day, yet most people choose to enjoy the company of family, friends, human beings who make us feel good about ourselves. Given the hard work that people daily carry out, today the very air brims with the consequential elements of our lives.

41

The Idea of a Mexican American/ Latino Exhibit

One Christmas Eve, First of the New Century

The night before Christmas Eve, several of us met at the house of Armando and Angelita to enjoy a few hours of good fellowship, as we have been doing for the last few years. Angelita, who recently painted the inside of her house with the most attractive Mexican bright colors that I can think of, à la Frida Kahlo (1907–1954), had been to my home town in Edinburg. Although she is from Mercedes, I believe she has an aunt or a relative in Edinburg, and she had returned with some great tamales that took me back to my childhood. I love tamales with the hottest green chile sauce I can find. After eating and exchanging remarks about our health, illnesses we have heard about in friends and acquaintances, and the progress and latest difficulties of our children, several of us began to talk about a subject that we have been discussing for a number of years. Led by Armando, a number of us have been talking about creating a traveling Mexican American exhibit that would bring national and regional attention to the presence of the Spanish-speaking people in the southwestern part of the United States. We have talked about the merits, but mainly about the difficulties of bringing together such materials, items that would highlight the last 480 plus years, that is, the time that has elapsed since Hernando Cortés conquered the Aztec empire.

Although the undertaking would require enormous effort on the part of many people at all sorts of levels and positions throughout the Southwest, including the national capitol, the need for such a useful recapitulation of the history of U.S. Hispanics is undeniable. Our group, at any rate, is convinced that in light of the changing demographics, nothing less than such an undertaking will do, if people in this country are going to have a good and true appreciation of the nature of the Latino contribution. Historians, anthropologists, and other scholars may know where such materials can be found. But, by and large, the rest of the American population knows very little about the nature of the lives and the contributions of the Spanish-speaking population to the history of the United States, especially in the vast southwestern region.

We spoke about the difficulties of initiating this daunting project, some of us saying that perhaps we should focus attention on the nineteenth and twentieth centuries only, either of which by themselves or together would certainly be challenging. But what about the eighteenth, seventeenth, and sixteenth centuries, others insisted, including yours truly. In order to provide exhibit-goers with a clear and better sense of the trajectory of the whole Hispanic/Latino/Mexican American history and presence, it would be necessary to think about how best to highlight the history of the region for the last five hundred years. Otherwise, several of us proposed, people would only have a truncated and skewed sense of the nature of the civilizations that have inhabited the large southwestern area. The terrain would include the current states of Texas, New Mexico, Arizona, California, and the southwestern, more Latino populated parts of Utah, Nevada, and Colorado.

This area was sold for 15 million dollars to the United States following the termination of the two-year war that President Polk waged against Mexico between 1846 and 1848. As in the case of the Louisiana Purchase, which President Jefferson bought in 1803 for the exact same amount, this vast southwestern territory actually comprised 55 percent of the land that Mexico owned at the time. I mention these facts not to lament a loss, as some people may suppose. Rather, such a history and the fact that Christianity was not introduced into the New World until the early sixteenth century, among other events, have significantly shaped the culture clashes that continue to prevail in the geopolitical areas widely recognized as the American Southwest.

The next day, the Texas newspapers carried the following Associated Press story: Readers were informed that the Bexar County Clerk is engaged in a struggle with the University of Texas-Austin central library over San Antonio's old Spanish records during the period before the Alamo indelibly benchmarked Texas history in 1836. A few historians know that this material exists, but no one has apparently brought out that treasure trove of materials in a way that compels unforgettable attention. I mention this information here to inform readers that this is a subject worth unearthing and disseminating to the four winds.

42

A New Language

S ometimes I dream of a language that employs well-used words to say
what needs saying, without, however, imposing upon the views and
beliefs of another person. I seek not only a utilitarian language, since there
is beauty in the idea, but words that are not ornate, or fanciful, but simple,
true, and appropriate, which is to say elegant and yet hardy. At such times I
look for a different rhetoric, one that does away with the fact that all languages are signs of communication. Human beings sometimes employ signs
to lay burdensome perspectives on other, less fortunate persons, who, for
one reason or another, do not know how to defend themselves, suffering
the consequences of seemingly innocuous but ill-intended words. The language I envision would not be prosaic, although it would have the common run-of-the-mill ways of signaling what we daily need, driven by human
desires. Such an encyclopedia of words would be used with precision, grace,
but most of all with sincere consideration, employed to discuss subjects
worth listening to and illuminating us, improving the world. Some days I
long for views illuminating novel ways of living and worthwhile ways of
thinking. We particularly need goals that require achieving, it being easier
these days to move in and to fit into a groove before spouting the restric-
tive, constraining words that almost all professions suavely practice.

Learning how to become an accountant, a physician, a lawyer, a blue-
collar worker, a secretary, or anything else connected with being a specialist
to earn a living requires learning a different language. But when a person
invests time in becoming something different, who can tell the result? Since
real improvements are difficult to invent in the United States, current practices ought to be studied and weighed. That would require true work. What
many of us have are similar mental pictures of what professional people do
and what they should be doing. Left alone, the great majority of people are
not going to discomfort themselves. Why should they? What would the gain
be for them? Students of many businesses today spend most of their time
concerned with the proper mannerisms, what cynics call the tricks of a trade.
When problems arise, we watch for the responses that the training and the

apprenticeships have taught. Often we see that is not enough, that we are measuring the wrong things, that we do not have a full appreciation for some of the things that really count, like love, friendship, family, religious scruples, weathering tough times, securing an education, and helping people in need every day of our lives.

The language I envision would begin by encouraging, insisting, or requiring students of all disciplines to spend a year, two, or three looking at how people in the field they would follow practice their business. The idea would not be to imitate, emulate, or to follow the best, leading practitioners, as students are naturally inclined or instructed to. The idea would be to work respectfully, sympathetically, and with understanding toward improving the actual substance, not the styles, and, most important, the actual languages of their professions.

These high-minded, idealistic propositions, I confess, appear attractive mainly because I think it is time to reintroduce what is desirable, especially when we endeavor to provide students of life with clearer purposes, purposes other than simply making money. Too long have people labored and lived without voicing ideas that might change lives, without motivating true leaders, leaving all of us to settle for what we see, for what is everywhere around us.

I would like to see a new race of human beings aware of how everything is related and interconnected. We need a new concern for how we might reconstitute society's infrastructure so that things might be made to work better for everyone, for the general welfare, instead of only for the few who have learned how to make the system work mainly for themselves. The U.S. Constitution is the greatest of documents, if only the courts were to follow what it says without changing the meaning of the words here or there. In a democracy like ours, I believe people need to be placed at the center of our interests, not businesses, people, not corporate interests. Goals and activities would then change, arise, and develop from such new centers.

American society has tried it otherwise since before the end of World War II. We have long been placing business and material interests at the center of our lives. Today, people simply do not matter much any more. The products manufactured by the companies we buy stock in end up being considerably more important than any one single human being. Hundreds of people can easily be recruited and persuaded, by paying them, to make commercials to which there is no personal or ethical connection. We need only to pay attention to how the young look at and treat people to see how dispensable and replaceable human beings are. Unfortunately, we have brought up the young to feel and to live by this distressing philosophy. They believe that their ways of being and thinking are correct, that how they see and deal with other people is fine, even natural, and no calls for changes are needed. Why should they? We ourselves do not even nudge them otherwise.

Being young is great, but youth is ephemeral, like all the material things we are encouraged to pursue. Flux, perennial flux is the one constant in our lives. Accordingly, when treated or seen in this fashion, people, too, fluctuate, appearing to become interchangeable. We morph into one another, and our technology celebrates that achievement. Individuality, the personal perspective and the personal attribute—how do we evaluate these contributions? Through surveys and polls, social scientists have effectively taught us that no one view is better than any other. But do we really believe that? Surveys are everywhere employed to help create and to justify laws and the policies that shape our lives, channeling and promoting certain realities, supposedly matching what people want and would like to see. Profits motivate too many companies and households in the United States and throughout the world, ruining many human lives adversely impacted in one way or another. People ought always to be considered first and foremost, not products and not profits. Through education we should strive to center anew the value and the importance of people above transitory things. Products and profits change, losing their significance. People stay and accrue or decline in perceived value.

43

Year-End Thoughts

It has been a good while since I have written anything more of these beachfront and backyard idylls. So much has happened that I now understand why, one day, when he was in the woods, Hawthorne despaired of ever writing again. One brings such high expectations to the task, being full of life and excellent intentions, but the writing product in the black and white of the words left in the *taraya,* the *chinchorro,* the net, sometimes discourage one from picking up the pen when the sun rises the following day.

Despite my better plans, there is still so much that has been left unsaid, so many subjects and issues I have not brought out or even alluded to in this work. All events and occasions are simply part of the rhythm of life, wherever one is, whether close to the edge of the Gulf, deep in the sagebrush country of the cities along the Rio Grande, in the larger cities like Houston, Austin, San Antonio, or Dallas, in rural central Texas, California, or elsewhere. I am, again, flying from LaGuardia returning to Houston's Intercontinental. I have been attending an academic conference in New York for the last several days. One afternoon, I went to Melville's watery shores, to see the Statue of Liberty with my family for the first time. I have "seen a lot," the Chicano poet Evangelina Vigil said, and everything depends on what we make of the life that we experience.

The airline captain has wished everyone a Happy New Year, and yes, I am very thankful for everything that I have experienced. When one is among one's kind, among one's people, one easily adjusts. I spent four years in graduate school at SUNY Buffalo, five years teaching as an Assistant Professor of English at the University of California-Berkeley, eleven at the University of Houston–Clear Lake, and now more than twelve years at Texas A&M. Although most people would say that I am well adapted, that I have proven I can feel at home in a variety of locales, I have learned that non-Latinos find it hard to warm up to ethnic people like myself. Occasionally here and there, yes, I have found good friends, but on the whole, living in the United States can be and often is difficult for Latinos. It is certainly a cultural issue, one shaped by our different educations, a matter of how we are brought up, a matter of with whom we feel comfortable. From that standpoint, all of our educations fail because they do not teach us to like, to feel comfortable with, and to appreciate people who are not like the people that we ourselves are. When we begin to encourage each other to live and to enjoy each other's company, at that point we will be on our way to better relations with people who are different. Not before.

And I do not think the issue is a matter of perspective. This is the response elicited from many Anglo people. I have seen the interaction among the different races of people in this country for many years while engaged in work and play activities, and I just don't see the warmth that Latinos tend to exhibit for one another. I invariably establish better relations with other kinds of ethnic Americans, be they Italians, Jews, blacks, Greeks, or of some other ethnicity. For all their education and civility, people can be very gracious to people of other races, but the difficulties appear when the challenge is to establish long-term relationships. At that point, many people tend to gravitate toward their own kind, where they feel comfortable. To do otherwise requires a real education, a real effort. Yet changing the ways that people relate to and deal with each other, regardless of differences, is not what our children are provided with every day in the schools.

On the radio the other morning, I heard that the Russian government is allowing fifty Russian immigrants in the United States—the largest number ever, said the newscaster—to return to Russia. The expressed reason given by the people who chose to return of their own accord was, America for Americans and Russia for Russians. This is a sorry, but unfortunately a quite commonly held perspective. Although, of course, one can talk about different ways to see this development, the bottom line is that the Russians wanted to return to Russia to be among people they know, even when they know that life will be harder for them in Russia in the aftermath of the cold war.

Such feelings, people will say, are a function of the person, of the many factors that go into creating the different personalities we all develop. Several years ago, I called at 9:30 a.m. to see if I could stop in to see the president and chief executive officer of the New York Public Library. Vartan Gregorian was my European History professor when I was an undergraduate at the University of Texas–Austin from 1968 to 1970. Even though I had not been in touch with him for eleven years, I had periodically caught word of his continued academic successes. Since graduating, I had only seen him once, when he gave the convocation speech commemorating the tenth anniversary of the University of Houston–Clear Lake in 1981. On reintroducing myself, however, he said he recalled me, one of thousands of his former students. That is the kind of impact power that the different student has, I remember saying to myself. People may not recall particulars about the different student, but they will remember something. We met after the reception at the local Nassau Bay Hilton by the lake, and, being gracious and generous, he invited me to visit him sometime in New York. One recent May, I wrote to tell him that I would be in town in December, and, after a busy, trying year I showed up at his door.

Part of the regard we have held for each other despite the years is based on the fact that as a former mentor he always gave me the space to be myself. He could have used his distinguished position and role otherwise, of course, but anybody who knows him knows that is not his style. He showed me a satchel bag with over three hundred letters, which, he said, he needed to answer. He was behind in his correspondence, but he nevertheless asked me about my pursuits, about what I hoped to do for the Mexican American student population of the great Southwest. I took a good twenty minutes of his time and could have talked for hours, but knowing that he would not hasten me out, I told him I had enjoyed our visit and left.

New York can be wonderfully exciting and frustrating. The place constantly enacts multidimensional scenes practicing that most venerated of American goals: making money. If there is money to be made, some enterprising New Yorker is at it. As I rode up Fifth Avenue and later down Seventh, I looked from the bus at the faces of the people on the streets. Everyone has a program, everyone is executing his or her purpose. The types of people, languages, and the signaling going on in the streets was visible everywhere. The grocer, watering his sidewalk, like the cop, the accountant, the city-wise kid, everyone was mainly engaged in doing what advances his or her agenda. I thought of Walt Whitman's love and acceptance for the foibles and accomplishments of everyone, and saw why Whitman, among writers, stays with us when we visit New York and when we think of what America could be. Everyone should be accepted for what he or she is, I said to myself again. Everyone I saw, with the exception of several down-and-out homeless people, who pained me, was up and doing. Unusually vibrant and accompanied by crisp 35-degree weather, everything was of a piece. It was wonderfully exhilarating to see New Yorkers about their business, sad as some of that business is.

Then I thought of the Rio Grande Valley. I focused attention on the education that we are providing for our little Chicanitos in Texas, and the education being served up to minorities everywhere in this country and abroad. Could the disenfranchised, ethnic people of America and elsewhere hope to make it in the teeming, competitive world that the twenty-first century is? That, I said anew, is why drugs and crime appeal to people with few viable prospects. Since we do not seriously invest in changing their futures, we can only expect more of the same. But if we were to approach Latino youths differently, perhaps they could help us achieve the full potential of the United States. Everything depends, I added, on what we do with our time, on whether we opt to do something good for everyone.

44

What Latinos Want

I wrote "Urban Renewal on the Hometown Block in Edinburg," the first and the one previously published piece in this volume, because I felt adrift after being summarily disconnected from everything that had been important during the first twenty years of my family's life. South Texas offered few career options for me, a reality that has not significantly changed for Latinos in Texas or elsewhere. Despite numerous pleas made every biennial legislative session from the citizens of the area for a few professional schools, for more education options, really for anything that will advance the social and economic livelihood of the citizens, the area is mainly interested in benefiting corporate America, from all the signs. This means that a few desirable jobs exist, but, by and large, the Valley is still in a minimum wage or low hourly pay environment. People manage to succeed mainly by leaving South Texas, by exploring prospects like the ones that I have described in these pages in other parts of the United States. Yet in mulling over the writing concerning the different doors on which life has made me knock in pursuit of a livelihood, I have gradually noticed a larger significance to my experiences.

Following the little diaspora of the neighbors who made up the barrio world of my youth, a bothersome suspicion gradually told me that the American side of my bilingual universe meant to deliver me a punishing blow intended to knock the Mexican American out of my way of life. Relations in South Texas between Anglos and the Mexican population, as writers have brought out, have not been as smooth and as Pollyanna-like as the schools taught us. Still, people generally respect each other and accept the separateness of their worlds, much as whites and blacks have uneasily learned to live in the South. I have lived through the civil rights movement, initially feeling jubilant that the world was on the verge of changing tomorrow and tomorrow and *mañana*. But that expectancy dims as changes continue to affect Latinos tangentially. More than forty years have gone by since John F. Kennedy was our hope, since César Chávez marched for the agricultural workers in California, and since Martin Luther King, Jr. uttered his famous words about seeing the mountaintop. The Supreme Court has lately reiterated the *Bakke* decision of 1978 supporting the recognition and the limited use of race in college admissions decisions, but the conservative criticisms continue. Affirmative Action, they say, unconstitutionally favors blacks and Latinos over whites. But in *Grutter* (June, 2003), the Supreme Court said that states have compelling interests in using race to obtain the educational benefits provided by diverse student bodies.

To make the decision more palatable, though, Justice Sandra Day O'Connor, the deciding vote supporting the *Bakke* position within *Grutter,* stipulated that she hopes within twenty-five years there will not be a need for Affirmative Action. Although I would like to believe that, I have doubts. For I have noticed that a number of the citizens who are most strongly opposed to considering race as a plus factor in applicants are in their twenties. In twenty-five years they will be in their forties and fifties, and, unless a concerted effort is made to change such thinking, why should things change? Without effective education in this area, we can only expect more of the same. In "A Dynamic Theory of History" (1904) in *The Education* (1907), Henry Adams said that the idea that "society educated itself" is a "fiction." Indeed, how can a goal in education be accomplished if its purpose is not clearly expressed and then consciously pursued?

During all of these years, I have remained discomfited about so-called social and economic improvements that have blatantly or subtly promoted the maintenance of the status quo for Latinos and other minority populations. I have always wanted to see the livelihoods of U.S. Spanish-speakers, blacks, Asian, and Native Americans improved because it is only by doing so that we are going to raise the quality of life for all Americans. Life in the United States should not be about preferring or favoring some groups of people at the cost or at the expense of others. Well-connected interest groups should not prevail at the expense of the common citizen. Such groups should not succeed in having the laws and the public policies of this country written mainly to promote their interests. Such interests are then expected to be borne on the backs of common people and paid for by people or other groups who do not have the appropriate representation, the necessary know-how for promoting their own welfare.

For years after Urban Renewal undid my corner of the world, I wondered where our neighbors went after their little houses were razed by the demolition engineers. People scattered, I later learned, just like I left for Chicago and Austin soon after. I remember being impressed by the words demolition engineers. The title sounded so important, so very American to my still untrained ears. I was impressed, until I found out that one of my friends was calling himself a demolition engineer because he had learned how to drive and handle a bulldozer. Demolition engineers, I learned, drove and destroyed houses and buildings with their bulldozers, but I also discovered, not just any Mexican American was allowed to learn how to drive one. My friend was hired to raze Latino barrios because his father was politically connected, and, politics matter throughout the world.

One evening, I remember rising before the members of the City Council to express the opposition of my parents and neighbors to their impending removal. The Council members beheld a strange sight: a young Mexican American publicly countering their decisions. All decisions, I have since ascertained, are political, everything can be changed or turned around, depending on the nature of the argument, the attack, or the defense launched against something. But, although I intuitively sensed that reality even then, I was not capable of fully understanding that fact, much less of formulating a useful refutation. I have since seen that usually we disagree about something among ourselves. We do not usually stand up to voice our views because we Latinos tend to hear an implicit: who do you think you are? To think of planning to be here explicitly to tell us what you want! Who do you really think you are? When I stood up to talk, they must have felt that they were witnessing one of Jonathan Swift's talking horses, a *Houyhnhnm*. Fully conscious of my actions, in turn, I recall thinking that I was talking to our local *Yahoos,* a metaphoric image that probably did not help my case. Talk about being on separate planets, democracy that I thought I was advancing! They thanked me "for my time," and proceeded with their plans, as if I had never said one word, like all of the older Latinos in the room.

I am contextualizing these closing remarks at some length because this is the best way to dramatize the paradox that I see when I compare events that happened nearly forty years ago to developments today. When Urban Renewal forced the dispersal of my Latino neighbors, who consisted of Mexican Americans, Mexicans, and one Puerto Rican family, our Anglo-American leaders summarily rejected almost anything suggested by our Spanish-speaking citizens. That, indeed, is how most of us Latinos felt then, for the people who controlled Urban Renewal were all Anglos. There might have been a Mexican American or two in the group, but we also knew that such Mexican Americans tended to act more *gringo,* as we used to say, than sometimes the Anglos themselves.

The irony is that nearly two generations later the United States is today experiencing the return of the same kinds of Latino residents who were dispersed by the Great Society idea of Urban Renewal during the 1960s. Like the people with whom I grew up, the resident Latino population is now being reinforced by other Spanish-speakers fleeing poverty or political unrest in their home countries. Legally and illegally, they are immigrating into this great country. Most of these Latinos are silent because they know they will not be heard. Nonetheless, we need to understand that the current demographic changes are not as new as some people believe. Indeed, Latinos have been in Texas, in the Southwest, and throughout the United States for almost five centuries, and considerably longer, if we include the indigenous people of the Americas, as we should. But only now are other Americans beginning to realize and internalize the fact that the United States has a sizeable Spanish-speaking population with needs that cannot be sidestepped any longer.

Over the years we have suffered all kinds of periodic dispersals, even though Latinos have been very good for the American economy for a number of generations. The Bracero Program showed that between 1942 and 1964. Still, Spanish-speakers have not been actually encouraged to remain in Texas, or in any other part of the United States. Like the Israelite and Palestinian refugees who perennially look for land on which to settle, Latinos today, whether long-time residents of more than ten generations, or newly arrived immigrants, have needs that can no longer be dismissed. To ignore such needs amounts to impoverishing American society willfully. The Hispanic population is now so large that the social and economic futures of all Americans are undeniably tied to the nature of our livelihoods and to the education that our children are receiving in the schools today.

For the Spanish-speakers I have in mind it is as if we have been living in a giant hole in the earth all of these years, a metaphor associated with some of the pre-Columbus Mesoamerican origin myths. And that is what our barrios have long been for Latinos: obscure, forgotten, passed-over places, whether in South Texas, San Antonio, Houston, Dallas, El Paso, Tucson, Phoenix, San Diego, Los Angeles, Oakland–San Francisco, Chicago, the Midwest, the Northeast, the South, or anywhere between rural and urban America. Like our mythical ancestors, today's Latinos have continued to wander from Mexico and Latin America to the United States and back. Where they can, they comply with border regulations. When they cannot, they disregard them, for the issue is a matter of feeding families, and of obeying and disobeying national laws and policies that impose hardships on otherwise good, dependable workers.

As generations have followed generations, each decade only a small number of Latinos, comparatively speaking, have discovered how to emerge from the forgotten obscurities of the barrios and close family lives. The insularity of modern life, largely created by air-conditioned homes, cars, and workplaces has kept mainstream Americans from hearing about Hispanic problems and concerns. Media reports are not the same as learning about troubles first hand, as my family and I used to hear when our Spanish-speaking neighbors told us about difficulties while they bought goods at our little corner grocery store forty years ago. But now that Latinos are increasingly aware of the superabundance of American life, gleaned from the ubiquity of the media, everyone has seen the Latino sun, rising for ourselves and our children. The challenge is to create and to invest in our communal future by helping America's Spanish-speakers. The objective is to challenge ourselves to develop an appreciation for people who have not traditionally been seen as Americans. If we do not, then the majority of Latinos will remain ethnic workers shut out from opportunities that our social infrastructure affords others, people who will continue to find it difficult to care for their needs and the necessities of their children.

The dictionary defines the word "ethnic" as a person who is "not Christian or Jewish," as a "heathen" and a "pagan." Although most progressive, politically conscious Latinos have boldly embraced the term "ethnic," we Latinos are far from being heathens, since most of us are Christians and members of other God-centered religions. And, despite the fact that too many Spanish-speaking Americans live without the modern amenities taken for granted by other Americans, Latinos are civilized and respectful enough to endure poverty and deprivation with admirable grace and social composure. Our everyday lives and practices have amply demonstrated that we Latinos are not a counter-culture or trouble-causing people, as we have sometimes been portrayed. No, Latinos essentially have inhabited what I have sought to describe as a parallel culture to mainstream America, one with different social infrastructures largely developed to define us as part of American civilization, primarily to help us succeed just like any other American. Individually we may seek all sorts of different things from the great cornucopia that is the United States, but as a group, being seen just like other Americans is what most Latinos seek and what Spanish-speakers want from the United States, no more, but no less either.

ISBN 1-58544-381-6